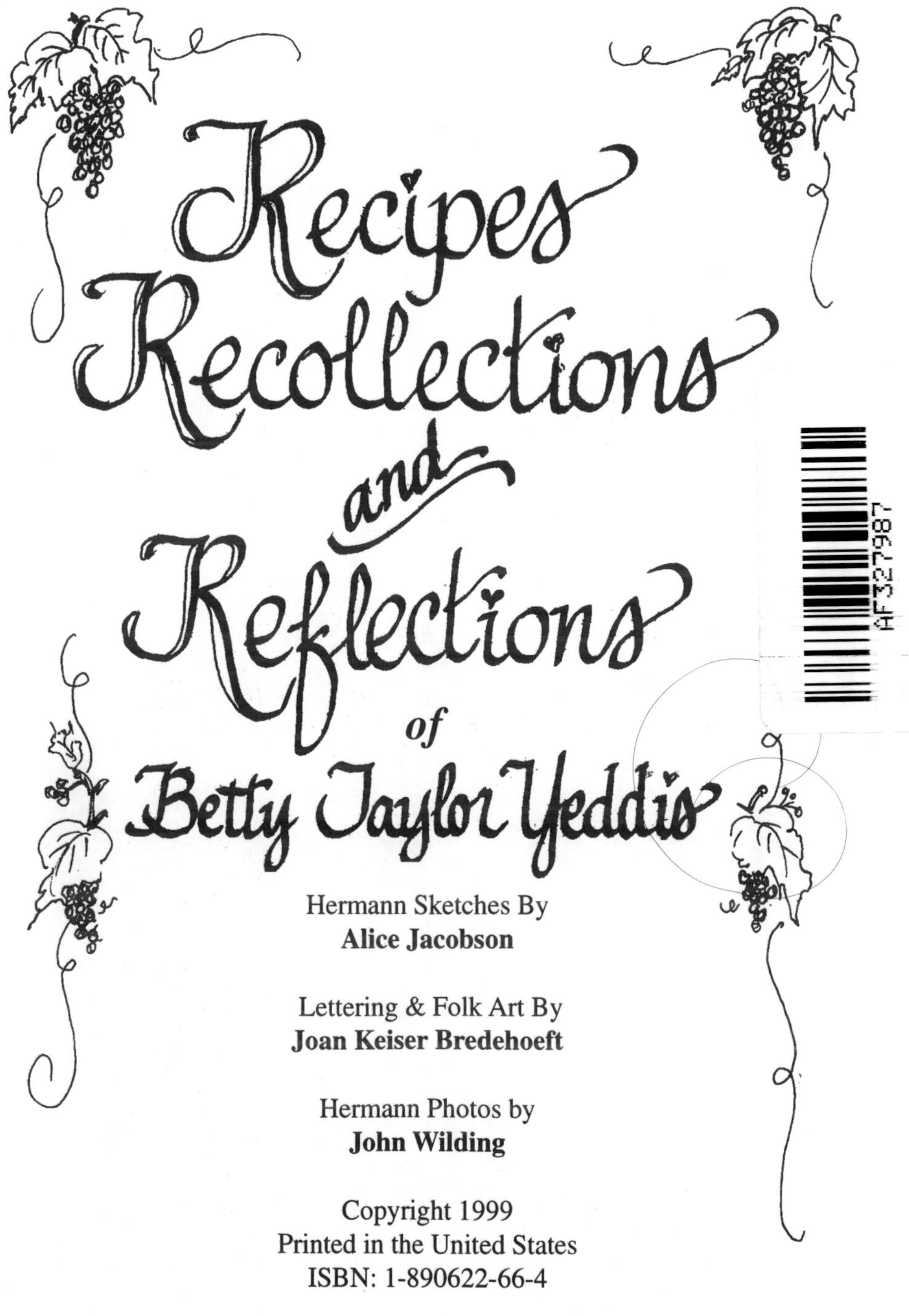

Recipes Recollections and Reflections

of Betty Taylor Yeddis

Hermann Sketches By
Alice Jacobson

Lettering & Folk Art By
Joan Keiser Bredehoeft

Hermann Photos by
John Wilding

Copyright 1999
Printed in the United States
ISBN: 1-890622-66-4

Leathers Publishing
4500 College Blvd.• Leawood, KS 66211
913-498-2625

DEDICATED TO
Morris Yeddis

*My sweetheart for 56 years
and my husband for eternity*

And to his parents
Jacob & Sarah Yeddis,
the in-laws I might have had

In Memoriam

William Albert Brackman
My devoted son

Max Koerner
Missouri Restaurant Association
"Your biggest fan."

Lee Kolterman
"The Gingerbread Man"

Dorothy Roe Lewis
Journalist and Mentor

John Lone
Loving Friend and Honored Guest

Bill Nunn
<u>Missouri Life</u> Magazine

Dr. Joseph F. Schmidt
Hermann's "Mr. Music"

Robert Weigel
Rhine Country Journalist

Today we laid to rest my best friend, Lois Hutson. She had been very ill for weeks.

In 1962, Lois' daughter, Sherry, was my 6th grade student at Peculiar. She told me I would enjoy meeting her mother. At the time Lois was "great with child", a month away from giving birth to her fourth child and second son, Dean. The following year her daughter, Lynn, was my student. Over the years Lois became my "sister" and Taylor and I became a part of the Hutson family.

Today, I was proud to be one of her loving friends who came to acknowledge her life and her dedication to Wilbur and her family. The service might also have been an "award for parenting" for both of them. The presence of her identical twin sister, Louise Wilson, added to the solemnity of the occasion. She, too, had touched my life in numerous ways.

Since I phoned her intermittently and she worried about me, I began signing off "I love you, Lois" thinking I might be leaving this world any day and I would have neglected to tell her how much she meant to me. You will find Sherry Hutson Staton among my "Missouri Daughters," but no one could fill Lois' shoes as wife – as mother – as sister – as neighbor – as friend.

As one left the funeral home for Peculiar Cemetery the automobiles stopped quietly alongside Harrisonville's streets mirrored Cass County's traditional respect for a departed neighbor and her grieving family. Lois did her part in keeping that respect alive.

Betty Taylor Yeddis
Nov. 20, 1998

Table of Contents

About the Motto

WE TWO!

The motto on the opposite page has added definition to the last fifty years of my life.

When our Calico Cupboard friends would see this plaque, their ready response was "You really do!" The original carved motto came from Alma Tarran in Irving, Illinois. I do not know how Taylor and I became acquainted with her but it was a lucky day. Her wood carvings echoed the flavor of our antique shops and we sold scads of this one. Everyone thought it was original with me and that it reflected my philosophy perfectly. Now her daughter continues her business at Irving and since I'm using this one in the book, I've ordered several more. Our collector customers said the motto added meaning to their collections and, for me, the "past" allowed me to include my recollections of Morris during these delightfully busy years. It still does.

We two kept house
the past and I,
I laboured while
it hovered nigh,
Leaving me never alone.

· anonymous

Preface

It was my mother, Winifred Jones Goby, who kindled my interest in the Doerr-Jones history as well as my interest in the foods they found on the frontier to nourish their families. From the time I could dry dishes (safely), she recounted happy memories of family. She talked about aunts and cousins; answering all my questions about who, where, and how things came to be. She always included memories of Park College and nearby Kansas City.

As the first Jones family grandchild, I also enjoyed the same recollections of people, places and events of an even earlier generation that had settled on the Illinois prairie. My great-grandmother, Johanna Vollbrecht Doerr, had passed away before I was born so my grandmother Jones probably felt even more obligated to make her memory a viable part of my growing up. In keeping with tradition, I have tried to acquaint my son and his children with these very influential ladies. Their different worlds, beliefs, and customs guided their efforts to make the world a more gentle place for all who came after them. I hope you will enjoy knowing these women. In reality, I shared many of their experiences. For instance, they all faced rigorous homemaking difficulties because of war-time shortages. For great-grandmother Doerr, it was the Civil War. For grandmother Jones, it was World War I. For my mother, Winifred Jones Goby, both World Wars I and II. I also experienced the hardships of those turbulent years.

Grandmother Jones and I were step-mothers before we became mothers. With the exception of great grandmother Doerr, we were all school teachers. As our family history reflects, Grandmother Doerr was very dedicated to educating the children. She taught them in her own home until a school could be organized on the frontier. We were all blessed with an entrepreneurial insight that found expression in the endeavors of our husbands.

I was not privileged to share the same detailed family history with my grand-mother Sarah Goby. Nor did I have the opportunity to learn of her recollections of her mother, Jane Jones Lisle. The Joneses in my father's family were from England. The Joneses on my mother's side were Welsh. Every generation adapted to its surroundings with grace. They survived war years, depressions, droughts and rainy seasons, epidemics and good health, rationing and surpluses.

So Recipes, Recollections and Reflections becomes a very sentimental journal of a very sentimental cook; for very, very loving friends and family members. Enjoy and, before it's too late, record the dreams of your family and pay homage to the people who dreamed them.

Acknowledgments

Veronica Brackman
Grand daughter-in-law and Counselor

Kimbra Brackman
Once my grand daughter-in-law, now my friend

Joan Keiser-Bredehoeft
Folk Artist and Friend

Carolyn Freeman
A Soul-mate

Alice Jacobson
Artist, Neighbor, and Friend

Chester Kaplan
Friend and Legal Counsel

David Nunn and The Nunn Group

Frankie Packer
"Inch By Inch" Ambassador

Karen Vogler
Candid Critic and Longtime Friend

Foreword

When my first grade teacher, Mayme Frey, told me how glad she was to have me in her tiny Vignos school, I told her I wouldn't be there long, for I was going to high school and then to the "Uni" where my aunts were. We didn't get to take the covered wagon trip that our teacher, Jesse McCullough, let us spend a month planning in the fifth grade; but I learned some very valuable lessons in planning, organizing and list making. I just may have used some of those skills in preparing this book. We really thought we were going to make that trip, at least I did. It was when I asked to take the family wash tub on the trip that my mother accidentally interrupted the preparations and then Gladys Herzog said she already knew. I am still naïve!

It was a dream come true in 1930, in the depth of the Great Depression, for me to be able to enroll at the University of Illinois and find a job to support myself there. After two years, I was thrilled to find a job that paid me more per month than my schoolteacher aunts were making, and they had Master's degrees. It was 27 years later that I got back to finishing college, this time at the University of Missouri in Kansas City.

My mother's recollections of Kansas City and Park College drew me to believe that Kansas City's streets were paved with gold. World War II took me to Kansas City and to Fort Riley, Kansas. It was in K.C. that I met Morris Yeddis. You'll get a full story on that fairy tale later in this book. The farther I got from home in Raymond, the more vivid my recollections of my mother and my grandmother became. The house I designed in my sophomore Home Economics class now exists in Peculiar, Missouri. My teacher, Ada Foster, another list maker, suggested that the house I designed would adapt itself nicely as a tea room. My aunt's summer excursions from one tea room to another nurtured my dream of offering my grandmother's Pennsylvania style food in a similar setting. That dream became The Calico Cupboard.

I had so much in common with my grandmothers, even though we lived in completely different generations. Three of us were school teachers. Two of us were step-mothers before we were mothers. Three of us had husbands with entrepreneurial skills that we quietly supported. We managed to sustain our families within the resources of our husbands. We contrived to put food on the table using what we had on hand. Fond memories are like "Prozac" without the nasty side effects. Remembering IS "alternative medicine."

Calico Cupboard

My favorite table at The Calico Cupboard with my birthday cake in the background, surrounded with violet leaves and violets. Only lilies of the valley were missing from my recollection of birthdays at Grandmother Jones'. In the background, the photos of my Great Grandmother Doerr (70), Grandmother Jones (67), Winifred Jones Goby (61), and myself (51) hallow the spot.

My grandmother was never without a dickey, except at bedtime. Her hair is parted in the middle, just like her mother's, Great Grandmother Doerr, except Grandmother Jones kept her hair dyed with a black walnut concoction that she kept in an old cupboard in the basement. She also saved her combings, as did my aunts, and when they had a sufficient accumulation they made hairpiece braids. Grandmother is wearing a braid in this picture. They learned how to do all this from their Kansas City cousins who were also adept at fashioning hair jewelry. You'll notice that Grandmother is wearing a brooch with human hair twined around a gold base. The first antique I ever framed was that pin and its display case in a shadow box frame.

I never remember my mother having short hair. Usually, she wore it in a French roll wound around a "rat" of her own combings. This portrait was made at the time she received national recognition for her role in developing a practical plan for rural health in Illinois.

Introduction

My mother cautioned me about revealing my personal life, my feelings, my goals, or my fears to "outsiders." RECIPES, RECOLLECTIONS, AND RE-FLECTIONS "lets it all hang out" in the same fashion that we now share the details of our lives with counselors. Originally, this book was to record Grandmother Jones' Pennsylvania style recipes. But how can you separate recipes from the women whose food found loving acceptance from their families, even when love was in greater supply than the food!

Whether this is a cookbook with a love story, or a love story with recipes, these recollections ARE my life. At the age of 86 years, they could also record an experiment in natural healing. I could have spent these years aching and complaining - but when your heart is full of loving memories and loving people, nothing aches.

I am reminded that when God sends us a dilemna, the solution that follows seems even sweeter. When Mother Nature gives us the beautiful purple, but prickly, thistles in June; we appreciate the Queen Anne's Lace in July even more. People, too, are sometimes thistle-like; they are beautiful but you can't touch. The Queen Anne's lace billows in the summer wind, standing tall and erect in profusion along every pathway, and we take them for granted.

So it has been, my first seventy years needed constant attention but that allowed me to cherish these last sixteen years that brought a harvest of loving recollections and an appreciation of God's planning for my life. I no longer believe in coincidences. What I have called my "scrapbook" life takes on plan and purpose as the past and present converge in this moment.

So join me in discovering who I was, who I might have been and who I am at this moment. We may get a glimpse of what is still to come.

About The Author
Our Grandmother

Recipes, Recollections and Refections was intended to record the simple down-to-earth foods of Grandma Goby and Grandmother Jones that her customers enjoyed at the Calico Cupboard in Hermann, Missouri. Her guests had no doubt of her dedication to the past, for the past was all around them in Hermann and in Calico Cupboard. With each visit, guests became more sensitive to the energy and love that found its way into what she and Taylor planned; her cooking, her decorating ideas, everything she did and everything she dreamed for Hermann, for herself and for Taylor. But she never provided us with any insight into the dreams she had put aside for a variety of reasons. I never realized that with two loving husbands and three hometowns, my grandmother was in a constant state of "becoming" until…

And that's where Recipes, Recollections and Reflections becomes a love story. Not "boy meets girl" stuff, but an unbelievable, fairy tale, made-in-heaven, romantic love story. What she called her "scrapbook years" found meaning, reality and purpose. As a fourth generation *magna cum laude* dreamer, she was alert to every incipient opportunity she found nestled in between life's predicaments. She still is. My brother, Tim, and I are so happy she decided to include Jacob and Sarah Yeddis in her dedication of the book. Their story is such an inspiration. They were the in-laws she might have had.

–*DeAnne Warren and Tim Brackman, grandchildren*

IN MEMORIAM

We sorrowfully mark the passing of

our son and father

WILLIAM A. BRACKMAN

January 13, 1993

We rejoice in recalling the enthusiasm and dedication he brought to each new day and each new undertaking. We are grateful for his constant love and affection and thank you most sincerely for the happiness your friendship added to his short life.

Betty Taylor - Yeddis

Timothy Scott Brackman

De Ann Brackman Gatten

5412 W. 104th Street

Overland Park, Kansas 66207   913 - 642 - 1163

Betty Taylor Yeddis

Winifred Goby

Henrietta Doerr Jones

.....to get a college degree
actually, the dream of
my grandmother and
my mother.

Joby Family

The Stork Brought Me!

I know because my mother told me all about it; how Doctor Kenton saw the stork flying over Raymond and got in his buggy, picked up Nurse White, and followed the big bird to see where he was taking that baby. And it was our house, not the big new house my dad built in 1920, but the old house that was on the farm when my mother and dad married.

My mother was twenty-seven and my dad was twenty-three when I was born. It was May 13th, 1912. My mother said I had been expected with great joy. I think she was just trying to make me feel good, for how could a twenty-two year old farmer look forward to supporting a child? Perhaps twenty-two year olds in 1920 were much like they are today in 1998, not entirely practical in their aspirations. But secretly, I bet my dad would rather have had a piggy sow. My mother had graduated from high school in Raymond, Illinois in 1903; in a class of three graduates. The years that followed had been busy, so I believe she really did look forward to being a mother.

It was only eighteen months later when Doctor Kenton and Nurse White caught the stork en route to our house with Sonny, my brother. I was named Grace Elizabeth for "Aunt Grace" Grotts and my mother's sister, Aunt Elizabeth. Sonny was named Albert William for my dad and by mother's father, Albert Milton Jones.

My dad was one of a family of nine children so the advent of a new baby never lacked for attendees to do what had to be done. No one ever used the word "pregnant" unless it was whispered. A woman was said to be "in the family way" and remained more or less house bound for the duration.

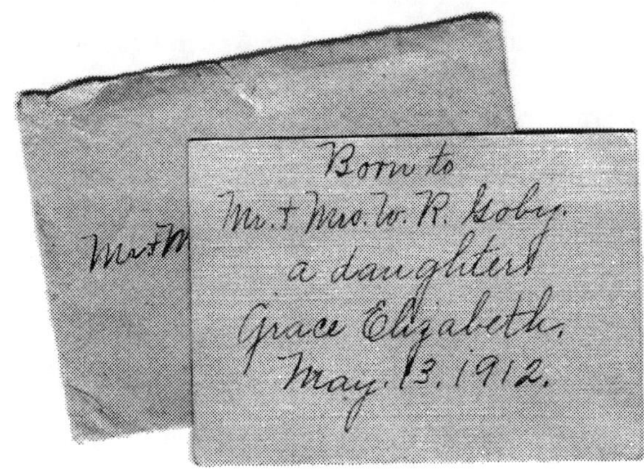

Reflections

My mother, Winifred Jones Goby, was my connection to the past. I fondly recall the time we spent together. She would relate bits and pieces of family history as she tidied up the kitchen. She answered my questions about who, why, where, and how things happened. Being the first Jones grandchild, I had even greater access to Grandmother Jones' version of people, places, and events. Great Grandmother Doerr was gone by the time I was born, so Grandmother Jones didn't get to share the blessing of great grandmotherhood with her. Perhaps that was why she felt so compelled to make her memories a viable part of my life. I do the same thing with my grandchildren, Tim and DeAnn.

I was a late arrival in the Goby family. My dad had five older brothers and sisters. Grandkids were no novelty by the time I came along. What I learned from the Goby family history, I gathered from my cousins and then went home to verify the information with my dad.

I have deliberately tried to keep my son and his children acquainted with these gentle ladies who were so influential in my life. Their very different worlds, their beliefs, their customs, and their efforts have made the world a better place for generations to come. I hope you will enjoy becoming acquainted with:

> Johanna Vollbrecht Doerr
> Henrietta Christina Elizabeth Doerr Jones
> Winifred Johanna Jones Goby
> Jane Butcher Jones Lisle
> Sallie Jane Jones Goby

I am finding that nothing has really changed. Grandmothers still maintain a vigil over grandchildren. Mothers still cuddle but find ways to guide unobtrusively. Great grandmothers are left to hope and pray that their efforts at parenting have not been in vain and that they will have the grace to keep their mouths shut.

GRANDMA AND GRANDPA GOBY

I never remember being alone with my Goby grandparents, either of them. My dad was in the middle of their nine children so they were seasoned grandparents when I and my brother and sister arrived on the scene. In fact, we were numbers 12. 13 and 14. No one ever entered the home from the front porch except Aunt Flora's and Aunt Alice's suitors. Everyone entered through the driveway porch. Grandma greeted us from the center of her large kitchen,

wiping her hands on her long calico apron. The fragrance of baking bread or baking pies preceded us so it seemed quite hospitable. Aunt Flora and Aunt Alice, who were the only Goby family members left at home during our childhood years, probably braced themselves for our visit. I know we interrupted their household chores, for they were always busy washing, ironing, sewing, or churning.

Grandpa Goby was seldom near the house, but when he was, he perched himself on the back two legs of his chair, leaning back against the porch wall. He spent hours there before dinner, relaxedly smoking his pipeful of Prince Albert. To his right, at the end of the porch, was a small boot closet. In it he kept overshoes or boots easily available

Anton William Goby at age 21,
11/22/1850 - 5/20/1929
A large framed copy of this portrait hung
in my Grandmother Goby's parlor.

with rows of empty tobacco cans lining the narrow shelves. If I had been taller or had more than a glance into Grandpa's private closet, I probably could have seen a fifth of whiskey high up in the corner for medical purposes, of course.

At mealtime, six big oak chairs surrounded Grandma's massive oak table. She would go out on the porch and blow on a steer horn to summon whoever happened to be working that day to come for dinner. They entered from the porch door and immediately took advantage of the washstand in the corner of kitchen to clean their hands before eating. They filled the wash pan from the water bucket alongside. That was the only place with "store bought" soap, usually Jap Rose. For every other washing chore, they used homemade lye soap, another of Aunt Flora's myriad skills.

No one vied for Grandpa's place at the head of the table, nor did they expect to engage him in dinner table conversation. The table was laden with big ironstone bowls of gravy, potatoes and home canned vegetables. Fresh baked bread was plentiful along with freshly churned butter, jam or home canned fruit. The bowls circled the table two or three times during the meal. No one would have attempted to fill their plate from the stove. Sometimes, there was dessert; Grandma's special rice pudding or Aunt Flora's angel food or devil's food cake. You couldn't miss, for if there was no dessert, you just might get to enjoy Aunt Flora's apple butter. Sometimes the dinner table silence was broken by Aunt Flora announcing who was coming down the road. She could identify every team and wagon from her place at the table, even if they were a mile down the road.

With dinner over, clean up was immediate. They needed the big table top for freshly ironed clothes. Without running water, dish washing required a big dishpan for washing, a small dishpan for rinsing and a large

Sarah Jane Jones Goby - my Grandmother Goby
(circa 1918) 1/23/1853 - 3/30/1935
Notice her brooch which bears a picture of
my Aunt Alice Stewart at age three.

shallow bread pan for draining dishes. Either Aunt Flora or Aunt Alice would separate the tableware to scour the metal fork tines and knife blades with Bon Ami. I always thought I could taste Bon Ami on my fork. Following dinner, while the oven was still warm, was a perfect time for making Grandma's rice pudding so that it would be ready for supper.

Grandma's kitchen was probably 20 feet by 20 feet. The linoleum on the floor originally had a pattern on it, but I never remember seeing anything but well-scrubbed brown linoleum with a fringe of lighter print around it. The print probably could not survive the lye soap scrubbing every week. In the corner of the kitchen was a pantry, about six feet square. One side of the pantry was a wainscot cabinet with storage and food supplies. In a lower part, there was space for the large utensils needed for a large family. On the other side of the pantry was a linoleum lined counter with a cheese wheel that supported Grandpa's huge wheel of cheddar cheese, just as he remembered from the old country. Beneath the shelf lodged his cracker barrel. The crackers drew moisture from the air and from the steam that came from the cook stove just outside the pantry door. The pantry always smelled inviting; not because of the oily cheese, but mainly because of Grandma's spice drawers just inside the pantry door. Grandma kept the crackers crisp as needed by putting a few of them in a bread pan in a cooling oven. In the summertime, the pantry held 100 pounds sacks of flour and sugar because there were more farm hands to feed and more garden produce to can.

The porch on the other side of the kitchen provided a leisurely place to stem green beans, hull strawberries, peel apples or peaches. All those chores offered a bit of privacy for girl-style conversation. In the summertime, the porch was an airy place to do the laundry with the hand powered washing machine and wringer. During the winter months, the laundry was relegated to the "old house" that remained in its original location. It housed outgrown furniture, old feather beds and the stuff of rug making. It was also next door to Grandma's smokehouse. I don't have a clue as to what went on in there, but I know we were threatened with extinction if we ever peeped in the door. I also know that what came out of there was delectable.

From My Mother's Desk:

Where do I go from here?

If I were younger, I feel sure I could find "service entrances" into many lives but I have to remember my limitation of age and position and also that I no longer have to earn a living. So, I may not contact those whose need is greatest and most urgent. I leave that to you younger people. But let's just talk about "service entrances" for a bit. Sometimes, they are so hard to find and are hidden by beautiful clothes, gracious manners and full purses. But the service entrance goes directly to the heart of human emotional need. It opens in the most unusual walls, back and front, and in any human facade.

Written by Winifred Jones Goby in the 1960's (she would have been in her late 70's).

UNITED STATES OF AMERICA.

STATE OF
ILLINOIS.

COUNTY OF

SS.

Be it Remembered, That on the _13th_ day of _September_ in the year of our Lord One Thousand Eight Hundred and ~~Eighty~~ _Ninety Two_, personally appeared before _Geo R Cooper_, Presiding Judge of the _County_ Court of the County of _Montgomery_ and State aforesaid (the same being a Court of Record, having and exercising common law jurisdiction, a Seal and a Clerk), and sitting judicially for the despatch of business at the Court House in _Hillsboro_ in the County aforesaid, _Anton W Goby_ an alien above the age of twenty-one years, and applied to the said Court to be admitted to become a naturalized citizen of the United States of America, pursuant to the several Acts of Congress heretofore passed on that subject, and the said _Anton W Goby_ having thereupon produced to the Court record testimony showing that he has heretofore reported himself, and filed his Declaration of his Intention to become a Citizen of the United States, according to the provisions of the said several Acts of Congress, and the Court being satisfied, as well from the oath of the said _Anton W Goby_, as from the testimony of _John Greene_ and _James D Kendall_ who are known to be citizens of the United States, that the said _Anton W Goby_ has resided within the limits and under the jurisdiction of the United States, for at least five years last past, and at least one year last past within the State of Illinois, and that during the whole of that time he has behaved himself as a man of good moral character, attached to the principles contained in the Constitution of the United States, and well disposed to the good order and happiness of the same, and two years and upward having elapsed since the said _Anton W Goby_ reported himself and filed his Declaration of his Intention aforesaid. IT IS ORDERED That the said _Anton W Goby_ be permitted to take the oath to support the Constitution of the United States, and the usual oath by which he renounces all allegiance and fidelity to every foreign Prince, Potentate, State and Sovereignty whatever, and more particularly to _William II Emperor of Germany_ whereof he was heretofore a subject, which said oath having been administered to the said _Anton W Goby_ by the Clerk of said Court, it was ordered by the Court that the said _Anton W Goby_ be admitted to all and singular the rights, privileges and immunities of a naturalized **Citizen of the United States**, and that the same be certified by the Clerk of said Court, under the Seal of said Court accordingly.

STATE OF ILLINOIS,
Montgomery COUNTY. } SS.

I, _Brewer A Hendricks_, Clerk of the _County_ Court of said State and County, do hereby Certify the foregoing to be a true and correct copy from the records of said Court.

IN TESTIMONY WHEREOF, The Seal of the said Court is hereto affixed, at the Clerk's office in _Hillsboro_ this _13th_ day of _September_ A. D. 189_2_, and of the Independence of the United States the _117th_.

By Order of the Court.

ATTEST: _Brewer A Hendricks_

Clerk of the _County_ Court of _Montgomery_ county.

Anton Goby's application for citizenship

8

Where Did "Goby" Come From?

Ost Friesland in northwest Germany was under the French rule of Napoleon. In 1811, Napoleon decreed that the patriarch of each family register a permanent surname for his entire family. Until this time, surnames had followed the Dutch custom of simply adding an "s" to the father's given name. Johann Friedrich Folkerts was the family patriarch at the time of Napoleon's decree. How or why he chose the name "Goebig" is still being researched. Within three years, Goebig had evolved into "Goby." By 1853, the name had become "Gobi." The first time the name Goby appeared in church records occurred when Grandfather Goby's sister, Johanna Goby, married Hillert Hidden in 1876.

(Adapted from <u>Letters From Home</u>, a publication of the Sonny Goby Family, Vol.1, No.1, January 1997.)

Anton W. Goby (From the Garrelt family notes.)

In 1815, East Friesland was part of the French empire. The North German state of Hanover, where Norden is located, was taken over in 1866 and became part of the German Empire, ruled by a Prussian king. Many young men left Germany to avoid forced military service at the age of twenty-one because they had no loyalty to the Prussian order.

At the time of Anton W. Goby's birth in 1850, Norden East Friesland had become a part of the North German Conference of States. Each state ruled itself under a Council. According to the Garrelt information, Anton crossed the Atlantic in 1871 by working on a cotton boat. These boats normally came to New Orleans port. He very possibly jumped ship there, since Immigration has no record of his entry. He made his way up the Mississippi River and the Illinois River to Eldred in Greene County.

Anton's sister, Grete Wilhelmina, also came to America. She married a Meyers and lived in Mt. Olive. She had three daughters and one son, Ferdinand. One of her daughters, Ali, married John Kruse. Grete died in 1908 of a heat stroke while her husband and John Kruse were in Kansas. She was buried from her home on June 26th and buried in Zion's Cemetery in Mt. Olive, Illinois. Our search did not produce an obituary covering her death.

MRS. SARAH JANE GOBY DIES

Mrs. Sarah Jane Goby, wife of the late Anton W. Goby died at her home northwest of Raymond on March 30, 1935, at 12:05 a. m., after an illness of eleven days, at the age of 82 years, 2 months and 7 days.

A daughter of Thomas and Jane Butcher Jones, she was born January 23, 1853, near Carrollton, Illinois.

In the year of 1873, on February 14th, she was united in marriage to Anton W. Goby, who preceded her in death in 1929.

To this union nine children were born, namely: Mrs. Lillian Swires, deceased; Mrs. Anna Boehler of Raymond, Illinois; Mrs. Frances Pearman, Springfield, Ill.; F. A. Goby, Springfield, Ill.; Mrs. Martha Jane Barnes, deceased; Wm. R. Goby and Gus T. Goby, of near Raymond, Ill.; Miss Flora Goby, at home, and Mrs. Alice Stewart, of Waggoner, Ill.

She is also survived by one brother, Richard Jones, of Divernon, Ill.; twenty grand children and nine great grand children, a number of nieces and nephews, and a host of friends.

Sixty years ago they moved from Greene county, Illinois, to the Raymond community. Here they founded their home and reared a family of nine children to manhood and womanhood. As a kind and loving mother her every interest was centered in her home and the well being of her family.

Through untiring efforts she mastered the many trials and tribulations accompanying home life, and won for herself the high esteem of the entire community in which she lived the greater part of her life

Funeral services were held at the Raymond Presbyterian church on Monday afternoon at 2:30 o'clock, with Rev D. A. MacLeod, the pastor, officiating. Interment was made in the Raymond cemetery.

The flower girls were: Mrs. Laura Stark, of Detroit, Michigan; Mrs. Elmina Hentirscher, Miss Martha Barnes, Springfield, Illinois; Miss Frances Jane Goby, St. Louis, Mo.; Miss Betty Goby, Champaign, Ill.; and Miss Ruth Boehler, of near Raymond.

P. A. Sellers, George Haarsuck, O. Ray Henry, Wm. Rhine, L. E. Hendrickson and Walter Wiegreffe were the casket bearers.

Mrs. Jane Jones Lisle

Mrs. Jane Jones Lisle was born at Yorkshire, England April 20th, 1818 and died at her home six miles east of Virden, Jan. 21, 1908 being 89 years, 9 months and 1 day old

Jane Butcher was married to Thos. Jones at the age of twenty years in Yorkshire England. To this union two children were born. In 1840 they came to America and settled near Alton, Ill. where the children died. They then went to Greene county, where seven children were born, Wm. Jones of Divernon, Mary Charney, Sumner, Neb, Martha Wertz, Scuyler, Neb., Sarah J. Goby, Raymond, Ill., Samuel Jones, of Woodbine, Iowa, and John Richard Jones, of Thomasville, and Frances A. Jones' who died at the age of eleven years

Mr. Jones died Dec. 21 1862 leaving Mrs. Jones to provide for her family which she did, keeping them together

Thirty five years ago Mrs. Jones was married to Thomas Lisle, in Greene county. They came to Montgomery county six miles east of Virden, twenty five years ago.

In Nov. 1886 Mr. Lisle died and since that, Richard Jones has made his home with his mother and by his care and devotion won the esteem of the community.

Grandma has been in poor health for several years and confined to her bed since last September. She united with the church in her native land.

She leaves to mourn her loss two sons, three daughters, thirty-two grand children and fifty-three great grand children. Funeral services were conducted by J. F. Howard at Bois d' Arc church Saturday Jan. 25, at 11 o'clock and the remains taken to Greene county for burial.

Dearest mother, thou hast left us
  O, 'tis sad to say farewell
But 'tis God who has bereft us
  And he doeth all things well

Dearest loved one, we have laid thee
  In the peaceful grave's embrace
But thy memory will be cherished
  Till we see thy heavenly face.

While no more on earth we greet thee
  Neath the circle of the sun,
Yet in heaven we hope to meet thee
  When our work on earth is done.

In peaceful are her slumbers now,
  Her days of suffering o'er,
Forever safe with God in heaven
  To rest for evermore.

Card of Thanks

We wish to extend our thanks to the friends and Neighbors for their kindness during the sickness of our mother Mrs. Jane Lisle, and especially for the flowers after her death.

    J. R. Jones
    Mrs A. W. Goby

OBITUARY OF ANTON WILLIAM GOBY

Anton William Goby was born in Norden, Germany, November 22, 1850, and died at his home west of Raymond, Ill., on Monday, May 20, 1929, at 10:30 a. m., at the age of 78 years, 5 months and 29 days.

He came to America at the age of twenty years and settled in Greene county, where he was married to Miss Sarah Jones on February 15, 1873.

Nine children were born to this union, namely: Mrs. Lillie Swires, deceased; Mrs. Anna Boehler, Raymond; Mrs. Frances Pearman, of Springfield; F. A. Goby, Springfield; Mrs. Jennie Barnes, deceased; W. R. Goby, Gus T. Goby, and Florence Goby, all of Raymond, and Mrs. Alice Stewart, of Waggoner.

Mr. and Mrs. Goby came to Zanesville township as pioneer tenants of land owned by the late Clark Sinclair. Later Mr. Sinclair urged them to purchase land and helped them to acquire the present homestead. Through long years of hardship they toiled, until the family was grown and two sons took over the tilling of the farm land.

Mr. Goby has been a familiar figure in Zanesville and Raymond for so many years that he was known to most of the older generation.

His pride was in the well cultivated fields, fine live stock, and the equipment of his farm.

He was reared and confirmed in the Lutheran faith, but never placed his membership in a church in this country.

Besides his devoted wife and children, he left nineteen grand children and five great grandchildren, also friends and neighbors acquired during the more than two score years spent in this locality.

Two daughters, a brother and a sister and many friends have "Crossed the bar" before him.

The funeral services were held at the home on Wednesday afternoon, May 22nd, at 2:30 o'clock, conducted by Rev. L. D. Lasswell, of Vincennes, Ind., assisted by Rev. D. A. MacLeod, pastor of the Raymond Presbyterian church. Interment was in the Raymond cemetery.

Obituaries of Sarah Jane Goby, Anton William Goby
and Great Grandmother Jane Jones Lisle

SARAH JONES GOBY

She was known in our household as "Grandma Goby." She was the only "Grandma" in my life, since my grandmother on my mother's side was "Grandmama Jones." Since there were Jones' on both sides of our family, differentiating the names avoided confusion.

I actually came into her life forty years after she married my grandfather, Anton William Goby. Five of her children had already married and established homes of their own. She had nine grandchildren by this time. Needless to say, I had the instant blessing of a seasoned grandmother who knew all about raising kids and bringing up babies; keeping them healthy or curing the ills that plagued farm folks. She favored poultices for everything from croup to respiratory congestion. Their effectiveness is attested by the fact that eight of her children lived to maturity. Only Martha Jane, my "Aunt Jennie," predeceased Grandma and she died of complications in childbirth.

Childbirth on the Illinois prairie seems frightening from this vantage point, but Grandma's first three children (all girls) were born in Carrollton; Greene County, Illinois. This all occurred before Grandpa Goby moved to Zanesville Township. In Carrollton, she would have been near her mother, Sarah Jones. Her Grandmother Butcher may have also lived nearby, but we have not been able to authenticate the Carrollton years to this date. Mid-wives served those early homesteads upon request and by the time her last four children were born, her older daughters were quite experienced in birthing routines. My father, W.R. Goby, told me that he remembered when my Aunt Alice was born. He was not aware that his mother was expecting but one day, they would not let him into her room. He was told she was sick. He began to cry when he heard his mother's screams and finally they came out and told him that he had a baby sister. He would have been about nine years old at the time. A couple of years ago, I asked my Aunt Alice who brought her into the world. She said it never occurred to her to ask.

Grandmother Goby was a sweet, gentle woman; a major accomplishment in the face of the rigors of early farm life. I really never recall seeing her seated. She would always greet us warmly, though not effusively, when we came in. Her daily attire was a blue calico shirtwaist dress with a full skirt. She also wore a blue calico apron which covered and protected her dress but also served as a spur-of-the-moment basket for garden produce, clothes from the clothes-line, or eggs she might have gathered. She was excessively neat about every detail of homemaking. She taught her daughters to be just as precise about sewing, ironing, cleaning, gardening, etc.

Anton Goby's family in Norden before he sailed for America in 1871

I did not get the impression that Grandpa Goby included her in his plans for increasing his land holdings or his financial planning. Just recently, someone in the family has said that she could barely read or write, which really surprises me because of her English background. Late in life, her mother remarried and became Grandma Lisle. She operated a tiny country store in Bois D' Arc Township on a corner now covered by the East lane of I-55. My dad recalled having driven his mother there to visit when he was a teenager. That would have been a 25 mile horse and buggy trip.

Her cooking was circumscribed by Grandpa Goby's likes and dislikes. She made pancakes with buttermilk, soda, eggs, and flour. They were large and flat and delicious. She also made her own sugar syrup and, of course, churned her own butter.

My dad's favorites, which became our family's favorites, were her gooseberry pie, rhubarb pie, and grape pie (which were made when fruit was available). Otherwise, it was her rice pudding which she made in a large round blue and white enameled pan that held about a gallon. She cooked it in the oven of the cook stove all morning, turning it and spooning it occasionally. Her white bread was superb and before we went home, if we would hint hard enough, we would enjoy bread and butter with white dry sugar sprinkled on it.

She did not think it was necessary for family resources to be wasted on education. My Aunt Alice, her youngest daughter, was the first child to go to high school. Since she lived in the country, she had to have the approval of the school board to attend high school in Raymond, three miles away. She graduated Valedictorian in her class.

I know just how quietly resolute Grandma Goby was. She must also have been quite patient, having a Prussian husband intent on accomplishing in America what neither he nor his family could ever have accomplished in Germany. Her large family appreciated her tireless efforts on their behalf and this, in time, replaced the support she had enjoyed from her brothers and sisters from whom she was separated when she moved to Zanesville Township with my grandfather. We remember her brother Richard, whom we knew as "Uncle Dick." There was also a brother named Thomas, and a sister named Mandy, but we are still in search of authentic Greene County records attesting to the Jones and Lisle families.

Written May 26, 1990

The A.W. Gobys with five of their nine children at the "home place"

My Grandmother's Kitchens

They didn't have counters. They didn't have plumbing. They didn't have outlets and they didn't have islands. They had a stove, a wash stand, and a kitchen table with six or eight sturdy chairs. There were always hungry people to feed and more in planting and harvesting season. The stove's needs were supplied from a coal and wood bucket near the stove. A water bucket served the tea kettle and the wash basin. A coal shed and a wood pile were replenished seasonally as needed.

In Grandmother Goby's kitchen, there was a low rocking chair by the window where she would rest while peeling potatoes or stemming green beans. She would use her blue and white enameled peeling pan that hung on the wall behind her chair. It hung next to a three-loaf bread pan that also came in handy for draining freshly washed dishes. Of course, if Grandad Goby came in the house, the rocking chair was his. The stove top was the center of activity each day until noontime, except on baking day when the kitchen table provided the only kneading and mixing area.

By noontime, the table would be cleared of any activities that had occupied the morning to accommodate six or eight people at "dinner" for it was the day's main meal. The table setting would include, of course; salt and pepper, a sugar bowl, the spoon holder, a syrup pitcher, and a vinegar cruet. Mustard, catsup and Tobasco were sometimes included and Aunt Frances Pearman always had hot pickled peppers from the grocery store on her table for Uncle Ed. Oh, I almost forgot the toothpick holder! It was always in the center of the table too. Food was always served in large ironstone bowls with the meat on a large ironstone platter. There was a bread tray and perhaps a bread cutting board, a large bowl of gravy and a butter crock. There was a pitcher of milk and a pitcher of water and glasses for each person. Clearing the table after dinner was a major undertaking by the time all these items were returned to their assigned storage spaces, which were very limited. Then the table cloth had to be removed revealing the oilcloth underneath. This cloth provided space for whatever chores were to take place in the afternoon; like ironing, darning or mending.

My Aunt Frances would leave all these supplementary items on her kitchen table, but would cover them with an appropriately embroidered "table cover" made just for this purpose. I remember reading the labels on some of the containers of store bought items and asking where D-e-c-a-t-u-r was and how to pronounce it. The syrup came from there. After I left home, in the interest of saving steps, my mother placed these items on a Lazy Susan that stored easily in a nearby cupboard.

Knives and forks were placed at each place on the table while spoons were in the spoon holder in the middle. We had a matching glass and gold trimmed sugar bowl, spoon holder and cream pitcher. Not too long ago, while I was still collecting, I ran across an identical set which was reported to have been given by Quaker Oats as a premium, with one of each item embedded in a package of rolled oats.

The syrup pitcher had a spring loaded cover and was not used for pancakes, for which we made our own syrup each morning. At the end of a meal, if my dad was still hungry and we didn't happen to have dessert, he would put a big dollop of butter in the middle of his empty and well cleaned plate, cover it with corn syrup, swish it around, and eat it with bread to finish his meal. If peanut butter was available, he just might add it to his special dessert. By the way, in those days, peanut butter was scooped out of a large tub at the grocery store and put in a meat tray for the trip home where you would put it in an appropriate container. It was not the least bit creamy, but very dry and solid.

The knives and forks Grandmother Goby used were metal with black wood handles. Once a week at least, they had to be scoured with Bon Ami to remove accumulated rust. I now use one of those three-tined forks in my kitchen to turn meat in the skillet. I think it is more effective but it just may be because of my sentimental memories of visits to my Grandmother Goby.

I really don't remember my Grandma Goby's china, for there was none of it visible except at meal time. I do remember Grandmother Jones' tea loaf ironstone china, in brown and white. There was only the brown band at the edge of the plate and in the center was a small brown leaf with three lobes. Taylor's old aunt called it "poor man's china" for theirs was much more effusive in blue and white with touches of gold. Buying a set of china in those days meant a service of eight which included: dinner plates, soup plates, pie plates, bread and butter plates, salad plates, butter patties, along with cups and saucers, sauce dishes, cereal bowls, platters large and small, a sugar bowl, cream pitcher, milk pitcher, gravy boat, and a round or oval covered vegetable dish. With breakage, you eventually ended up with a lot of mismatched dishes. Grandmother Goby kept her old dishes in an old dish cupboard in the old house, which she used for laundry and storage. My cousin, Ruth Boehler, and I always enjoyed playing with the old dishes and wondering why they abandoned those pretty plates and cups.

While Grandmother Goby had large sacks of flour and sugar in her pantry, our new house built in the 20's had a floor to ceiling cabinet with a bin for 25 pounds of sugar and a bin for 50 pounds of flour. It also had a pull-out board for kneading or rolling out pie dough or biscuits. There was ample room for spices and cereals in the cupboards above for we didn't have boxed foods to take up space. Now there are so many boxes of various heights and shapes that the pantry has returned to kitchen design, however, I doubt that they will ever include room for cracker barrels, cheese wheels, or vinegar kegs.

FERDINAND ANTON GOBY
"UNCLE TONE"

Uncle Tone was my dad's oldest brother. He married Lucy Richards. They had one son, Lee Goby. He started first grade when my mother taught at Lily school. My father's oldest sister, Aunt Lil, was married to Jim Swires, a well respected building contractor who recognized Uncle Tone's interest in construction and included him in his crew of workmen. As they finished an assortment of building projects on nearby farms, they were given the contract to build the Presbyterian Church, our family church in Raymond Illinois.

With the church completed, Uncle Jim Swires returned to his home in Virden. Uncle Tone, Aunt Lucy and Lee moved to Virden too. They continued to work together until the Swires family had grown to two sons and a daughter, at which time they moved to Detroit, Michigan. Their son, Raymond, was born after they moved. Uncle Tone moved to Springfield to work for Crawford Construction. I do not know that he ever worked for anyone else. He and King Crawford became as brothers and he enjoyed the security that a faithful, skilled employee deserves. Without any other skill, he found it expedient to be a strong union member. Unions were just beginning in these years and needed members.

Uncle Tone had an automobile as soon as they were available. I can recall his having a "Reo" and a "Hupmobile." He drove to Indianapolis for the auto races every year and he traded cars every year. If you asked him why, he shrugged and said "Why not?" Aunt Lucy did not interfere with his interest in automobiles. If she felt neglected, she would simply ask for a room to be added to the house or ask for more cabinets to be added. She spent hours sewing in her well-designed sewing room. In those years, it was impossible to buy clothing sufficiently large for her needs so she made them.

When they would drive down from Springfield to Raymond, Aunt Lucy would bring a big enamel roaster full of Jello fruit salad. We Goby kids really enjoyed it, for we did not have access to fresh fruit in our small town country stores, nor did we have a refrigerator to cool it. I remember she told my mother she should try fixing it for us sometime.

When I was in business college in Springfield in 1928 and scuffling for every penny, they invited me to stay with them during the winter months. Lee and the beautiful Helen Chittick had married and had two sons, Jack and Bob. They were there many evenings and I joined them around the radio listening to Amos and Andy. Uncle Tone would be convulsed with laughter and he slapped his knees with enjoyment of their black humor and dialect. Of course, our daily lives at that time did not include any black people, either at work or at home.

Every morning, Uncle Tone would leave in his car of the moment; always with the same lunch box, his thermos bottle of A&P coffee, a Velveeta sandwich, and a homemade cookie or piece of cake. Velveeta was new on the market then and he preferred the Velveeta with red pimentos in it. He came home every night to a tasty meal and often home baked bread if Aunt Lucy hadn't been too busy sewing that day. My favorite recollection of her cooking style was her wintertime vegetable soup. After Uncle Tone had gone to work, she brought a three gallon blue and white enamel bucket out of her

Uncle Tone and Aunt Lucy at the back of her mother's log house in Petersburg, 1920's I always wondered if Lincoln had been there.

pantry. The pantry was another one of Uncle Tone's creations. She began with what she called boiling beef cut in chunks about two inches square. Actually, it was what we now call brisket. She would fill the bucket about two-thirds full with water, put it on the back burner, turn the gas on low, and go back to her sewing or whatever she was doing. By noon, the water had cooked down to about a half gallon of broth. The windows were frosted and the house smelled great. It was time to add the vegetables: dry onions from her garden or pantry, home canned tomatoes, turnips from Uncle Tone's postage-stamp garden in the back yard, and carrots, cabbage, and celery from the grocer. Just before Uncle Tone walked in the door, she sprinkled the slowly cooking accumulation with a handful of elbow macaroni, a partial handful of parsley flakes, and she tasted the broth for saltiness or a need for pepper. With her homemade bread, what a feast!

In the 1970's my grandson Tim and I visited Jack Goby and his wife, June, in their home in Rochester, Illinois. At dinner that night, Lee and Helen, their parents, joined us. They commented on how fortunate it was that I had been a part of Uncle Tone's household at that particular time, for Lee and Helen had just left to establish their own home.

I was always in awe of Helen's beauty. She suffered through many illnesses but always seemed radiant. Lee was a very competent shop teacher in the

Springfield schools and was later selected to be superintendent of building and grounds for the Illinois State Department of Education. He always reminded my mother that she was his first teacher. There is a picture of him at Lily School in this book.

My dad's 80th birthday photograph with his remaining brothers and sisters; from the left: Aunt Flora, Goby, Aunt Alice Stewart, W.R. Goby, Uncle Tone, and Uncle Gus Goby

AUNT FLORA AND AUNT ALICE

I really can't separate recollections of Aunt Flora and Aunt Alice. Really, I can't separate them from my memories of Grandma Goby; for where they were, Grandma was.

Aunt Flora was next to the last child and she was six years old when Aunt Alice was born. Alice was the last of nine children and after 25 years of child-bearing, Grandma was 45 years old. Only Aunt Lil was married and away from home. The whole family could enjoy a baby sitter and at six years old, Aunt Flora became a "little mother."

As the family grew smaller with the departure of each married son and daughter, Aunt Flora took on more of the household responsibilities. She did the milking, helped Grandma with the chickens, tended the garden and the yard, did the laundry, and in her "spare" time, did the family sewing as precisely as if she were a trained modiste.

If we were fortunate enough to get to spend an afternoon with her, she frequently found time to subject us to the "egg shampoos" which she recommended so highly. She maintained huge stacks of magazines - Pictorial Review, Ladies Home Journal, Needlework, and Woman's Home Companion. If we were good, we just might get to cut the paper dolls out of the Pictorial (an old one). In the summertime, she introduced us to spearmint in our iced tea, which she picked from the garden near the fence where her sweet peas grew rampant year after year. Not that these peas were perennial, but she wanted them there each year and saved the seeds from one year to the next.

Aunt Flora and Aunt Alice were as quiet as Grandma Goby. I never remember any of them sitting down with us at the table. They were always waiting on everyone, particularly Grandpa Goby, and then eating later. All three of them were good listeners and seldom interjected unless it was to correct a date. Aunt Flora remembered everybody's birth, the year they built the barn, the spring they didn't get corn planted. You sometimes wondered if she was listening to you at all and then she would come up with some terse statement that condensed everything you had been saying.

Aunt Flora was so fortunate to have Aunt Alice Stewart's grandchildren to enliven her last years. Aunt Alice was fortunate to have Aunt Flora to share her grief when Carl was accidentally killed. Aunt Alice never failed to remember my birthday, even if she had to phone. She also kept me in touch with the goings on of each of my cousins. After my parents were gone, Aunt Flora and Aunt Alice were "home." They still kept an immaculate house and their big kitchen was the center of the household, just like Grandma Goby's and the home place. They were truly great aunts and everybody should be as blessed as I was.

The W.R. Goby farm home, 2 1/2 miles west of Raymond
and 1/2 mile east of I-55 at Hwy. 127

This is America to Me

The farm house that we live in
The fields, the barn, the stock
The milkweed at the roadside
The garden at the back

The cars and trucks that travel
At speeds we know unsafe
The friends who come on visits
From every distant place

The busy days of crop-time
The harvest's golden glow
The peace of quiet evenings
When winter brings us snow

The rush of children's school bus
The drivers - had you thought
How much you give unto their care
Each morning? Well you ought!

Our schools, our church, our fellowships
All are a gift from those
Who labored years ago, and left us
Things they never knew, but
Hoped for with their love

This is America to me.

Winifred Jones Goby
In the 1940's, Age 55

Doerr and Jones Family

Johanna Vollbrecht Doerr, 1890 (age 70) and Phillip Peter Doerr

GREAT GRANDMOTHER DOERR

My great grandmother, Johanna Katherine Vollbrecht, was born on October 16, 1819 in Muehlhausen, Schwartzburg, Germany. In 1845, she came to America. She sailed on a ship for nine weeks to reach her destination. The monotony of the voyage was broken somewhat by the porpoises that followed and played about the ship. Having lost her mother at the age of four, she traveled with a married brother, Henry Vollbrecht, who located in Pittsburgh, Pennsylvania. Later, she came on to St. Charles, Missouri where she was married to Phillip Peter Doerr. In 1851, they moved to Edwardsville, Illinois. During this time, my Grandfather Doerr sustained the family by doing brick and stone masonry. The sale of the Edwardsville home and the removal to the prairie occurred in1858. They left for their journey in wagons. The condition of the country was primitive in the extreme. The farm where they hoped to settle was in Township 10, Range 4, West of the 301 principal meridian, in Montgomery County. This was about twelve miles north of Hillsboro, the nearest church. A small settlement then existed in Butler, Illinois. The land office was in Edwardsville. Prairie land was sold mostly in fifty acre tracts and the price had gone to $1.25 an acre. Some of the land was so badly drained that they called it swamp and in 1854, this land was sold under the so-called "bit act" at 12 1/2 cents an acre. The individual purchase limit was 160 acres. My grandfather purchased 120 acres at that time and later purchased another 40. At a future time, he bought another 80 acres, at $10.00 per acre.

In the fall of 1857, Phillip Peter Doerr built a clap-board house, about 36 feet square, planted an orchard and sowed a field of wheat. The next year, the family moved out from Edwardsville. He later erected a clap-board granary, a barn, and a rather large blacksmith shop and tool shed in one. The first prairie wheat crops were always very good, though it was hard breaking up the soil. The war between the States brought up grain prices. Late in the war, Phillip Peter Doerr was drafted. The war ended before he had to serve.

During these years, there was much game in this low, flat prairie land. Several horses were lost to rattlesnakes and at about twelve years of age, Grandmother Jones was bitten on the foot by a rattlesnake. Dogs were often bitten, but after a few days of bad going, they would recover. Only the most industrious and frugal habits enabled settlers to make any progress.

Henrietta Christina Elizabeth Doerr,
1870
The "DD" appearance was achieved
with puffs of tulle.

Albert Milton Jones in his
blacksmith shop in Raymond in 1890 and
a photo from before 1882

GRANDMOTHER AND GRAND DAD JONES

You can detect the difference between my relationship with my Goby grandparents and my mother's parents. I was their first grandchild and, being a daughter, my mother was very close to her mother. There were five Jones children: Uncle Milton being the oldest, then Mother, and then Uncle Lloyd. Aunt Elizabeth and Aunt Florence came somewhat later. Grand Dad Jones was a blacksmith and a wagon maker. My mother wrote about him from her own memory so you'll find her account elsewhere, in her own handwriting. I'll confine my recollections to what great grandparents they were.

My personal recollections are of the "old house" at the north edge of Main Street in Raymond. My grandfather had a huge grape arbor with a carpet of blue violets in between the weathered posts that supported the heavy vines. The grape arbor separated Grand Dad's big garden from the yard. There was an outhouse at the far end of the yard, but it had been supplanted by Grandmother's new bathroom, carved out of a back porch (The water closet hung high on the wall so that gravity facilitated the flushing process). An apple orchard separated the yard from the pasture as the five acres made their way to the creek.

There was a small two-story barn at the end of the driveway that sheltered Grand Dad's buggy and provided feed and hay for his Jersey cow. Just at the edge of the orchard and outside the yard fence was a small shed roof pig house that I imagined was the original home of the three little pigs. After all, I had heard the ones my grandfather fed huffing and puffing! There was every kind of flower along the driveway. I particularly remember the daisies, bleeding hearts and big red poppies whose seed pods we used as pepper shakers when we played house late in the summer - in leaf houses.

By the time I came along, Uncle Milton and Uncle Lloyd were both finished at Lake Forest and were enrolled in Engineering School at the University of Illinois. They found time, however, to help care for the old house and to fashion such changes as to make it more comfortable for my grandparents. A right-angle porch surrounded the front of the house and Grand Dad built a porch swing from wagon building materials. He made hand wrought bolts to be sure it was sturdy and safe. I remember hours with him in the swing, mainly on Sundays after church, while we waited for dinner to be ready.

Every night, Grand Dad wheeled a two-wheeled cart carrying cow feed and

A.M. Jones with helpers Paul Angle and Heine Bergman

Henrietta Doerr Jones near a favorite pear tree in her
back yard at the "old house" on the north edge of
Raymond, the Convery home is seen in the background

supplies home from his blacksmith shop. You could hear the grinding of the metal wheels on the sidewalk two blocks away and I would run to meet him if I was visiting them. I always wanted to push the cart and he would let me until I ran off the sidewalk, then he would take over.

My Grandmother Jones' kitchen was as small and dark as my Grandmother Goby's was light and large. She had the same type of wainscot cupboard between the chimney and the corner of the kitchen. With the bathroom, my uncles had installed a sink with a pump so that she did have water handy. All preparations took place on the kitchen table which was covered with "oil cloth." I remember baking cookies with Grandmother Jones and her springerlie operation every December was carried on for years after she was gone. I've already written about her door-yard garden. She could find something good to make with a handful of vegetables. With no more than half a cup of green peas, she would serve peas and dumplings. I still love them; you'll find the recipe here. When she thinned out the carrots in the garden, as tiny as they were, she washed them and creamed them.

A few years ago, I gave Grandmother's cookbook to my youngest Goby niece, Jayneece, along with the oval shaped chopping block my grand dad had made for my mother when she married. It was made out of wagon-making materials, of course, and was built to last a lifetime. In her cookbooks, Grandmother had my aunts write down some of Mrs. Carter's recipes, for my grandmother's script was a definite reflection of her early German upbringing.

I don't recall her ever telling me how to cook anything but she was very explicit about what kind of kettle to use for this or that and she explained what went on under the lid with a hot fire or a slow fire.

I was about ten when the Jones children conspired to build a new house for their parents near the Raymond grade school. There was the same type of storage for dishes and utensils, a Hoosier cabinet for preparation, and a big cast iron sink with a drain board, and running water. My uncles insisted that Grandmother have an electric stove, one of the first ones in Raymond. It had three burners with a tiny oven up on legs. The big Monarch coal range went to the Goby kitchen in the country, for sentimental reasons, and my mother used it for years.

They didn't move the old grand piano Grandmother Jones had bought from the Hugg sisters. I hated to practice on that piano, for it hadn't been tuned in years and some of the ivory was coming off the keys. Aunt Elizabeth and Aunt Florence would punish me for not practicing and make me sit on the cellar steps. I will always think I learned to read on Grandmother's cellar

Henrietta Doerr Jones with her daughters Florence, Elizabeth and Winifred

Henrietta Doerr Jones with her Kansas City cousins Jennie Bonn and Nell Kundegraber

steps, for there was a Wise furnace (with an owl on the door) and clippings on the stair wall about how to cure your chickens and pigs of sundry diseases, in case my Grand Dad needed them. I also had to sit on the cellar steps if my aunts caught me reading the funny paper. They objected to the language the cartoon characters used. These were the World War I years and the Katzenjammer kids spoke in English fractured by German backgrounds. From my present perspective, I am surprised the comic strip appeared. I

Albert Milton Jones in 1893 when he was the mayor of Raymond

was fascinated by their antics and also by Powerful Katrinka and the Toonerville Trolley. My aunts succeeded in dulling my interest in comics for my lifetime. They also dulled my interest in piano lessons.

Aunt Frieda (Uncle Lloyd's wife), Grandad Jones and me on the front porch swing, 1914

Winifred and Milton Jones, 1886

Henrietta Doerr Jones, 1880, the teaching years

Winifred (age 8) and Elizabeth (age 3) Jones in 1893;
William R. Goby (age 4) and Gus T. Goby (age 2)

Albert Milton and Henrietta Doerr Jones' 25th wedding anniversary, 1907

Winifred Jones, 1903, graduation picture
She made her own graduation dress.

Grandmother's 25th wedding anniversary postcard to send to relatives

Picture post card of Wiesbaden-Sonnenberg, Germany; Great Grandfather Doerr's homeland

The Doerr family reunion in 1911
You'll see Grandad and Grandmother Jones in the front row
(second and third from the left),
Winifred Goby in the center back row with
Uncle Milton, Uncle Lloyd and my dad at the far right.

My grandfather and grandmother are in the front row at the far right.
My mother and dad are both missing for at the time of this picture,
1916, she was "great with child" awaiting my sister's arrival.

Reflections

My mother, Winifred Johanna Goby, graduated from high school in Raymond, in 1903. We know that between 1903 and 1907 she attended Park College for a year in Parkville. Missouri. She also worked at Gus McLean's Dry Goods Store in Raymond from time to time.

It would be difficult to determine which made the greatest impression on her future life, for she always had loving memories of her days in Park College and Kansas City. But she also appreciated fine lace, buttons, trimmings, and materials that she had access to at McLean's. In those days, there would only be one dry goods store in a town the size of Raymond. Of course, the grocer might decide to stock a few bolts of calico for his customers. The findings of a skilled dress maker were Gus McLean's chief concern as he made his intermittent trips to wholesale houses in St. Louis.

In 1907, Mother earned a teacher's certificate issued by the county. Her first teaching assignment was at Pleasant Hill School where she resided with the Bandy family. Until I-55 obliterated all the landmarks that remained of the Pleasant Hill community, they would remind her of students and their families that she had known there. Her next school was Lily. It was nearer to Raymond and though she often boarded with the Flint family, it was within walking distance from her home.

There are twelve students in the photograph of Lily School and, in all probability, there were no more. In the first row, second from the left, is Mary Bowsher. Next is my Aunt Alice Goby and next to her is Louise Flint. I recognize Hazel Paden, second from the right in the first row. Behind her is my cousin, Lee Goby, the son of Uncle Tone and Aunt Lucy. At the far left of the back row is Earl Boehler.

Lily School Cousin Lee Goby - back row, far right; Aunt Alice Stewart - front row, third from left. I also recognize Earl Boehler, Mary Bowsher, Louise Flint, Hazel Paden, and Walter Wiegreffe.

The A.M. Jones family
This is a steroptican viewing. Uncle Milton always loved photography and no doubt had a friend take this picture, for he is to the left of the porch post with my mother on the right. Aunt Elizabeth is standing.

Park College dormitory, 1904

Park College friends visit Winifred in Raymond, Mabel McGowan house in background

Residents of my mother's dorm at Park College.
Mother is in the standing row on the far right

Mom and Dad's wedding picture

Wedding announcement of
my mother and dad's wedding

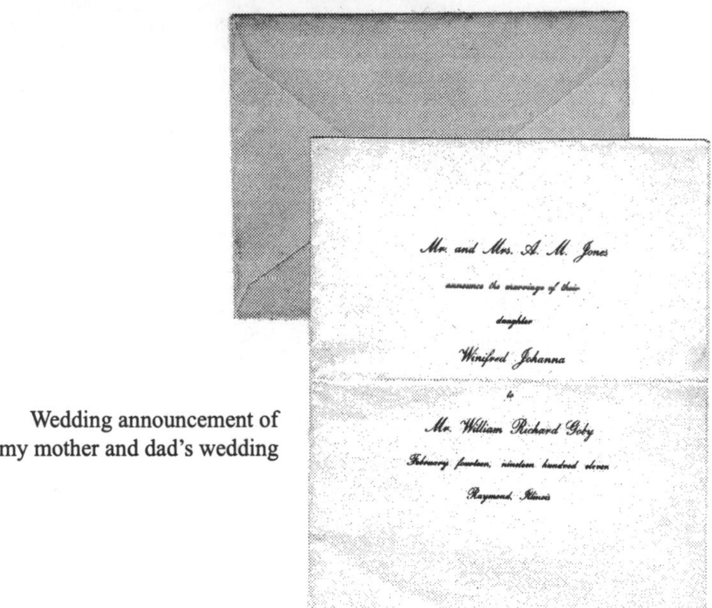

Mr. and Mrs. A. M. Jones

announce the marriage of their

daughter

Winifred Johanna

to

Mr. William Richard Goby

February fourteen, nineteen hundred eleven

Raymond, Illinois

Mom, Dad and me (at 8 months)

Albert W. and Grace Elizabeth Goby, 1916

Grace Elizabeth and Dorothy Foster with my brother (Sonny) in the swing.
He always wanted to wear my hats

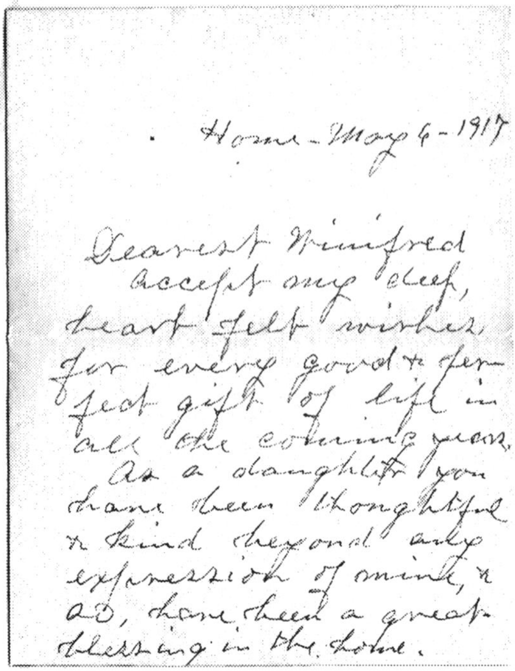

Home - May 6 - 1917

Dearest Winifred
Accept my deep, heart felt wishes for every good & perfect gift of life in all the coming years.
As a daughter you have been thoughtful & kind beyond any expression of mine, & so, have been a great blessing in the home.

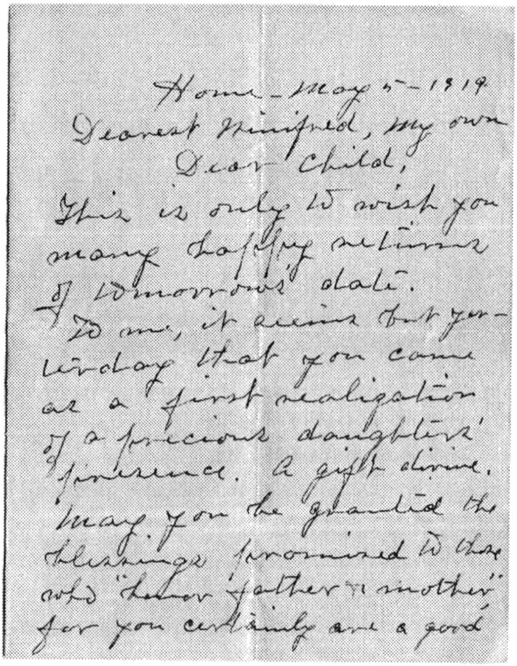

Home - May 5 - 1919
Dearest Winifred, my own Dear Child;
This is only to wish you many happy returns of tomorrow's date.
To me, it seems but yesterday that you came as a first realization of a precious daughter's presence. A gift divine.
May you be granted the blessings promised to those who "honor father & mother" for you certainly are a good

My Grandmother Jones' birthday letters to my mother, 1917 -1919 Grandmother Jones lived within 2 1/2 miles of my mother during these years, but with no telephone service. At this stage, my mother nurtured three children under the age of seven with only a horse and buggy to get her to Raymond and her parents.

Death Notices

In the early settlements in Illinois, the only way to notify the community that one of its citizens had passed away was by word of mouth. There was no telephone and, of course, no TV or radio. The community's general store became its communication center and the doctor or the undertaker would make it known to them knowing that the grocer would convey the word to those who came in.

With the establishment of a newspaper, "death notices" were printed immediately and given to local merchants who posted them near the cash register for all to see. My Grandmother Jones' youngest brother passed away in a state hospital in Lincoln, Illinois. His "funeral notice" appears below. To have sent someone to bring his body back to Raymond and to have his funeral within three days is almost unbelievable under the conditions that existed in the 1910's.

Strangely; when I was in Hermann, Missouri a few weeks ago I noticed just such a card near the cash register listing the passing of a Hermann resident just two days earlier. All the notices bore a black border that attracted the attention of anyone who came near. The undertaker is still a part of a community's network.

FUNERAL NOTICE

———

DIED—At Lincoln, Ill., on Saturday, April 1, 1916, at 2:00 o'clock p. m.,

Gustave Doerr

Aged 57 years and 28 days.

———

Funeral services will be held at the Presbyterian church in Raymond, Ill., on Tuesday, April 4, at 1:00 p. m., Rev. G. C. Alexander officiating.

Interment in Asbury Cemetery.

Friends invited.

Death notice for Gustave Doerr

Downtown Raymond, Illinois - 1920

Our favorite grocery store at Raymond belonged to A.W. Foster. The "uptown" area, across from the railroad track, was divided in half by a cross walk between Foster's Grocery and G.C. McLean's Dry Goods Store. My mother had worked at McLean's in her high school years. When you went to the grocery store, you bought what you hadn't raised. You took your accumulated eggs and whatever else - like lard, fresh fruit, home-made apple butter - and local people who had a reputation for being good sausage makers or experts in some other field, like home-made yeast, could leave their produce at the store knowing that Mr. Foster would tell everyone he had their products on hand. Peanut butter came in large crockery containers and was scooped out and sold on paper trays like we now see raw hamburger in. Dry yeast was displayed on the counter. A Mrs. Chambers had a reputation for good yeast. Occasionally, the grocer would find that some of the eggs you took in were too old to sell and, if the grocer wasn't too scrupulous, he could reduce your credit more than you normally expected. Of course, you would find another grocer if this happened too often and the disparity was too great.

Most grocers had a shelf of dry goods such as calico, flannelette, and muslin; along with hem tapes, braid, thread, hooks and eyes, and elastic. Only oranges and lemons were available all the time, but bananas were available on the weekend. My dad always took advantage of the grocer's prospect of over-ripe bananas and picked up a good supply at a bargain. It was even a better buy if he happened to be in Litchfield on Saturday night, for they had a fruit market with a greater variety. When you remember that we had no refrigerator at home, all foods were perishable. Even after we had an

Letterhead for Grandad's wagon and blacksmith business

ice box, it was only stocked with ice when we had harvest men to feed or on a special occasion. I never remember feeling that there was a shortage of food. Of course, the cellar was full of vegetables that we had canned the summer before. I remember being with my cousin, Ruth Boehler, when we returned to school in the fall. Even though we lived only two miles apart, we bragged about how many quarts of food we had canned the summer before.

Occasionally, my mother could get a freight order of foodstuff from Sears Roebuck and we'd have to pick it up at the railroad station. She always took advantage of those opportunities to get dried peaches, dried plums, raisins, prunes, and figs. I hated figs. She could also include dried fish in these selections, which we soaked in water to remove the salt and then prepared in a white sauce. Of course, we always had plenty of milk on hand. P.A. Sellers had a grocery store on the other side of town and Walter Molohon had a meat market with a few staple items in addition. The store served the farmers who brought their horses to the blacksmith's shop or wagon dealer. P.A. Sellers had a regular card playing group nestled near a heating stove and Frank Harris had a barber shop with bathing facilities. Of course, there was a pool hall on both sides of town. Lem Potts had the newspaper on the second floor of a pool hall.

There were livery stables on both sides of town, with nearby blacksmith shops and wagon and buggy shops. The livery stables housed the horses and buggies of the town residents, particularly the doctors and the bankers. My grandfather, A.M. Jones, was a partner in one of the early wagon-maker shops. This was when he came to Raymond in 1881 with his six year old son , George, after his wife died of tuberculosis. He married my grandmother, Etta Doer, a teacher in Raymond, in 1882. At first he was a partner in business with a Mr. Kennedy. The Haarstick Implement Company occupied that location for many years. My grandfather moved his blacksmith shop across the street beside Molohon's meat market. The railroad station was central to life in Raymond; as was the telephone company later, where Emma Yunker was central to everybody.

Faith Starts Here

"I can do all things through Christ which strengtheneth me." That was the first Bible verse I remember learning in Christian Endeavor meetings at Raymond First Presbyterian Church. It has probably been my most quoted Bible verse. L.D. Laswell was our minister at that age and his wife was our children's leader. They were an Eastern couple and they filled our Presbyterian pulpit admirably for several years. They were highly educated and did much to elevate the role of our congregation among other Presbyterian churches. Their son, Harold, was in an Eastern college at the time and went on to become a world renowned economist. His parents were nearing retirement during their Raymond years.

Rev. Laswell was followed by D.A. MacLeod who also had been educated in the east. His leadership allowed his congregation to personalize their faith. At this time, I was finding an active spiritual life in McKinley Foundation at the University of Illinois. Until Taylor and I moved to Peculiar, I did not feel an identity with any church or congregation. In Peculiar, we found inspiration in John Pihl's sermons and pastoral interest in his members. He had been a local farmer, trained in Methodist theology, but his pastoral concern came from his heart. He was casual in his manner and in his dress, but not in his philosophy. He died a short time after Taylor and I moved to Hermann, but he remains my ideal of a minister.

My grandchildren and I have frequent conversations about our beliefs, the role of prayer and how meditation makes its way into our busy lives. Our early lives might have presented a conflict, but when Morris and I were married in 1986, many of those issues had been resolved. I share Morris' membership at B'nai Jehudah. I have no plan to convert, for I find little at odds with contemporary Protestant religions. In fact, I find much of what I was taught as a child had its genesis in Judaism.

I still find Philippians 4:13 a solution to many of life's problems. The more I read, however, I feel that Judaism predated all the other theories. For it was Judaism that gave us the concept of one God and the freedom to make choices and find a personal relationship with that one God. I never could quite understand the painting on our Sunday School classroom wall. It was a painting of Christ among His elders all in rabbinical dress. My questions were answered but the answers never quieted my thinking. At least I was allowed to question. That doesn't happen in some denominations.

Sunday always meant a hurried breakfast in order to get to Sunday School on time. Church followed in only a few minutes, so if I saw Aunt Flora in her "chosen" pew across the church from our "chosen" pew, I would race across to ask her if I could go home with her. She was a tall lady and she would continue speaking to others as she made her way to the door, seemingly oblivious to my request. About the time she reached the vestibule, she would say, "Go ask your mother." And I would. In most instances, mother consented and I would be on my way to Grandmother's.

When we arrived, I headed straight for Aunt Flora's stack of old Pictorial Review magazines, for they had Dolly Dingle paper dolls in them. If I was lucky enough to find a magazine that my Goby cousins overlooked, she might just let me cut them out and add them to my collection. Believe it or not, kids used to brag about how many paper dolls they had. Dolly was a chubby little girl but she had beautiful clothes with matching hats and coats. By this time, I was becoming "chubby" too so I felt a particular kinship with her.

Communion

Today is Palm Sunday and I spent the breakfast hour with my loving brothers-in-law at Ari's Pumpernick Restaurant in an area that once was "up-scale" but now serves octogenarian Jewish and Gentile families who are still independent of the comfortable retirement villages nearby.

Next Sunday will be Easter Sunday and my recollections of this holy day in our Presbyterian church at home include weeks of planning and preparation. My earliest memories include Mr. and Mrs. Fensterman bringing quart jars of homemade grape juice and home-baked white bread which had been carefully cubed for communion service. The minister would repeat the Presbyterian liturgy to emphasize the symbolism of the wine signifying Christ's blood, shed for each of us and the yeasty cube of bread symbolizing Christ's body "broken" for us in the crucifixion. I was always impressed by the solemnity of the occasion, but I also felt that there must be a special place in heaven for the Fenstermans who prepared months ahead in order to supply these occasions. Today's communion service is no less symbolic nor solemn because of my recalling the dedication of the Fenstermans.

My mother's recipe box contained a not-too-old recipe for Communion Bread - 100 pieces. I assume that the Fensterman provision for communion gave way about the same time women found it practical to buy bread at the grocery store. I do recall that Paul Angles had furnished communion supplies for a few years. The Fenstermans are gone, the Angles are gone, Schulte's Bakery is gone, but communion Sundays still inspire dedicated believers to accept today's symbolic wafers in contemplation of communion's real meaning to each of us. Here is my mother's recipe:

Communion Bread (100 pieces)

1 scant T. Spry
4 T. water
Pinch salt
Flour to make stiff dough

Roll out to thickness of pie crust. Mark in squares and prick with a fork.
Bake very slowly, without browning.

The L.D. Lasswells

. My Sunday School class with my friend, Ada Foster, to the far right

I Didn't Learn to Cook on the Farm

The first day of my freshman home economics class in high school remains a bright occasion in my life. Hildegarde Haarstick (Folkerts) was my "stove-mate" and Ada Foster was our teacher. I already loved Ada because she was also my Sunday School teacher, not to mention the friendship of our mothers. Our first assignment was to make a white sauce in preparation for Eggs a la Goldenrod.

At that date, 1924, we prepared everything that needed cooking on a two-burner hot plate. There was a coal fired cook stove in the Home Economics laboratory for use when an oven was needed. I can recall one other duo in class, Blanche White and Catherine Welsh. I can recall Helen Luking, but not her laboratory mate.

White sauce was really nothing new to our cooking experience, but with this lesson we learned to begin with melted butter as a base, adding flour and milk. At home, we simply added thickening of flour and stirred it in the milk as it heated. Now it had a

Ada Foster; my Home Economics teacher, Sunday school teacher, and friend

name and was probably the most used method in my lifetime. It is also the most versatile, equally adaptable with vegetables or meats. With white sauce, you also had the beginning of tasty casseroles. I still make a white sauce with cheese when making macaroni and cheese where my mother layered the cheese and macaroni in a casserole, covered it with milk and bits of butter and expected the same result.

A buttery white sauce with extra milk to reduce the thickness becomes the basis for many soups. Whether or not Ada knew how basic this lesson was to our culinary future, it was a well chosen first lesson. I recall no other recipes, but I always felt I got an "A" in Home Economics for the simple reason that I could build the best fire in the cook stove. I always had the oven at the right temperature at the time the class arrived. Ada Foster was more than a teacher to me, and her mother was more than an "aunt." If there are lumps in my white sauce now, I know I didn't follow Ada's directions.

Alleys

When I think of all the things that are not a part of my life today, but were significant in my early life, I have to catch myself or I am tempted to say they are missing. They are not missed. The world has just managed to find alternatives, and in most instances, for very good reasons.

I am thinking particularly of alleys. The alley behind my grandmother's house in Raymond was a ribbon of lush grass. Each home owner took the responsibility for the tidiness of his own part of the alley and had no doubt that his neighbor, across the alley, would do the same. A few of the neighbors had small outbuildings abutting the alley for a few chickens or for garden tools, but they too were always neat.

The alleys were very important in facilitating deliveries to homeowners. Coal was the most immediate need, for most homes had a coal shed in the alley that provided coal and kindling for the cook stove or heating stove. The milkman came down the alley early in the morning and filled the blue enamel milk bucket my grandmother put out for him each night. Sometimes, she put out a quart bucket. If she was expecting company, she would place the half-gallon bucket that provided a recessed space at the top where the cream could accumulate. Without refrigeration, this daily service assured her sweet milk in the summer months. In the winter, she need only use her back porch. Eventually, she had an ice box and the ice man used the alley to deliver ice. She would indicate her need for 25 pounds or 50 pounds by displaying a square card the ice man provided to be placed in her kitchen window. In wintertime, the ice man became the coal man so he provided for his family year round. The coal man I remembered was Lee Gilbert.

As the automobile made it possible for larger dairies in nearby towns to supply milk in glass containers, the milkman disappeared from the picture and milk was delivered from the front street. The electric refrigerator replaced the ice man and, gradually, gas and oil replaced the coal man. By this time, the alleys were becoming extensions of lawns and flower gardens. Grandmother had a pussy willow tree at the edge of her alley and an assortment of iris that continued up along the sidewalk to her back door.

Hermann, Missouri had the most interesting alleys and some of them were actually still needed to provide access. Our bed and breakfast homes were located on Second and Third Streets and backed on an alley lined with hollyhocks. We always called it Hollyhock Alley.

Saturday Nights

If you've ever been cooped up in the house for a week, you'll understand just what a treat it was for us to go to town on Saturday night. Of course, the stores were about ready to close before my dad would get cleaned up and in the car. We usually had to take the hired man home and occasionally my dad would have an errand to run.

By the time we got to town, there would be no place left to park on Main Street, so we had to park around the corner where there were no street lights. While Dad would get out and chat with whoever he ran into, we were left to swelter in the car. Parking around the corner also meant that we were parked by a hitching post. By late evening on a summer Saturday night, we were exposed to the fumes arising from the waste deposited by the horses that had hitched there earlier in the day.

After an hour or so, we would have convinced my mother that we were desperate for a drink and reluctantly she would let us go to the town pump in front of George Back's ice cream parlor to get a drink. There was a tin cup always available on the pump and that was what everybody used. I'm getting goose bumps writing about this. To think we were exposed to all those germs (without antibiotics) and survived! Rugged characters.

When we were lucky enough to get in town earlier in the evening, we could park on Main Street and we would see friends and relatives on the sidewalk. Sometimes there would be two or three girls (or boys) walking up and down the street, seeming to enjoy it. But my mother told me we must never do that because the girls were only doing it to attract the men. I was interested in the girls' pretty clothes and at that age, I didn't know what the men were interested in.

I sometimes think of all the things we were told "nice girls" don't do and wonder why they didn't spend that time telling us about life or about boys. Then we would have known what was naughty and what was nice, or at least acceptable.

As we would leave for home, my dad just might get us a lollypop at George Back's Ice Cream Parlor. A lollypop consisted of a dip of vanilla ice cream on a lollypop stick that was stuck through a milk bottle cap, dipped in dark chocolate, and frozen until solid. Of course, they would melt fast and be dripping on our clothes by the time we covered the two and a half miles home. We'd all race for the well to get a cold drink. It took me a long time to realize that the longer I waited my turn, the cooler the water would be.

The Chautauqua Lady

In our small town of Raymond, in the 1920's, the local merchants would underwrite a Chautauqua program during the summer season. For a period of two weeks during mid-summer, an entertainment group would come to town with a variety of evening and afternoon performances, as well as morning activities for children under the supervision and direction of "The Chautauqua Lady."

The community furnished volunteers to assist her in the morning programs, which varied from music appreciation, to art instruction, dancing, public speaking, and other skills. The families who had bought season tickets would take their children for morning sessions and at the close of the season, their children would perform in some way to justify their parents' support. The evening sessions brought skilled artists, speakers, and humorists to entertain the adults.

To this day, when I see a stately middle aged woman, I recall the Chautauqua ladies. They were impeccably groomed, had perfect manners, and I always wished that we lived in town so that the Chautauqua lady could stay with us. My mother managed to get us to the morning sessions in spite of the fact that this was the busiest season of the farmers' year.

There were prizes offered for all kinds of activities, but the only prize I won was for identifying classical music played on a portable Victrola. That attested to my listening skills and the Chautauqua ladies' ability because we were never exposed to classical music at home. My dad did buy a Cable player piano. Mable Sharp and Jesse Bently tried valiantly to teach me piano. Occasionally, my mother would have Cecil Marten (a girl) help her during harvest time. Dad would always encourage Cecil to play her, and his, ragtime favorites after lunch.

Dooryard Gardens Made Cooking Fun

My recollections of my mother's birthplace are limited. I know it was a two room German style brick home flush against the sidewalk with a two room loft above. More importantly, it backed up to the railroad track. In fact, it was probably there when the railroad was built. The tracks separated Raymond into two areas, "this side of the tracks" and "the other side of the tracks." The Jones place was directly across the tracks from the Bowles place, so Mrs. Bowles and my Grandmother Jones became good friends. With a growing family, however, the Jones family moved to the north edge of town where they could have a pasture, a garden and an orchard. While Grandad succeeded in growing food for his family, Grandmother was equally diligent in maintaining a dooryard garden of herbs to season whatever produce Grandad grew in the garden or stored in the cellar.

With luck, you would have a dooryard garden on the south side of your house, in which case you could gather herbs until Christmas and you would welcome the first green sprigs of spring. Parsley dominated the dooryard garden and was Grandmother's first choice of seasoning. Chives, thyme, sage, rosemary, and marjoram filled in near the steps and petunias took over beyond that.

When I visited Hugo's mother in Concordia, Missouri, there was another south side dooryard garden. Garlic and sage dominated her assortment, for she enjoyed making sausage and needed both in quantity. She, too, had little bouquets of herbs tied with string drying behind the cook stove each fall.

My Grandmother Jones loved parsley, not just because of its flavor, but because it made everything else look so pretty when she served it. Her mashed potatoes were always fluted with a table knife into a sort of volcano with a dollop of butter and a sprig of parsley at the apex. The parsley was her "signature."

The Telephone

I can't remember when we didn't have a telephone. It was a long apparatus connecting two boxes, one of which held batteries. The space in between provided the mouthpiece and a slanted shelf for writing easily. The receiver hung at the side in a special hanger and when you removed it, you could hear any other conversations on the line. Calls were so infrequent at the beginning that if you took your receiver down to answer your call, you would hear receivers in other homes coming off too. There were usually eight or ten other people on your line… You did not have a telephone number identification. Instead, each home had a certain telephone ring like a long, short and a long ring or two shorts and a long. But you soon learned to identify the ring that was intended for you.

If you wanted to call someone on a line other than your own, you had to go through "Central." Central on our telephone system was known as Emma Yunker. Central facilitated all the mechanical operations incident to a small switchboard. She also knew of any emergencies in the homes of her subscribers as well as the doctor's visits and the progress of his patients. Emma had very able assistants and she confined her activity to the night shift. Grace Luking was a sister of my best friend, Helen Luking. It was a real treat to go to the telephone office, taking lunch for Grace, for she just might let me call my mother and tell her I was at the switchboard making the call. I remember that my grandmother's first telephone number was 31.

Earlier, I remember my mother calling Dr. Lipe, the local veterinarian, asking him to come and attend to one of my dad's cows or pigs. One time, when I would not take the medicine my mother wanted me to take for a cold, she threatened to have Dr. Lipe come and give me some calf medicine and she picked up the receiver to call him. When Dr. Lipe asked why I had started avoiding him at church, she had to admit that she had used his name in vain. She didn't do it again.

Stitches in Time

Elsewhere, I've told you I was named "Grace" for my mother's best friend who became a skilled dressmaker in great demand. In addition to all the accouterments of dressmaking that most families had, Aunt Grace had dress forms matching the measurements of the ladies for whom she was sewing at the time. She had the added advantage of her mother's skill in dressmaking also.

When she was busy making the garments her customers ordered, as she finished the machine stitching, she would throw the garment toward her mother's rocking chair by the window. There, her mother would begin the fine hand finishes: hooks and eyes, buttonholes, and stays to support the high collars. I can still hear the swish of the taffeta or silky fabrics in vogue at that time.

Most often, however, the customer would have more than one person for whom she wanted clothes made and would arrange for Aunt Grace to come for "two weeks in March" to do her sewing. Pre-Easter sewing was heavy, as well as preparation for school. Then there were weddings. Beading was still done by hand. Not only was the wedding gown a masterpiece in stitchery, but the petticoats underneath were equally ornate. The dress-form holding a wedding dress was draped with a sheet when not being worked on to be sure no one got a glimpse of the bride's dress before the wedding day.

Later in life, after the death of her parents, Aunt Grace married an older widower, Albert Chapman. I happened to be in Raymond the weekend his estate was auctioned. I hope the four Eastlake chairs I bought were Aunt Grace's. They surround my Grandmother Jones' drop leaf table now, for sentimental reasons.

Another Stern Taskmaster

I was on the phone the other day with the Alumni Office of the University of Illinois checking on their latest information on Meyer Abramovitz. I took advantage of the office to ask them for the phone number of the Zoology Department. When I was a freshman, in 1930-31, I had worked in the Zoology Department office. I did not work for Dr. Henry B. Ward as emeritus head of the department, but for him in his capacity as the head of the American Association for the Advancement of Science.

Dr. Ward had had twenty-three secretaries in the last twenty years, I was told, and was quite a "stern taskmaster." For the outer office secretary, her assignment was simply "a job" in a time when jobs were scarce. In fact, she was back home in Urbana because she had lost her job in New York. She tolerated Dr. Ward. For me, having been assigned to him by the Dean of Liberal Arts, I felt very fortunate. I had also been alerted to his idiosyncrasies because my Aunt Elizabeth had been his student in Graduate school.

It wasn't long before Dr. Ward wanted me to work more hours each week and at thirty-five cents an hour, I wanted to work all I could. I went to Dean Browne again to see if I could get excused from P.E. because that would free up two hours a day, three days a week. Dean Browne told me: "If you stay with Dr. Ward until he retires, I'll excuse you from P.E. for good. No one stays long." But by that time, Dr. Ward and I had a very comfortable relationship; mostly because I'd grown up with the same type of taskmaster in my family... my dad. You'll understand why I'm including this when you reach Dream IV.

In 1933, the American Association for the Advancement of Science planned a "congress" of scientists from all over the world as a part of the Chicago World's Fair which would mark a Century of Progress. The Washington office of AAAS was busy making all the arrangements, but they hadn't reckoned on pleasing Dr. Ward. Dr. Ward, on the other hand, took a dim view of these "illiterate" clerks in the Washington office. His physique was overpowering. Slightly more than six feet, he paced back and forth as he dictated, looking across the campus as he chose each word. He was doddering but not palsied and, in his well hewn professorial voice, he painstakingly assured his readers of his position on matters of interest to the Association. He would bellow as he became emphatic, reaching to remove his glasses as he felt he'd done justice to his responsibilities with the Association. All octogenarians doddle but when Dr. Ward doddled, he also jingled for the watch chain stretched across his vest carried so many "keys" and medals they almost played a tune when he was agitated.

One day, when he was writing an associate, he dictated: "I know as much about what is going on in the Washington office as if I lived in Kamchatka." When I asked how to spell Kamchatka, he bellowed: You don't know how to spell Kamchatka? Do you know how to spell Los Angeles?' I nodded. "Then put Los Angeles!" he said. As soon as he finished dictating, I hurried to the huge dictionary in one of his laboratories and looked up Kamchatka. "A sable bearing peninsula off the coast of Russia," if my memory is correct. So I used Kamchatka in the finished letter.

The World's Fair arrived and Dr. Ward was in Chicago to do the honors to his scientific colleagues when Sam Woodley, from the Washington office, telegraphed me to come to Chicago forthwith because Dr. Ward was "confused." I was to receive $12.50 for three days work, in Chicago, and I did as I was told. I took dictation from a variety of scientists whose names I don't even recall, but I do remember Robert A. Millikan whose achievement with Mt. Palomar was current in 1933. Later that year, Dr. Ward was selected as the "world's most famous zoologist" and this was reported in <u>Life</u> magazine. Our computer carries no biographical material but we did find reference to the Henry Baldwin Ward Medal Awards for the American Society of Parasitologists. I had pasted his picture on the inside of my closet door at home, thinking it would not be disturbed… but it was. At the University, Dr. Ward was banished to South Campus in the third floor laboratory upon retirement. Occasionally, he called to ask me to help him catch up on correspondence. As I breathlessly reached the third floor, he would smile and greet me as "My Elizabeth." Strangely, he's still my Dr. Ward. There is no Zoology Department now. It's Ecology. Dr. Ward wasn't ready for such inclusive recognition.

(My great granddaughter asked me if I remembered the Depression)

Dear Catie:

I'm so glad you asked me if I remembered the Depression. Of course I remember those years, but at the time, I didn't know it was a depression! We didn't have daily newspapers, we didn't have TV, and radio was limited. You see, we were used to doing the best we could with what we had to do with. According to our parents' occupations; they encountered more or less difficulty in conducting their business, getting financing for large expenditures, and selling whatever it was they produced. My dad was a farmer. We always had plenty to eat. Mothers did not work outside of the home so my mother could make over hand-me-downs and if she was fortunate, she could find dress material in a remote corner of the grocery store, which was no super-market. Every family raised everything they could and bought factory made products only when necessary.

The stock market crashed in 1929, and I was just out of high school. That year, I got to go to business college in Springfield, Illinois. It was thirty-five miles from home. The college would find room-and-board jobs for its students. A year later, when I finished the secretarial course, I got a job that paid $12.50 per week. Out of that, I paid $3.50 a week for my sleeping room with breakfast. You walked every place you went or took the street car which sold you three tokens for twenty-five cents. A movie was ten cents and, on certain nights, they might also give you a piece of china or colored glass; enticing you to come frequently so that you could accumulate a whole set... hence, today's "depression glass" collectors. You did your own hair with a "water wave" or a "marcel" which required a gas heated curling iron. Cosmetics came from the local pharmacy, who occasionally got a supply of teensy Tangee lip-sticks that turned an appropriate color when they were exposed to air on your lips. The worst part about lipstick was that your parents thought it was wicked, so you used it away from home or put it on in the back seat while your dad drove to church.

As I said, we really weren't aware of the depressing part of the Depression. By 1930, my family insisted that I enroll at the University of Illinois but they left it to me to figure out how I could afford it. All of my mother's brothers and sisters had graduated from Illinois and all were teachers. Again, I worked for my board and room, but I also worked as a secretary part-time in the Zoology Department for thirty-five cents an hour. At Champaign, I became more aware of the economic upheaval, for the campus was crowded with Chicago students whose parents could no longer afford to send them to Northwestern or the University of Chicago.

When Roosevelt was elected president, he surrounded himself with scholarly advisors in all fields and the picture began to change. The press referred to his advisors as his "brain trust" and he founded the HOLC, Home Owners Loan Corporation. This enabled home owners to refinance their homes with low-interest loans which they would be able to repay over longer periods of time, if they had a job. Since there were no jobs, he founded the WPA, Work Progress Administration. With this, small and large communities found it possible to build libraries and court houses, as well as to update their sewer and water systems. He also founded the REA, Rural Electrification Administration, which brought electricity to rural areas where utilities had not wanted to invest. We had telephone service at my home as long as I can remember, but it was 1941 before my folks had electricity.

I left the university with seventy-four hours as a pre-legal major and went to work for the local power and light company at $100.00 per month, much to the disgust of my school-teacher aunts. With Master's degrees, they were teaching school for less than that and every move they made was scrutinized by the local school board or the wives of the board members. As a teacher, you could not marry, could not date, could not wear lipstick, could not wear high fashion clothes, and could not leave town over the weekend without the permission of the local school board.

Had it not been for the desperation of the Depression years, the changes Roosevelt effected would have taken years. For, left to their own energies, the states would not have taken the initiative. We always had "poor houses" and "poor farms" where counties would reluctantly dole out a modicum of food and clothing, but not with the idea of helping you redefine your life so as not to continue the problem. Roosevelt's "brain trust" served his administration for $1.00 per year. Hillary Clinton should have asked her healthcare advisors to be as generous. When we each received a social security number in 1936 (another Roosevelt idea), everybody said it wouldn't work. But it has and it does and your generation will have to see that it meets your needs too.

While I was a student at Illinois, I was secretary of the newly formed Young Republicans. It didn't take long to find out that the "old" Republicans weren't interested in the ideas of young people. I hope, and I truly believe, that attitude will change with a lowered voting age and the advantage of the evening news keeping everybody informed. During the Depression, families looked out for their own, shared their homes, their belongings, and their hopes and dreams of a brighter tomorrow. That brighter tomorrow is NOW! We now have excellent public education, health insurance, social security, equal opportunity, nation-wide transportation, mass communication, and the freedom to set our own goals. I was 84 this week and my goal is to be 85 this time next year and still believe in this great country finding the most compassionate solutions to its problems.

Betty Taylor-Yeddis
May, 1996

11 October 1959

Dear Winifred, Will et al:

George telephoned me from Cleveland that Milton
had gone. It seems that their son Johnnie came over from
Milwaukee at once - he was there at the time she telephoned,
and I got to talk with Johnnie too. Bob was expected in from
Chicago soon; but it has been several days now and I have heard
nothing since.

It was very fortunate indeed that I got to go to
Cleveland last May and to spend some time with Milton and George.
It was as much of a visit as I could make without imposing on
them quite unduly. I realized that it was just possible that it
might be my last chance to talk with Milton - and it was very
difficult to hold much conversation at that time.

Now, one can take pleasure only in the memories;
and there are many and pleasant ones. Actually we were reasonably
close, considering the fact that so many years and so many miles
have separated us during the past thirty years or so.

During the early years it seemed to me (then) that
I was at a great disadvantage in being the younger and necessarily
looked upon at times as a tag-along-kid. Not that such was too
often the case - nor that it bothered me; it did not. It was just one
of those fleeting conditions that exists in a family of children.

As we grew older I encountered many advantages in
having an older brother. Milton always possessed a skill in drawing
and in such things as whittling with a pocket knife. I remember so
distinctly the set of chess men that he whittled out and with which
we learned to play chess - reading the rules from that old cyclopaedia
which you too may remember. You see, Milton was able to read the rules
and show me how the game went; I supplied the raw material to try the
game on. Nevertheless, I profited greatly by having him to associate
with in such activity.

Of course there were times when, as little brother, I
felt very much imposed upon; since I was so often cast in the role of
a mere helper; Milton being the one to initiate and carry on the
immediate project, whatever it may have been. I remember once how he
shouted for me to "come here"."hen I got out of the house and to where
he was busily working at something or other he said "hand me the hammer".
It seemed such a preposterous request that I shouted "NO", and then ran
like the devil - expecting the lightning to fall on me. I remember that
he merely laughed; seemed preposterous to him too, I guess. Strange
what inconsequential things a kid remembers! Sometimes I learned from
him too. I remember once, when I must have been about eight or ten,
that I placed a chip (an actual wood chip) on my shoulder and cockily
told him to "knock it off". Kid like, I had thought he might merely
tip it off. Instead he just hit me a good wallop - and it fell off.
I learned a lot in that minute; probably has stood me in good stead
ever since.

It was probably during Milton's High School days
that I profited most from his more advanced views and greater
intelligence. He and Mr. Thacker were greatly interested in
things electrical, and I did valiant work as a helper in the
things they wished to make. Needless to say I probably learned
a great deal more than they did - which is just another way of
saying that I had so much further to go. Anyway it gave me an
interest in things electrical, which I followed throughout the
days I spent in University physics; and which has led to the bit
of success I have had in life.

When I was at Lake Forest, and the year Milton was
there too, I was working with a light sensitive material on a
laboratory project. I still remember that Milton told me to keep
in mind the possibility of development of television. I must have
looked quite nonplussed at his suggestion, because I still
remember that I had not even thought of such a development; he
was just that far ahead of me in thinking.

The time I spent in the two wars, slight though
the participation was, produced a bit of a change in my own way
way of looking at life - bringing a view that I think has helped
in my general outlook; fatalistic though it may be. Two flights
in particular helped form the viewpoint. Two days after Pearl
Harbor I was given the chore of flying the extreme west coast-
line as far up toward Alaska as gas capacity would permit; to
determine whether there was a remote sandy beach from which the
Japs could operate a fighting squadron. Flying along there 100
miles from anywhere one just naturally gave up worrying about
whether or not there would be a return to base. The second time,
in late 1944, I was 500 miles out over the Atlantic with a four
engine bomber - and one engine showing sickness. Since I was
doing the flying at the moment I was more aware than the crew of
the possibility that there might be no return. Well, that led to
the view that if one does not get back just what difference does it
make? Actually it makes no difference! Just an other way of saying
that one might well look at life as all velvet from here on out.
Personally, I think I have lived long enough. True, there are a lot
of things I wish to get done and I'll do my best to get them done;
but I am just not able to do any worrying.

Milton and George were most fortunate indeed in
having Bob and Johnnie firmly ensconced with wonderful families.
What more can a parent wish than to see his children well on their
own road through life. Parents may then feel quite justly that
their mission in life has been accomplished.

Ann and I made a very, very hurried trip to San
Francisco a couple of weeks ago. The trip was so hurried, and so
unpredictable and unpremeditated that I did not even get to see
Bobbins and her family inBerkeley. I was in Berkeley for a couple
of hours (Bobbins was away at the moment) and did get to see the
Berkeley High School people. Although I had arranged for the
gold key awards that now accompany the cash benefits that are
awarded under the Florence D. Jones Memorial Awards the School was

careless enough that not even I had seen one of the gold keys.
I suggested to them that it might be a clever idea to send one of them
to each of Florence's brothers and sisters; which they have done. Thus
the reason you, too, should have received one.

The awards have been paid out at the rate of about
a dozen or so each year; and we can have some reason to feel that
a bit of good has been accomplished by them. That bit of help in
encouraging academic effort is as Florence would wish it, I believe.

Ann and I are both enjoying reasonably good health,
although either one or both of us is on a diet now and then for
reasons that are all too indefinite. Also the success of the diet
is usually quite indefinite. Anything unusual about that?

A letter from Elizabeth a few days ago tells that
you, Winifred, are able to carry on more and more of your many
activities. More power to you.

Please give our very best to Albert and his family.
I shall never forget the pleasure in the dinner they arranged for
us when I was there in May. What a wonderful family!

With live from the both of us.

Lloyd

Uncle Lloyd's reaction to the death of his brother, Milton.
Uncle Lloyd developed "Mountain View Garden of Memories."

9 February 1950

Dear Elizabeth & Emory:

As a matter of fact I think that I have not written for so long that neither of us can remember when. You and Winifred are so much more energetic, and accomplish writing while I do not.

We have not been up to Berkeley since last July, at the time Florence was operated on - although I was there then. We had hoped to get together with Florence at Christmas time. However, she did not feel up to traveling. On Christmas Day both Ann and I found it advantageous to remain in bed - with quite unusual colds. Mine ran a couple of degrees temperature for a day or two - but nothing came of it.

It was nice of you to send me the book. Ann had got copy of General Arnold's Global Mission. I was so glad to have it. On Pearl Harbor day I had picked up General Arnold at the San Francisco Airport and brought him up to the Presidio to see General Dewitt. Arnold was as surprised as anyone else that day, and had asked immediately "what is the news"? I talked with him several times both before and after that. He was exceedingly capable. I had a very nice letter from him at the close of the war, in appreciation of the work I had done as a Base Commander.

You and Winifred are skilled in ceramics in a way that I shall never be able to duplicate. The things you have made are perfectly beautiful. Up to date I just have not found a clay in this region that has ceramic possibilities. During the past year, however, the search has not been so diligent. Other activities have intervened. A fellow named Gowen and I own some two or three thousand aces of the surrounding desert, some of which is capable of being made into an alfalfa farm, I mean ranch! Of course the problem is water.

You just would not believe that we have not had so much as an eighth of an inch of rain during the past twelve months. It means of course that there is always a dearth of water - although there is a fair supply of water by drilling wells; until the population gets to be too great. For the one alfalfa ranch we drilled a well which turned out to be most excellent. Had to drill 1254 feet but have a well that flows (artesian) some 340 gal/min. This is suitable for irrigating about 34 acres. We have some fifteen acres of land all cleared, levelled and wetted - so that it is nearly ready for seeding. Since we can not do all the work personally we are hoping to carry the project along sufficiently to attract a lessee; so that we can start another project.

The second ranch, two miles from the first, on another section that we own looked very promising at first. However, we are drilling a well there that is not turning out well at all. We are down 1100 feet and have no water - just almost exactly none. Very unusual to encounter no water, but life is like that! Costs about $5000 to drill such a well. That particular ranch may have to continue to grow sage brush.

Lots of other pieces of property that we have are for home sites and such, and always have a bit of a market; enough to bring in a few pennies now and then.

The 160 acres next to the Golf Course, which Ann and I own is continuing in absorbing development work. We have not yet been interested in disposing of any of it - since the price will be a great deal higher a little later. We have a couple of wells on it, a lake-swimming-pool-reservoir and some bits of landscaping done. We have variously considered building our own home there, but lack the incentive to start soon. Costs are so darned high - but they are not going to be any lower, it seems. All the trend is quite the other way.

It was certainly unusual for you three sisters to be in the hospital at one and the same time. I think that Florence is getting stronger continually, but the recovery rate is always so much slower than one can desire. I hope that you and Winifred are recovering at least equally well.

Wishing all of you the best in the world. Love.

Lloyd

Uncle Lloyd at home with his sister, Florence D. Jones, in Berkeley
Uncle Lloyd's letter records purchase of two or three thousand acres –now Las Vegas
(See obituaries p. 68.)

66

Obituary for Lloyd T. Jones from the Las Vegas Sun, 2/9/64

Lloyd Jones, LV Investor, Dies at 76

Funeral services are pending for Lloyd T. Jones, 76, a prominent Las Vegas real estate investor.

Dr. Jones, who held a Ph.D. as a physicist, was born Feb. 20, 1889, in Raymond, Ill. He was a retired Air Force colonel and was commanding officer at Fort Dix, N. J., from 1941 to 1945. He held a number of patents on inventions.

Dr. Jones lived in Las Vegas since 1945, and had extensive real estate holdings in Clark County. Jones Boulevard was named after him, and Jones Road was named after his widow, Ann Greta Jones of Las Vegas. He was chairman of the board of Real Estate Investors Corp. of Las Vegas and was a member of the Las Vegas Chamber of Commerce.

In addition to his widow Dr. Jones is survived by a daughter, Mrs. Margaret De Roche, Berkeley, Calif., two sisters, Winifred Goby and Elizabeth Reish, Raymond, Ill., and two grandchildren.

Obituary for Col. Lloyd T. Jones from the Raymond News

Col. Lloyd T. Jones Commanding Officer At Fort Dix, N. J.

Col. Lloyd T. Jones, former commander of Olmsted Field, Penn., has been named commanding officer of the Fort Dix Air Base. He succeeds Col. William H. Garrison, who was transferred to Memphis, Tenn.

A native of Raymond, Ill., and a former professor of physics at the University of California, Colonel Jones began his military career in 1917 with the royal flying corps of Canada. He studied the Canadian system as a pattern for the U. S. army air forces ground schools. Upon the entrance of this country into the World War, Col. Jones served as an instructor and at army air forces headquarters in Washington before being discharged in 1919.

Following his release from the army, he was professor of physics at the University of California until 1928 when he entered a private engineering business. His company was a pioneer in the unionmount welding process, now used in nearly every American shipyard for heavy steel welding.

Colonel Jones is a son of the late Mr. and Mrs. A. M. Jones of Raymond. He was born and reared here and graduated from the Raymond High school. Mrs. William Goby and Mrs. Emery Reisch of this city are his sisters.

JONES, Col. Lloyd Theodore, 76, 1812 Goldring Ave., retired physician and engineer in research and Army Colonel, died Feb. 7, at Southern Nevada Memorial Hospital. A resident of Las Vegas for 18 years, he was born Feb. 20, 1887 in Raymond, Ill. He is survived by his wife, Ann Greta of Las Vegas; a daughter, Margaret Jean DeRoche of Berkeley, Calif.; two grandchildren and two sisters. Winifred Goby and Elizabeth Reifh, both of Raymond. Funeral services were held Feb. 11 at Bunker Brothers Chapel with Rev. Walter Hanne officiating. Burial followed at Mountain View Garden of Memories.

Las Vegas Review-Journal,
Tuesday, February 11,1964. p. 30

February 11,1964

Lloyd Jones Funeral Set Today

Funeral services for Lloyd T. Jones, 76, a prominent Las Vegas real estate investor, will be 2 p.m. today in Bunker Brothers Mortuary with Rev. Walter Hanne officiating. Burial will be in Mountain View Gardens of Memory.

Dr. Jones, who held a Ph.D. as a physicist, was born Feb. 20, 1889 in Raymond, Ill. He was a retired Air Force colonel and was commanding officer at Fort Dix, N. J. from 1941 to 1945. He held a number of patents on inventions.

Dr. Jones lived in Las Vegas since 1945, and had extensive real estate holdings in Clark County. Jones Blvd. was named after him and Jones Road was named after his widow, Ann Greta Jones of Las Vegas. He was chairman of the board of Real Estate Investors Corp. of Las Vegas and was a member of the Las Vegas Chamber of Commerce.

In addition to his widow, Dr. Jones is survived by a daughter, Margaret De Roche, Berkeley, Calif.; two sisters Winifred Goby and Elizabeth Reish, Raymond, Ill.; and two grandchildren.

I've Had Three Home Towns

I grew up in the 1910's and 20's near Raymond, Illinois. We lived in central Illinois, 35 miles south of Springfield and two miles from Raymond. Going to town always meant hitching up the horse and buggy, unless the men weren't busy in the field and then it might be ready for my mother's trip. She always had errands to run, but I'll bet it was more important for her to see my Grandmother Jones. We didn't have to plan to see Grandad Jones, for his blacksmith shop was right at the corner when we turned onto Main Street. In summertime, we started out nice and clean. But with an inch of dust in the dirt roads, it didn't take long to get dirty. There were no safety belts in buggies and one day, on a return trip, my brother fell asleep and fell out of the buggy. He was about two years old. He wasn't harmed, but my mother chided herself for allowing this to happen.

Hometown I - Raymond, Illinois

Raymond was established as a stop on the Wabash Railroad with stockyards and pens for shipping cattle and hogs. The business area reflected the farmers' needs. Early on, it had a telegraph station and I remember Mr. Nettleship and Percy Greenfield as operators. Townspeople had easy access to St. Louis, Chicago and Decatur. Farmers would drive their animals to the railroad by guiding them down the road with enough helpers from the neighborhood to keep them headed in the right direction and not allow them into neighbors' driveways or other roads. Someone from the farm would have to be on hand when the freight train pulled into position to load its cattle cars the next day. Someone usually rode in the cattle car sleeping compartment to be with the animals at market time the next day when their animals would be sold at prevailing market prices.

Services for farmers, implements and repair, were at each end of Main Street with long hitching rails to accommodate customers' horses while they contracted their business. Individual merchants of other supplies might have single hitching posts in front of their stores. Primarily for horses, the town provided watering troughs in some areas. In front of George Back's Ice Cream Parlor was such a watering trough but it also had a shiny tin cup for those who wanted a drink.

You always referred to merchants as Mister, even though once back home you might use their first names. I don't recall a merchant who was disrespected, but some bore more scrutiny than others. Women were happy to have Dessie Leitch in town with her millinery shop. She actually made hats from the bolts of braid and veilings she kept on hand, but since she wasn't married, they worried about their husbands! She did marry - our hired man. By the time Mary Poggenpohl opened her Variety Store, people no longer worried about women merchants.

In the summertime, the local merchants would sometimes present open air movies to bring people to town. Sometimes, there were band concerts on the band stand that also filled the needs of local politicians. I can still recall the names of everyone who lived along the street from the high school to down-town. Some were referred to as "aunt" and "uncle" because you grew to have a sincere love for these aging residents; many of whom had moved in from the farm and turned their acres over to younger family members.

No one had credit cards and few people "ran an account" with individual stores. In an emergency, a merchant would voluntarily extend credit. Seymour Drug Store had a few chairs around a heating stove for customers with a few min-utes to talk. P.A. Sellers, on my Grandad's side of town, had the requisite chairs but also a wooden barrel that supported a large wooden checkerboard. Of course, the barber shops provided conversation and on Saturdays, they pro-vided a bath for regular customers.

There were two banks on the far side of town, across the railroad; The State Bank and The National Bank. While Lem Potts published The Raymond In-dependent, the telephone held the town and outlying community together with Emma Yunker as "central." Central equaled 911 in many instances, alerting neighbors when help was needed.

Our school teachers were revered for being so dedicated to the village's chil-dren. Few were from a distance. We had basketball only for sports, in the wintertime. Most teachers "roomed" with local families. Women teachers dressed very conservatively; no bright colors, no makeup. They did not date. If they wanted to leave town for the weekend, they sought the permission of the school board in advance.

The churches maintained their own identities and, in most cases, were founded by early families. Next to the banks, they exerted the most influence on the town. Raymond was typical small town America in the 1920's. Though I lived two and one half miles out in the country, Raymond was my home town; my first home town.

Kansas City never earned the role of home town, in my thinking. Taylor had grown up near Warrensburg but came to Kansas City in 1921 after service in World War I. He found work with a cab company in an upper-class area known as the Hyde Park / Valentine area. The cabs were all Cadillacs. The owner paid for full lunches for his drivers, but would never pay for a sandwich.

I came to Kansas City as my jobs in wartime construction wound down in the early 1940's. It was in those years that I met Morris, who was on deferment from military service because his employer had wartime construction contracts. Kansas City never became a candidate for "hometown" in those years.

I don't know how I survived the next fifteen years. I married Hugo Brackman, had my son Bill in 1947, and was divorced in 1951. With Bill as the center of my life, I managed to stay alive. No job I had provided a future and every time I changed jobs, I was reminded by my family that I had not finished college nor had I prepared myself for a satisfying occupation. I had gone to business college and was an expert in shorthand with above average speed. I also felt I had let my mother down, but she knew she hadn't been able to offer me any alternatives. It was in connection with a kitchen remodeling firm that I finally found acceptance. My boss accidentally told me one day that I sold more than the men in the department, and I had always been in awe of them. I had never thought of myself as a salesperson. It turned out that it wasn't the kitchen equipment that I was selling, but the decorative millwork that I suggested to my customers. This would increase the value of my sale.

I was in Topeka at this time and I would come into Kansas City to get estimates for counter tops and louvers, etc. On one of those trips, Norris Limpus at Limpus Woodcraft mentioned that if I was using this much of those special items, other people must be looking for them too. He offered me a job in his operation in Kansas City. He said that if I would come, he would inventory the materials from the suppliers I referred him to. He kept his word and anything he didn't want to inventory, I was free to sell from some other source. Finally I had a job I could enjoy, and I

Residents of Alpha House,
University of Illinois, 1931

could be in Kansas City again. And I was selling. Mr. Limpus had an almost uncanny ability in sizing up customers. One time, he told me that he never wasted any time on a prospect until he could see the palms of their hands because they weren't in the mood to be sold until they relaxed. If there was a problem in the shop, he would lean back in his chair with his feet on his desk, toying with a pen or pencil, and finally go out to the shop with a solution for a better way of doing things. I left Limpus Woodcraft when I married Taylor, but Taylor went to work for them and remained there until his retirement.

I became executive housekeeper at Menorah Hospital shortly after I married Taylor. The administrator insisted that all of his department heads have degrees or be in the process of getting them. With the University of Kansas City right across the street, I took my twenty-six year old transcript from the University of Illinois to the College of Liberal Arts. In Illinois, I had taken classes that were offered at the time I could take them, for I was working for the head of the Zoology Department for thirty-five cents an hour. Without too much time reviewing it, they said, "The only thing you can do with this transcript is teach." I always felt this statement revealed the respect they had for the School of Education! Fortunately, a mature Dr. Marksberry led me into the exciting field of remedial reading and school librarianship.

The Brackman Years

At my mother's death, there was a large brown envelope in her desk labeled "The Brackman Letters." By that time, Hugo and I had been divorced 14 years. Since our son, Bill, was 18 at the time, I put the envelope aside thinking he and I would read them together at an appropriate time. They were my letters to my parents. In preparation for this book, I thought it an appropriate time. After weeks of searching, we have not been able to find these letters. I know I saw them when arranging my lower level family room since we moved to Barrybrooke in 1995. At this stage, I feel that I wasn't supposed to include them. I don't know whether mother saved them because they revealed my rationalizations about deciding to marry Hugo - and ten year old Richard - so soon after breaking up with Morris. She may also have saved them to record the mental anguish I endured for years before asking for a divorce. Anyway, it spares me the necessity of explaining details of what the letters said. The fact that she saved them is a compliment from her. Perhaps they will be found after I am gone.

Hugo Brackman February 21, 1907 - 1970

Hugo Brackman was one of the pharmacists in Brecklein Drug Store at 9th and Grand. My court reporting office was in the same building, the Rialto Building. Doctors and insurance companies occupied a large portion of its offices.

Pharmacies had soda fountains for the convenience of their customers and other drop-in business from the street or nearby offices.

I had just broken up with Morris Yeddis because I was not Jewish and his parents objected to his "keeping company" with me, particularly since his military deferments would soon come to an end and he would be going to the service. I spent hours transcribing courtroom notes and mopping away tears. Before the drug store closed, I would get a bite to eat at the soda fountain and perhaps another box of Kleenex. Hugo told me that his wife wanted a divorce. She had already moved in with friends and his ten year old son, Richard, was with his Grandmother Brackman in Concordia, Missouri. I referred him to an

The Goby Family Tree as designed by Winifred Goby

attorney for whom I worked frequently and he proceeded with the divorce.

Richard came to spend the weekend with his father frequently and on some visits, the pharmacy would let him deliver filled prescriptions to doctors in the building. If he had time, he sometimes stopped in my door and asked if he could read the funny paper for a few minutes. By late summer, Richard realized school would soon be starting and the trips would be less frequent. One

Betty Brackman's TV show, "Home and Garden Time" Topeka, KS at WIBW

day, he asked if I would go to the show with him, but that day I couldn't. However, I said perhaps I could another time. We went to the show two or three times on subsequent visits. On one occasion, he asked, "Why don't you marry my dad so I can live with you?" He also told his dad he had asked me. Obviously, my next purchases took a little longer.

Morris and I had stopped dating eight months earlier. I was thirty-one years of age. My family doctor had always said I could have no children. Perhaps this was the only son I could ever have, I thought. Hugo was an honor graduate pharmacist. That ought to please my parents, at least my dad. My mother hoped I would marry Morris. "Jewish men make such good husbands," she said. "Aunt Christine was so happy with Ed Leberman." Hugo and I talked it over several times in the next few weeks and Richard kept asking us to listen to him. We finally decided to marry on October 23, 1943, in the Chapel at Park College where my mother had been a student. In that way, she might feel a part of our planning even though none of our family would be there.

TV Guide magazine, Week of March 19-25, 1954

Richard's mother had remarried but he had never asked to be with her. She drove by his school playground at recess, and he was gone. I was heartsick but I felt I had made the right decision and I knew Richard had not been deprived of anything or our love. It was a real blow to Hugo. At the time, I was getting medical help for my weight and it was working for a time. I sought my regular doctor's advice and learned that I was pregnant, about four months pregnant. My son, Bill, was born April 23, 1947. We were both overjoyed.

Hugo's dependence on alcohol became more noticeable and since my family had always considered drinking a sin, I was reluctant to tell them. My mother and my aunt visited us and were shocked at Hugo's behavior. Of course, he blamed me for his drinking. His bosses called me to tell me their experiences. As a result, we were divorced in 1951. He and Bill remained close the rest of his life. His health became worse and worse and he died of cirrhosis of the liver in November, 1970 at the age of sixty-three. His father had died in 1914, during the flu epidemic when Hugo was seven. I often wondered if that was a factor in Hugo's use of alcohol. Tearfully, it is time for me to say that Bill, my son, also died of cirrhosis of the liver in 1993.

Hugo Louis Brackman, 1907 - 1970

Darling Baby Billy & Mama Betty –
We are so happy to know you two have met and been formally introduced at last. We hope you really like each other a lot, and even things up for Papa Brock, who loves you both so much – Then I hope you have a "wee love" left for the rest of us. Oceans & mountains of love & good wishes – Grandmother and Grand daddy –

Grandmother Goby welcomes Bill Brackman to the world in a postcard

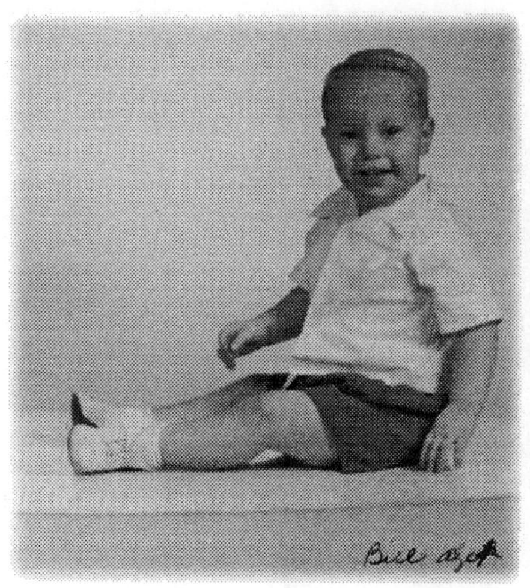

Bill Brackman at age 1, 1948 and age 3, 1951

Dear Billy –
I am so glad I told you what a fine doggie Boots was and how much Grandaddy loved him for he was struck by a car and killed instantly later that morning. He is buried in our garden. He was always alert to Grandaddy's needs and so happy when he came home after a few hours away. We miss him and wanted you to know he has gone to be with all good doggies.
We hope the weather will be good so we can see you Thanksgiving day.
With lots of love,
Grandmother.

Grandmother Goby tells Billy that his dog has been struck by a car

Hugo, Alvin and Elmer with Grandma Brackman

Four Brackman Brothers: Walter, Hugo, Alvin, and Elmer

Larue Brackman Welch and VonCile Brackman Heerman
with Betty Taylor in Hermann at Der Klingerbau

William and Winifred Goby on their 50th wedding anniversary in 1961
Winifred passed away in 1965 and William in 1970.

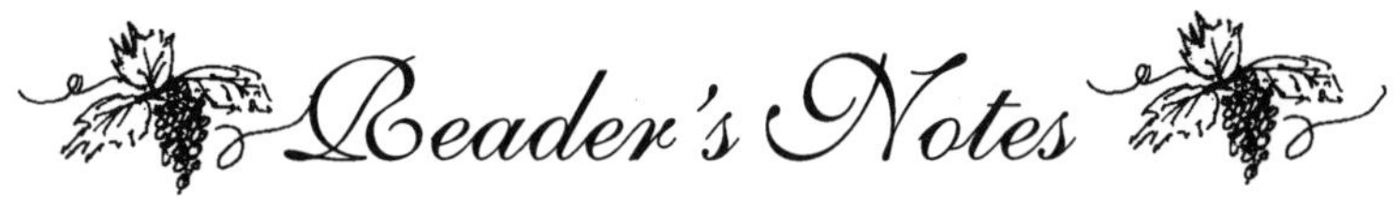
Reader's Notes

Reader's Notes

Reader's Notes

By now, page 84, you realize that there really isn't
an established sequence to these vignettes of the
people, places and events recorded in RECIPES,
RECOLLECTIONS AND REFLECTIONS. In fact,
you may have already encountered a repetition here
and there. These recollections began with a packet
of materials I provided for a family reunion…our
first family reunion of the Goby family. They were
MY recollections then and they have not changed.
Some of my cousins would no doubt have recollections at variance with mine…or their memory might
be more exact for I am 86 years old, 300 miles from
home, and memories become idealized under such
circumstances. The longer I live the memories seem
more vivid…like yesterdays.

At this time, the adjectives and verbs appear more
accurate and the pleasure of remembering more
idyllic. Taylor never realized that his happy devotion
to our daily activities would find its way into print.
Morris knew that he had lived up to his father's and
his family's expectations. Was there more?

Yes, there was…and because of Morris' careful
planning for these late years of my life, I'm able to
assemble these wonderful recollections and share
them with you.

Fondly,

Betty Taylor Yeddis

A hillside home beside
a babbling brook......
... Brockwood

Dream II

1958 to 1973.....Brockwood,
Peculiar, heritage, Belton,
the Antique Taylors.....

The Taylor Years

When Taylor came back from military service in World War I, the Roberts family no longer needed his services on the farm. Some of the Roberts children had moved to Kansas City to find work, At their invitation, Taylor also went to the city to look for work.

At that time, the hub of Kansas City was in the Armour to 47th Street area. The Armour-Valentine area was home to many wealthy families and several upscale residential hotels. Few people owned automobiles and many of those who did had chauffeurs. Many of the people who did have automobiles did not have garages, so they housed their vehicles in public garages. These garages were called "liveries" because they operated much like the old livery stables had.

Taylor was employed by Armour Auto Livery at 3125 Main Street in Kansas City. He would have been just as much at home with

William M. Taylor: 1960
Taylor joined a Walnut Grove school photo evening. He was at home in any world and Walnut Grove was no exception. Any man who survived the Battle of Verdun in WW I could easily adjust to being a school teacher's husband.

horses as he was with cars. The owner used all Cadillac equipment and catered to a Cadillac-style clientele. He insisted that his drivers eat a full lunch or dinner at his expense but would not compensate them for sandwiches or between meal beverages. From the perspective of 1997, it is also interesting to see his business card emphasizing careful drivers serving the Hyde Park and Westport areas from a Home Bell Phone 123.

Taylor worked intermittently after the Chevrolet plant opened in the Leeds area. Their production, however, was sporadic and completely at the mercy of the market and the economy. At the time I met Taylor, he had a tractor and a team. He served the area around Waldo and 75th Street, which was then the southern edge of Kansas City. Hugo and I had just acquired a lot on 84th Street and, in this post-war era, were allowed to build what we could afford. The lady next door referred me to "Taylor" who plowed gardens on request and could be reached through the McCall Filling Station on Wornall Road. I contacted him and drew a scale drawing of our lot. I was expecting Bill any day.

While I was in the hospital, Taylor plowed the garden. Years later, when we were married, when Taylor cleaned out the garage in preparation for moving, the scaled drawing fell out of a box.

On May 20th in 1958, Taylor and I were married in the Presbyterian manse in Excelsior Springs, Missouri. Small Presbyterian churches are rare in this part of Missouri where Baptist and Christian congregations compete with Methodists to serve the spiritual needs of the community.

Taylor had been a long-time friend of the Brackman family. He was always responsive to our calls to fix this or that. He was equally accessible to South Kansas City families, an area that was still outside the Kansas City limits.

Hugo and I were divorced in 1951 when Bill was four. We lost track of Taylor. When we stopped for gas at McCalls, I learned that he had gone to Florida. One day when I was working at Miller Screen & Door, Taylor stopped in to see me. He said he had seen Hugo at Parkview Drug on Wornall Road and he had told him where I was working. He asked where I was living and I told him that I had bought a co-op apartment near the VA hospital after Hugo and I had divorced. He was surprised by the news of our divorce, which by that time had occurred six years prior. He stopped by again, unannounced, about two weeks later. I invited him to come back the next week and said I would fix a fried chicken dinner for the occasion. He always talked about the impromptu chicken dinner that he had enjoyed at our house years earlier.

My mother was always concerned about my driving back to Illinois with Bill, fearing that in a hurried trip I might fall asleep or have an accident. So, as her birthday approached, I asked Taylor if he would make the trip with us and he accepted the invitation. My folks were relieved to know that I had such a gentle, helpful friend. I didn't read anything into our friendship; for I really didn't know if Taylor had been married, who might be back in Florida, or who "Aunt Em" and "Aunt Lou" were. I didn't even know where he lived or who the lady was that occasionally answered his phone.

When Taylor asked me to marry him, I was peeling potatoes in the kitchen while he leaned on his elbow and watched my every move. Without too much hesitation, I told him that I would not make a good wife, for I had been in love with Morris Yeddis since my late twenties. Morris and I could not marry because I was not Jewish, but he still filled my heart and I told Taylor this. (I believe that for the same reason, my marriage to Hugo didn't have a chance.) I kept on peeling potatoes. He repeated his suggestion and finally said, "Let's try." When I got a quiet time to talk things over with Bill, he was so enthusiastic about the prospect of having Taylor in our family. I decided to put my own reservations aside for his sake, not without some apprehension, but having no idea of the great life that lay ahead.

Taylor was sixteen years older than I was. He had an eighth grade education but had been educated by a vigorous life, including military service in France in World War I. He was at ease in any group of people, was a loving companion, a perfect collaborator, a great host, an in-house handy man, and a lousy cook. He was a 62 year old bachelor, never married. When I told him that somebody had to have had a hand in making him such a mellow fellow, he

Armour Auto Livery business card, front and back

told me of Daisy. She was the niece of Aunt Em and Aunt Lou. Daisy had died of breast cancer about ten years earlier. He never told them he had married until he took me to Bentonville, Arkansas to meet the Aunts. They weren't exactly delighted. Aunt Em was a widow whose husband had been a railroad engineer. She was a matriarch-patriarch, if there is such a thing. She had a prize-winning herd of goats that Taylor always helped her show in livestock exhibitions. Aunt Lou had been a modiste in ElPaso where she had a workshop of Mexican women who made wedding gowns and bridal parties. By this time, she was bent double and her hands were so gnarled with arthritis that she could barely busy herself in the kitchen. They purchased the Pickering lumberman's home on Janssen Place and they enjoyed every morsel of its elegance next door to Notre Dame de Sion Academy.

Today, Taylor and I would have been married 38 years. I never cease to be thankful for our 27 years together. Clyde and Ruth Parker, his friends, witnessed our wedding in1958. When I called them at the time of Taylor's death, Ruth explained that Clyde was very ill and they wouldn't be able to attend services. I remember what she said, "I just want to tell you what a great life you provided Taylor." And what a great life he provided me! With the stability of his companionship, I got to go back to school. I finished a BA and MA degree. I spent seventeen years teaching and retired in 1977 to realize a lifelong dream of having a tea room to serve my grandmother's food. In press materials about our restaurant and our subsequent bed and breakfast efforts, Taylor's gentle and happy "hosting" received as much recognition as my culinary efforts.

I am so glad that I can not only remember, but can put these recollections on paper. I've shed a tear or two in the process of recalling these years. As you know, Morris and I became reacquainted and later married. It was he who suggested that I keep Taylor as a part of my name, because the Taylor years had been the most creative part of my life. Retrospection fills my days and keeps me healthy, if immobile.

Taylor's home at 7919 Mercier, Kansas City, Missouri It had been outside the city limits when built, but by 1958, the city extended much further south.

William and Betty Taylor with son, Bill Brackman: 1959

Monday

Dear Mother and Daddy:

If one could only know what the good Lord has in store for you
it might be simpler to arrange your day-to-day life but that is
impossible so I've found your prayer to "show me the way" more
satisfying than to attempt your own solutions and find your
prayers unanswered. Last fall I felt a real "glow" to think
that after all I'd been subjected to in recent years it might still
be possible for me to make a happy home for my Billy boy to
make up for the omissions up to date. Then the surprising thing
to me was that when that dream faded I was mentally equal to
the ordeal without it's taking my heart with it. Billy and I both
feel that all of this has been preparation for a happy family life
with Taylor and that while making him happy, we will really be
a "family" for the first time.

While we've known him for years and grown to have the greatest
respect for him, the idea of sharing our lives and my son has
developed in the last two weeks. It was nothing I knew or even
thought possible when I was home for I felt that after having
lived serenely all these years, he could never find it in his heart
to assume the responsibility for our happiness. To see him in
my own home, however, made me very receptive to the idea .
So far as I am concerned, the difference in our ages is no factor
knowing what a wonderful outlook he has on life for, certainly, he
has not "aged" as much as Bill's father. While I am considering
my own happiness, too, I probably wouldn't be concerned about
remarrying if it weren't for Bill's future, but I feel that the next
few years are the critical ones and I need the help of someone as
understanding and stable as he. Too, Bill is still boy-ish enough
in his outlook to appreciate Taylor for what he means to him where
later on it would only be a source of happiness for me .

In the last few days I've met his closest friends and "family" and
truthfully, I wasn't so sure they'd be too happy about the idea of
Taylor taking on a ready-made family but they had nothing but
the nicest comments and think it is wonderful for both of us.

I hope you will find it in your hearts to accept him as your
son-in-law with the same love and grace that you accepted Betty
and Al for he is just as "real" a person as they with the most
wonderful philosophies to smoothe life's "bumps." To know that
he loves me and my son is ample reward for the problems I've
had thus far. I hope I can make him a good wife and that in time
I can inherit some of his quiet, stable manner. I'm glad that
over a period of months I've had the opportunity to look at life
as it can be and that I was mentally ready to make this decision.
Please grant us your love for at this stage, that is the only
assurance we lack. Had it not been for the trip home, however,
I think things would have progressed along an entirely different
pattern...if at all.

We are to be married Tuesday at 5:30 at the Presbyterian Manse
in Excelsior Springs with a man and wife who are his closest
friends for our attendants. We plan to have dinner with them
afterward and be back home about 8:30. Billy was going with us
but has decided not to and some friends of ours in the Village
where we live are "minding " him for me. They had a little
"girl" party for me Friday night to mark the occasion. We
decided on my birthday to be married so I had an opportunity to
announce it at sorority meeting the Wednesday night following and
they were so happy. Most of them know Taylor or his family and
it just seemed there was a real "ripple" of approval as Betty
Burkett did a beautiful job of the announcement. Everyone thought
the box of candy she had wrapped and beside her was a secret pal
gift so it was a real surprise...and of course, the next meeting
is at my house so it was much better to do it then. Mr. Crawford
thinks it will be wonderful for Bill but thinks Taylor must be a little
"touched" to go overboard at 60. This morning when I came in he
told me to take the day off tomorrow and when I told him I wanted to
go home after school was out and would rather take the time then,
he told me I could take it then too.

We are going to live in my apartment but will probably dispose of
the house on Prospect and probably Taylor's property too, however,
there are some trafficway changes that may influence the value of
his property and he may rent it for the time being. At any rate,
we are going to be "at home" at my house.....and now I know why
I've loved fixing it so.

Needless to say, I'll be anxious to hear from you. Believe me when
I tell you that Billy and I are not only as happy as can be but feel
that we"re mighty lucky to have Taylor love us so much that he wants
to be part of our family. As you know, this decision has been months
in the making...but never believed it could have such a happy ending.

Please remember us in your prayers for Bill and I both believe
this was God's plan and realize he does "work in mysterious ways"
to accomplish his plan.

With all our love,

Betty & Billy

Dear Mother and Daddy:

All day Monday I wanted to call you but decided it was best to write
for we're always so inhibited on the phone. Now, having talked to
you I feel a great deal better but I still want to get home again as
soon as I can, for I had no idea this would happen when I was home
and, yet, Taylor has been so thoughtful of Bill and me for so many
months that I certainly could not help but listen when over Mothers
Day weekend he told me just how he felt about Bill and me. He said
that if he had come back from Florida and found us living on Prospect
under the same circumstances, he probably would have just gone on
back, but after having heard about what had transpired and knowing
that I felt nothing would ever develop to my advantage from the
recent associations I had had, he felt that he could properly explain
his feelings.

Up until then nothing had been said except that one day he told me he
felt that perhaps he had lived 60 years just to look after Bill and me.
At that stage I felt it would probably develop into something more if
I could get my mental "house" in order to accept the idea. I was
afraid that after having been alone allthese years it would be hard
for me to please him but we discussed that all the way through. We
discussed the fact that it would mean new financial responsibilities
for him for no doubt he has had such minor demands on him that
he could work when and if he chose. He has always worked hard until
the last seven or eight years with tractors and trucks and headaches
but in recent years he's been working almost entirely with TV and feels
he can continue in that now that we can be settled down. We have decided
to live in my apartment and to sell his house and my house as we feel
the market develops but in the meantime to rent them. Everyone
asks if I am going to keep on working but I feel as long as my work
associations are so pleasant I will feel much better for, after all,
we will be raising my son and I think he needs him now and not ten
years from now.

Last weekend after we had our license he took me to meet his "family"
and some of them are blood relatives and some are families with whom
he has been associated just as he has with us for years. They were
all very pleased, it seemed at least, and all spoke about how wonderful
he had always been with children and how much Bill and he would mean
to each other.

He hasn't paid any attention to clothes for years but instead of
being hidebound about his ideas in that respect, he has followed
my suggestions oompletely and I was quite proud of him yesterday
afternoon. Clyde and Ruth Parker who are in their early 40's were
our attendants and R .th cried after it was all over.   Taylor kept
expecting the "part" where you're supposed to get nervous, he said.
He had picked out my ring by himself and did a real nice job of it.
I had asked to be married in Excelsior Springs since the license
wouldn't appear in the KC papers and there would be fewer explanations
and questions asked.   Then I looked up the Presbyterian minister
there to be sure it wasn't a dilapidated old church since this is such
a Christian and Baptist area, and it all went off very well. We had
planned to have dinner at The Elms in Ex. Spgs. which is the " spa"
hotel of national note, but we drove in rain going over and were through
at 6:00 so drove on back to have dinner here afterward. Clyde and Ruth
brought me a lovely white corsage with sprays of rhinestones in it
which seems to be something new in corsages. Then our neighbors in
the Village had a little get-together which lasted until about 9 p.m. and
Betty Murdock and her husband (a sororitysister of mine) had baked
a wedding cake and decorated it for us and that was quite a gesture on
her part for she is five moths pregnant, has just had the measles
herself and now her 7 year old has chicken pox with a 2 year old in
line next.   So I felt we had to go out there and so it was about twelve
when we finally got back to my house. Bill, in the meantime, had been
with his buddies for dinner and then had been home with us until we
went out to Betty's . When we got back he was sound asleep on the
davenport and I couldn't help but enjoy watching Taylor take his shoes
off and get him to bed just like he was a little baby.

So much for the details until I can get home to talk to you. The main
thing is this......please bear in mind that it is my happiness and Bill's
that is at stake. Taylor is giving us the opportubity to live a healthy
family life and I'm going to work at making him never be sorry that
he gave up so called "single bliss" to nurture a ready-made family that
is slightly battle scarred. Everyone who knows him and who knows me
thinks it is wonderful for all of us. The only omission in my mind to
date is yours and Daddy's blessing. Without that I couldn't be happy under
any circumstances but I think I deserve it this timewithout its being
coated with austerity. If it hadn't been for the trip home I think I would
have delayed until I could have made one but that is behind us. Someday
I will have to be without you and Daddy and surely you will allow me to
share you with a man who is determined to make me and Bill forget
the nightmares of the past. Bill and I are starting this new life without
reservations.   Please go along with us.

Love to you both,

Original letters from Betty to Mother and Father regarding her decision to marry
Taylor: May 1958 Hoping for approval from my parents, I try to explain my decision to
marry Taylor. Dad never read my letters. Mother read every word and in between the lines.
(She had hoped that I would marry Morris years ago.)
At this time, she was not only concerned about opening her heart to Taylor,
but reluctant to acknowledge that Morris would not be a part of my future.

Recollections

Shortly after Taylor and I were married in 1958, I became executive house-keeper at Menorah Hospital, which at that time was located just across the street from The University of Missouri at Kansas City. The hospital administrator was a very well educated man who had great goals for Menorah, as well as his own career. He wanted all of his department heads to have college degrees, at a time when few colleges offered programs in institutional management. Dutifully, I arrived at his office with a twenty-seven year old transcript from the University of Illinois that showed seventy-three credit hours.

Actually, those seventy-three credit hours were an exaggeration so far as academic work was concerned; for when I entered college, I had to find a job as fast as I could. In 1930, the prevailing wage on campus was thirty-five cents an hour. So you took the job and rearranged your class schedule to provide the most hours for working. As a consequence, my transcript really did not reveal any academic goals. It said I was a pre-legal student. I did as he suggested and took it with me to have it evaluated by the Liberal Arts College at UMKC.

They told me the only thing I could do with those credits was teach. They didn't refer me to the School of Education or make any other suggestions. I really had the feeling that because I was referred by the hospital, and perhaps because I was forty-six years old, they thought I was not a viable candidate for admission. A few days later, I called for an interview with the School of Education. Dr. Marksberry, a mature lady, questioned my motivation but she did say that with my previous experience, she thought I would make a good elementary teacher.

I knew my family would be glad to know that I was going to try again to finish school. My grandmother had taught, my mother had taught, and my mother's two brothers and two sisters were either teachers or administrators. Now I had to convince Taylor, and he was most agreeable.

Dr. Marksberry became my advisor and we became good friends. By the next fall, she had referred me to a teaching position in a rural school just outside Harrisonville. I started teaching in a one-room school, just like my grandmother and mother had. In the same period of time, the role of the school librarian had become a requirement of Missouri schools. My degree in remedial reading would be an asset. From the rural school in Cass County, I joined the Peculiar school system. At the same time, I completed a Masters Degree. In 1963, I became the Junior High Librarian in the Belton school district. I retired from there in 1977. The emphasis on education had shifted markedly since I was told that all I could do was teach.

Walnut Grove School near Harrisonville: 1961
My grandmother, my mother and I all started teaching in a one room school.

Belton Junior High School, Study Hall and Library: 1963

As I reflect on my University of Illinois pre-legal transcript, if I had had the resources to continue in law school in 1933, I probably would have found the fulfillment I longed for. In legal practice, every case would have been a new experience and every verdict an achievement. A failure would be experienced as the basis for further study. But in 1933, I was only interested in a job with a living wage.

Reflections

In the late 1960's, I traveled from South Kansas City five days a week to teach at Walnut Grove school. The daily trip became monotonous, but as I learned more about Cass County and its heritage, I became curious. And then there was Peculiar, a tiny town just large enough to make you slow down as you negotiated the two curves in the four blocks that brought you in town and took you out of town.

Since Taylor was more familiar with this part of the country, I asked him where the blacktop road next to Raby's gas station led. He told me it wound around over the hills and ended up just east of Raymore. When the first mild days of February assured you that, in spite of the wintery weather, spring was not far off; I decided to venture through the hills. In a short distance, I came upon a quaint country cemetery surrounded by a beautiful Victorian iron fence just a few hundred feet off the blacktop. As I paused to soak up the environment, which reminded me of Asbury Cemetery in Raymond, I noticed a real estate sign for Y-Lane Acres just across from the cemetery entrance.

As I turned the corner to continue my journey home, I found myself at the top of a steep hill and at the bottom a not too sturdy rustic bridge. The bridge crossed a small meandering creek that made its way between natural rock outcrops bordering a much wider creek bed. Continuing home, I couldn't wait to tell Taylor that I had dared to venture over the hills.

Where I grew up in Illinois, there were few creeks because the level farm land was drained by drainage districts. The few creeks near Raymond were a place for picnicking and wading during the summer months. Taylor joined me on the trip one day and together we visited Y Lane Acres and the beautiful little cemetery. By this time, the woods were alive with red-buds so the hillside was even more fascinating. This time, we drove down the hill and loitered on the rickety bridge long enough to look back up the hill to assess the corner's possibilities as a home site.

I had put the idea of building out of my mind, for I was still working on my degree. Taylor's buddies at the doughnut shop in Belton had told him that the "Y" in Y Lane stood for a Mr. Young, who lived in Belton. We spent the next Saturday morning walking from the cemetery road to the creek, counting the red-buds and wild crab apple trees while watching our step to keep from crushing the carpet of violets in our path. By this time, we knew there were five acres in the lot, including the creek and a half acre across the creek. We were both in love with the lot and Taylor could identify every bush and tree. I could visualize a hillside home with tall white columns, a beautiful view of the woods and the winding highway. We had everything but the money.

A week or so later, a Realtor called to tell me that the doctor next door to my rental house on Prospect would like to buy my property to expend his parking area. Taylor's tenants had told him several times that they would like to buy his house, so we knew it was marketable. On March 1, 1961, we celebrated the purchase of the lot by clearing it sufficiently to let Taylor in with his truck so that he could trim the remaining trees. Within six months, we traded Taylor's house to the builder for the plan on our lot. It would eventually be ready for us to finish the interior and arrange for the mechanical trades.

In our dreams of the future; my son, Bill, and I had always talked of a country place called Brockwood (for Brackman). By this time, Taylor was such a great part of our life that we decided to call it Brookwood, and so it is. Taylor rests in the little cemetery across the road and the tombstone says they are expecting me some day.

Hometown II - Peculiar, Missouri

My first teaching assignment as I worked on my degree was at a country school near Harrisonville. As I drove back and forth each day, I wondered where all those country roads led. It also occurred to me that I was the third generation of country school teachers in my family. My mother had met my dad when she taught Lily School near Raymond. My Grandmother Jones had been a teacher in a two room school in Raymond when she met my Grandfather Jones and his six year old son.

On a slightly springy evening, on my way back to Kansas City, I ventured down one of those inviting country roads and came upon Peculiar Cemetery with its beautiful wrought iron fence and entrances. Just like Asbury Cemetery in Raymond, I thought. Across the road and at the corner, someone advertised five acre tracts for sale. Taylor searched out the owner. By this time, I had a degree and a contract to teach a split 5th and 6th grade in Peculiar. We closed the deal on March 1, 1961 and spent the weekend cleaning up the lot. By the summer of 1962, we had a beautiful new home on the lot exactly like the one I had planned in Sophomore Home Economics class in Raymond. Peculiar would be our next home town and my son, Bill, was ecstatic at being in the country.

In 1965, I lost my dear mother who was part of every dream I ever had. I finished my Master's Degree and Taylor and I now had time to enjoy life. My students had asked so many questions about local history for which we could find no answers. As I searched where I could, I found Carrie Nation and Missouri's struggle during the Civil War as the "burnt district." With Irene Webster of Harrisonville, who lured others with similar interests, we organized The Cass County Historical Society. We found every little town had a story.

Brookwood - The Peculiar Home: 1962

In a speech one night to the Lion's Club, I said, "A year from tonight, Peculiar will be 100 years old," and I continued with its history. As I sat down, G.C. Wills sprang to his feet and moved that the Lion's Club sponsor a centennial celebration. Someone else stood immediately and moved that G.C. Wills serve as chairman of the event. Three months later, when they had asked me to write the history of Peculiar, I complained that I was an outsider. "But you'll research it," they said. And for the next eight months, our dining table was covered with notes and history books. <u>A Peculiar Heritage</u> remains to document a lively community and, as the book says, in the process I became a Missourian.

Taylor now rests under that beautiful old pine tree on the lot he picked out in the happy years. When Taylor and I were putting <u>A Peculiar Heritage</u> together, we became known as The Antique Taylors. Our interest in

The "babbling brook" in the winter snow

early history had given us an appreciation of what it took for early settlers to tame the countryside so that it would provide a living. Our collection of Missouri primitives was enviable. Our appreciation, even greater.

Peculiar was never our "hometown" in the Raymond sense, but Ed Ullery's lumber yard, Jack Braun's Meat Market and Grocery Store, Raby's Gas Station, and Ed Schug's bank were the town's cordiality committee in uptown Peculiar. "Hometown" changes its meaning with each decade. Our family still compares round steak to what we got at Jack Braun's but Ullery's lumberyard has no counterpart now.

With my dad's passing in 1970, we no longer needed to make the trips to Raymond. But we did get to mid-Missouri to Kallmeyer's Auctions frequently. Joy referred us to other sources of handmade German primitives. One of these collectors was Doone Jackson in AuxVasse. Not only did she educate us to the identification marks of true primitives, but she referred us to printed sources describing these early furniture making techniques. She showed us true primitives in an old bank building in McCredie, just north of I-70. She also told us she was going to have to vacate the building, for the whole property was for sale.

With the help of a local bank, we arranged to buy the property that had been the town of McCredie. Only the half lot that had been a community hall remained, but it was held in trust by several elderly ladies for the McCredie community. We had little hope of getting it but we made an offer to their attorney. By now (1970's), it had no windows left in it and the doors stood open all the time. Our offer was accepted. As we finished renovating the house so we could overnight there instead of at a motel, a thoughtless paper-hanger stuffed the heating stove with wallpaper scraps and burned the house down. Our insurance left us with the property clear, a bank building and a community hall.

As I did needlework in my living room in Peculiar, Calico Cupboard Antique Village became a dream, and later a sketch. Calico Cupboard gave life to the tea room dream of my mother's and mine. We put a double-wide trailer in between the bank building and the community hall. It would just be for week-end dining because I still had three years to teach at Belton before retiring. In 1974, <u>Missouri Life</u> found us and did a great article about us with beautiful photos by a great photographer. Hermann's historic leaders visited us one Saturday evening and, as they helped themselves to food from our quilt covered buffet table, they said, "You belong in Hermann." Shortly after that, on a trip to Hermann, Wilford Kallmeyer stopped me on Wharf Street. From his truck window, he said that he had heard I was looking for a building in Hermann. I could see his building in my rear view window. When I asked when it would be available, he said two years. That would be 1977 and I would be retired.

CHRISTMAS GREETINGS from Peculiar, Missouri!

Last year we looked forward to 1968 as "the Peculiar year"...and so it was! We never thought we'd write a book but we did...and it's over...with A Peculiar Heritage, hard-bound, 387 pages, available from the Lions Club of Peculiar at $7.75 postpaid.

The newspapers kept you informed about our Centennial which far over-shadowed the community's expectations. The Historical Society's antique show - another first for the Taylors - yielded $900 for our museum fund.

Bringing our antique shop home to Peculiar has been a great blessing. After the Centennial we built a "French barn" type shop, surrounded it with stockade fence and a brick courtyard and now we have a most appropriate setting for the antique business nestled among the trees on our hillside...which is disappearing daily with the advent of a new highway back of us which will join new 71 Highway and leave us about half a mile from the exit.

Taylor still enjoys his school bus duties and, of course, I'd be lost without the Junior High Library. My father seems much improved this fall and his companion has recovered sufficiently to be with him again during these confining winter months. Bill is still with Art Bunker Volkswagen and he, Joan, Timmy and DeAnn are looking forward to a countryside home of their own before too long.

We hope the sketches 'longside will clue you in to what our surroundings are at present....and just in case you overlooked the postmark, be assured that we overlooked nothing in Taylor-ing this message to you for 1968. (We found this teensy spot and a dear friend was our accomplice.)

It is an extreme pleasure to thank you for the part you played in making 1968 great. We wish for you a joyous Holiday Season. Quoting from the Heritage, "Let us ...put aside personal prejudice and tradition, as we seek the common good..'one world' under God... in which all men are equal."

Sincerely,

Bill and Betty Taylor

P.S.: Just after writing this Betty suffered a severe whiplash injury in an accident near Columbia. How extensive the damage is will be determined by tomorrow"s x-rays and examination but she is most uncomfortable just now...and slowed down to a "crawl."

Peculiar newsletter: "Christmas Greetings from Peculiar, Missouri" 1969

The Younger Family

When the Cass County Historical Society was organized, we came face to face with the role of the Charles Younger family in post Civil War history. Their abandoned home remained a stark monument to the turmoil of the area alongside the 71 Bypass (now 291) as it led from Harrisonville to Lee's Summit. The owner was offering the farm for sale with the house, but we did succeed in getting him to let us show the house to the public and to televise it. At the beginning of his career, Wendell Anschutz presented the old home on TV. Concurrently, we arranged to hold a Younger family reunion knowing that many of them only knew the lore of the house and not knowing how many would care to be included. We had about twenty relatives attend.

We made an initial effort to have the area between Harrisonville and Lee's Summit designated Cole Younger Country. We prepared place mats for the restaurants along this route that gave complete historical data for all communities. But when we presented the idea to a group of Lee's Summit city leaders, they were not interested in any effort to memorialize these unsavory ruffians. Later, the house was salvaged by someone in the movie industry. For years, Lee's Summit celebrated Cole Younger Days; but beginning this year, it will be known as Lee's Summit's Fun Fest.

The "Younger Home" at Lee's Summit

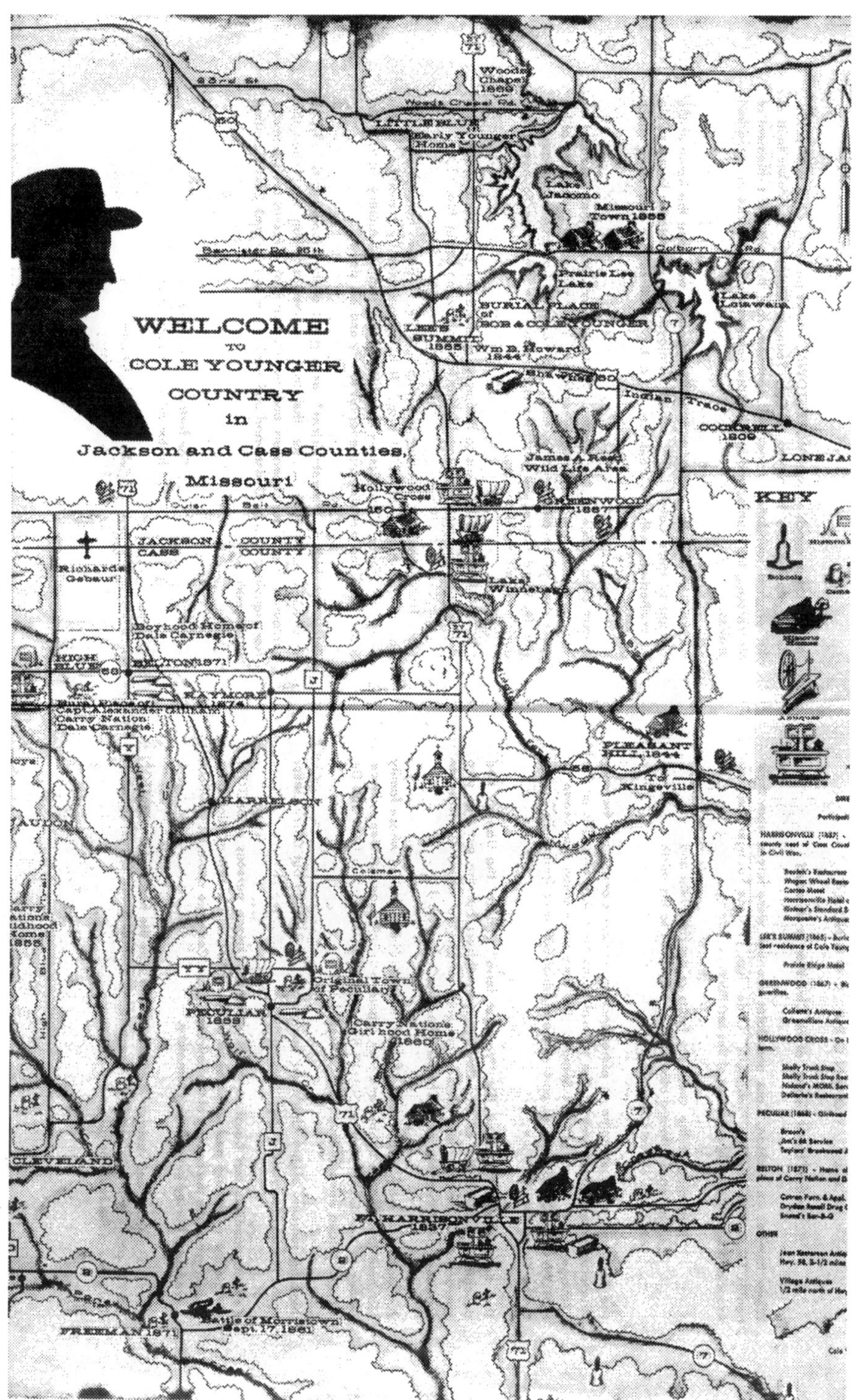

Historical Map / Place mat of "Cole Younger Country"

A Peculiar Heritage

With Brookwood a reality, in 1962 Taylor and I had time to phase some other personal interests into our schedule. I was still teaching at Belton and Taylor was driving a school bus. We became curious about the history of Peculiar, where we lived. Among other things, we wondered why the area had been known as the "burnt district" of Missouri. In pursuing an answer to that question, we encountered references to "Old Peculiar" and the Moore family. Finding Old Peculiar was no problem, for it was just down the road about a third of a mile. People gladly let us see the abstracts for their property, for whatever information we could glean from them. Taylor sought out people by day and arranged for me to visit them on weekends.

By the time I finished my Master's degree in 1965, we had accumulated a lot of local history. Then we stumbled onto some papers from 1868 that documented the creation of the town of Peculiar. The Lion's Club asked me to present my findings to the group as a program. When I told them that a year from tonight, Peculiar will be one hundred years old, I had their rapt attention. G.C. Wills, Jr. moved that the Lion's Club sponsor a centennial celebration and someone else moved that G.C. Wills, Jr. be the chairman of the celebration. Taylor and I kept researching the subject everywhere we could. One day in November, Taylor told me that they wanted to see me at the bank that night. That could have meant anything. When I got there, I was asked to write a history of Peculiar. I questioned their judgment as I said "I am a newcomer." But they expressed their confidence in me by saying that I would research the history, whereas anyone else would just rely on hearsay.

Of course I was flattered. We worked out the details, got cost estimates, and we never saw the dining room table again until we took the manuscript to the newspaper office in Clinton for printing. Kathleen White was publisher then and I knew I had no worries. Her daughter now leads the *Clinton Democrat*. The Cass County Historical Society was founded within this period and blessed our efforts. Irene Webster has led its growth all these years.

Just this week, I've had inquiries from Virginia wanting to know if there were copies of "A Peculiar Heritage" still available. Local residents were invited to have family photographs made for inclusion in the book and they were allowed to reserve copies for their own use. I'm sure they are proud to have them. I know I'm proud to have our photo in it. When I see it, I sigh as I did when "A Peculiar Heritage" was a finished story. It was one of those things that comes once in a lifetime, that you somehow manage to find the energy for.

PLEASE RELEASE AT YOUR EARLIEST CONVENIENCE

There's an air of hospitality along 71 Highway just south of Kansas City and it starts around the stove in Ed Ullery's lumber yard at Peculiar, Missouri. The bare brick walls echo the jovial "Good mornings" of generations and the empty buggy whip holder suspended from the ceiling seems a kind of "halo" for those who have gone before.

The calm of a century is rapidly disappearing as newcomers, in search of what remains of rural life, bring the bustle of the suburbs. Change had been a way of life in Peculiar… but things were not always calm. Early Southern settlers were forced from their farm homes in the 1850's by the border wars and "infamous Order No. 11" which depopulated the "burnt district" of the Civil War in Missouri. Following the war, settlers came from the North and the East and exiled Southern families returned, with faith and courage, to build anew from the rubble of the Jayhawkers and the Bushwhackers. Among these families were the Moores, parents of Carry Nation, noted temperance crusader, who grew to womanhood in the family home nearby.

The coming of the railroad changed the location of the town and the coming of the highway changed its economic life. Today's changes are less evident… or, perhaps, we grow to expect them… but nothing has changed the friendliness and hospitality of this rural Cass County community that was founded June 22, 1868.

A week long celebration has been planned to commemorate 100 years of Peculiar history. The program includes a parade on July 6th followed by a rodeo, the Bushwhacker Antique Show and Sale, pony-pulling matches, and Carry Nation Day, which will be attended by members of her family. A chronicle of persons, places and events has been compiled by Mr. and Mrs. William Taylor, titled <u>A Peculiar Heritage</u>. G.C. Wills is coordinating all phases of the program for the Peculiar Lions Club, sponsors of the event.

First press release, announcing centennial celebration of Peculiar and the introduction of the book "A Peculiar Heritage" authored by Betty and WilliamTaylor: 1968

Preface

If I had never had the good fortune to assemble these facts, this lore, these personal experiences that make A PECULIAR HERITAGE, I would never have "become" a Missourian.

If I had never had the good fortune to listen to the facts, the lore, the personal experiences of my Illinois ancestors, their coming to America, quarrying the stone that fashioned the earliest buildings in St. Charles, Missouri, homesteading Illinois prairie lands and using "old world" tools to build a "new world," and living a Faith that brings any people nearer its goal -- I could never have appreciated the courage and determination those earliest settlers brought to Peculiar. My ancestors weren't threatened by Border Ruffians. . .nor the dissolution of families as they took their stand with the Union and against the centuries-old institution of slavery. Courage, in the face of those odds, has no modern American counter-part.

While researching the events and circumstances recorded here, I've been reminded that certain things "weren't history," "happened in the last twenty years," or "wouldn't be of interest to anybody," but this record of the first hundred years in Peculiar and West Peculiar Township is prepared primarily for the grandchildren of those persons who view with disinterest the significance of these everyday happenings.

For instance, I believe there's a message for future generations in the devotion of "Miss" Helen Thompson, who went regularly to the Peculiar Methodist Church early each Sunday morning to ring the church bell and wind the clock. . .a Peculiar type of "angelus." There's also a lesson in the integrity of those early bankers who were not successful, but who used their own wealth to assure every depositor a full return of his money. Communities today could use hundreds of "Aunt Dode" Wills to serve humanity's needs from birth through death.

In these days of legislated security for the elderly, perhaps we should explore how the "uncles" and "aunts" of Peculiar earned the love and respect of the community. With "conformity" the watch-word, it might even be important to know that people once felt so strongly about their convictions that they were willing to suffer humiliation and public ridicule -- as Carry Nation did.

Peculiar's past has much to say to its future. Most memorable, perhaps, is the faith and courage with which the exiles of Order No. 11 returned to build anew from the rubble of the "burnt district" the farms, homes and communities in which Cass County takes pride. Let us learn from those "exiles" to put aside personal prejudice and tradition as we seek the common good of "one world" under God--in which all men are equal.

—Grace Elizabeth Taylor

Peculiar, Missouri
April 15, 1968

Preface from "A Peculiar Heritage": 1968

Appendix

It is with regret that we bring this task to a close. From the inception of our inquiry into the history of the George Moore family and their famous daughter, and later in the history of the Younger family in Cass County, we learned that the gathering of historical data has no "dead end" streets. Each new insight into the life and times of a people only whets your enthusiasm and compels you to dig deeper and dig continually.

To credit the scores of persons who contributed to our search for facts and photos would require another chapter and the "Heritage" has far outgrown the 200 pages we anticipated at the outset. We are proud to have had this part in the celebration of Peculiar's founding, particularly since we have lived in the community only six years. Perhaps this "labor of love" will in part compensate for the warmth and friendliness Peculiar has shown us during these years.

Our task will not have been completed until you use the scrapbook pages that follow to record your personal and family history. Over the years you will find the "index" page a convenient place in which to list the page numbers in which your family has particular interest. In short, this printed history provides for its own personalization and continuing growth.

Many persons have asked how we became so interested in the history of Cass County and the Peculiar area. Since completing the manuscript we have reflected on these past six years and have established these sources of inspiration:

The Class of 1969 of the Raymore-Peculiar High School, as fifth grade students in my classroom, constantly sought answers and information about the history of the area. When we learned that no county historical society existed and when their questions continued to come, we sought the advice of the State Historical Society of Missouri, followed it, and we now have a three-year-old Cass County Historical Society already on the threshhold of a museum project for the area. This group of youngsters can take pride in having this small part in an organization that should bring pleasure to the community for years to come. Let's hope that youngsters continue to ask questions and prod oldsters into activity.

A second source of inspiration was a series of letters written by my mother, and a childhood acquaintance, David Sorrell, now of Houston, Texas, in an effort to stimulate the recollections of a former classmate who had been confined in a mental hospital for years but who, when near 80, regained her mental facilities almost as a miracle, and sought to learn about her family and friends through one of the few names she remembered - that of my mother, Winifred Jones Goby. These letters found their way into our hometown paper and set the entire community to "recollection."

Among the countless persons who shared in the mechanical details of the manuscript, photography and interviews, I want to particularly thank Edna Wills, Louise Harper, Mrs. Clara Brierly and Mr. Ed Schug. Special thanks go to Mrs. Dorothy Northrup who caught the spirit of the Centennial in her title page illustration.

Little did I realize in 1961 that one of my sixth grade students at Raymore would one day proofread the manu scipt of a history of a Peculiar that I didn't even know, but as I bring this acknowleagment to a close, Sherry Hutson is performing this final ritual.

The Lions Club of Peculiar has been a most understanding taskmaster, asking only for the "best" history rather than holding to the format we planned at the outset. As a result, we think it will be unique among local histories and justify the enthusiasm manifested by the orders that have accumulated even before publication.

Finally, we want to thank the people of Peculiar for making their personal recollections and possessions available to us without hesitation. Sometime ago we prepared a letter for the hometown Heartbeat column of "Capper's Weekly." We presume it was too personal for we have not seen it in print, however, we think it best expresses our personal feelings about the Peculiar community. We therefore include it here:

"They say that adopted children are more loved than natural children. Perhaps the same may be said for "adopted" home towns. Our friends shook their heads questioningly when we announced we were moving to Peculiar, Missouri - asking what we expected to find "there." And the adjustment wasn't an easy one - giving and forgiving - getting and forgetting - but that was six short years ago.

"This year 'our' home town celebrates its 100th anniversary July 5-13th. As we prepare "A Peculiar Heritage" to record this century of history in what was the 'burnt district' of the Civil War in Missouri, we're happy God drew us to Peculiar, just as he did countless other families in the past - among them the Moores, parents of Carry Nation who grew to womanhood here.

"What did we find in Peculiar? Friendliness, thoughtfulness, sincerity and love. It might just be coincidental, but that is what we've tried to give!

We thank you, Peculiar.

William M. and Betty Taylor

Brookwood
Peculiar, Missouri
June 6, 1968

MR. AND MRS. WM. M. TAYLOR

Appendix from "A Peculiar Heritage": 1968

The Antique Taylors

While we were immersing ourselves in Peculiar's history, we were grooming ourselves to present other historic items to the public. With the encouragement of Irene Webster and the Harrisonville Chamber of Commerce, we endeavored to present the Cole Younger home to the public. It stood as a great memorial to Missouri's role in the Civil War. The owner at that time wanted to maintain the home on its acreage. It was located on the 71 Bypass (now 291) near an intersection with Highway 150, known as Hollywood Cross. We did succeed in getting a local TV station to present it. Wendell Anschutz was the host and he was just entering on what has been a very rewarding career.

The summer that we toyed with the Younger home, we accumulated Missouri primitives to offer antique buyers. We had already done a reproduction of my Grandmother Jones' kitchen in a room at the back of our garage, but it was not for sale. The next year, we built a "Dutch style red barn" to use as an antique shop. We surrounded it with a stockade fence which also provided display space for antiques. With the red barn, we became known as the "Antique Taylors of Peculiar." Now we could tread Missouri in search of the primitives that Taylor and I remembered using on the farms where we were raised. Taylor grew up in a much more rural environment than I had, but we both remembered the hard work of gardening and canning that provided for farm families. The first advertising I ever wrote was for "The Antique Taylors" in Peculiar, Missouri. It truly presented us as we were and we were successful and happy.

After my father's death in 1970, we no longer made the trip to Raymond; but we remembered the very German communities we loved visiting in mid-Missouri: Hermann, Warrenton, Aux Vasse, and Kingdom City. We followed the Kallmeyer Auctions and they referred us to collectors who also frequented their auctions and were knowledgeable collectors of truly primitive furnishings from early Missouri homes. That's how we met Doone Jackson. She was in the process of reconditioning an old house in Aux Vasse, Missouri. In the process, she personally found time to refinish early primitive pieces that Homer Coil and Dennis Scholes found at the auctions they attended as a pastime. Doone's husband traveled for a national appliance manufacturer and they had moved out of the suburban St. Louis to Callaway County.

Because her collection was larger than her house possibly could accommodate, she had rented an old bank in McCredie (population 12) just off 54 Highway, a mile from I-70 and five miles from Fulton. After a few month of acquaintance, Doone told us she was giving up the bank space because the whole block was being sold. We were informed that the owner wanted $6,500 for five and one-half lots. That included an old home that had been converted into two rental units. Since we were weekend-ing in the area at a motel, we decided to buy the property. An aging paper-hanger lived nearby and we sought his help in preparing the house for occupancy. As he hurried to get our place ready for our impending weekend visit, he stuffed the heating stove with trash and scrap paper and lighted the fire. By the time I got home from school that day, Taylor had gotten the word that the house had burned to the ground.

As I scanned the insurance policy, I learned that all of our insurance was on the house, which more than paid for our indebtedness on it. We still had five and one-half lots and the bank building, all debt free. The half lot we didn't get had been the old community hall. It was in the hands of four aged trustees whose attorney was in Fulton. Everybody said they would never sell the old building but, as it stood; it had no windows, hadn't been painted in years, and had become a local hangout for kids. We contacted their attorney, made a bonafide offer of $450.00 and were advised within the week that we had bought the building.

Taylor and his old friend, Charlie Richardson, delighted in restoring the old building. I occupied myself dreaming of a collection of small antique shops called "Calico Country Antique Village." I named it for Callaway County, but also because calico was very popular at that time. By the next summer vacation, it was pulling antique lovers into McCredie and I was speculating on how I could add food to the Village. In late summer, we brought in a double-wide trailer and parked it between the bank and the old community hall. The Volney Hildreths stopped by regularly to see how we were progressing. They had had a restaurant at one time. Finally, they said they would be there in three weeks and they would be coming to eat. And Calico Cupboard became a reality.

We hired local kids to help us and a few mothers. Debbie Daro, now Craighead (and one of my Missouri Daughters), joined us with her brother, Mike, behind the scenes. It was fun from day one. We served a buffet, specially set up for each reservation, on my grandmother's kitchen table. It was covered with a well-worn quilt and food was served in dishes that would have been at home in her kitchen. Columbia newspapers found us interesting, if not unique. Hermann diners found us too and some of their historic group told me that I belonged in Hermann.

. . . . a chubby old lady and her little old husband decided to settle down in a remote corner - far from the hustle and bustle of the city - and retire quietly. The chubby old lady had dreamed for years about a house on a hillside beside a babbling brook with rocks and trees and wildflowers everywhere. The little old man had just dreamed of a homey spot where he could putter leisurely. He, too, loved the woods but he also loved the chubby old lady and what made her happy made him happy.

They looked far and wide, up and down the most remote by-roads, miles away from the city. They had almost given up when they came upon a beautiful tree-studded hillside - just like the chubby old lady's dream - beside a creek and near a quaint rural village named "Peculiar."

Within a few months the chubby old lady and her little old husband nestled down for "the quiet years." At least, that's what they planned. They had rocks and trees and wildflowers everywhere, and the little old man had time on his hands to putter around. It was just about this time that they discovered the fascinating history of Missouri's "burnt district" oozing out from under every rock. In 1860 Carrie Nation would have been their neighbor . . . and the Younger family might have tarried at the creek to water their horses on the way home from Hickman's Mill.

With so much history at their finger tips, the chubby old lady and the little old man began collecting morsels of Missouri's heritage. First they filled the house. Then they filled the barn. They built another barn and in a short time it was filled. And that's when the little old man put his foot down "kerplop!" "Woman," he said, "it's time yu'all was getting shed of some of this here stuff."

So the chubby old lady "got shed" of everything but the hand-made pine and walnut furniture crafted by Missouri's early settlers and, of course, she couldn't part with those quaint home-made gadgets the menfolks made for the women they loved. Together they have accumulated these gems of the past in a cute, cozy, but "country-style" Home Sweet Home Shop in the loft of their red barn. This crafty old couple's ideas have made these unique pieces Peculiar-ly (pardon us!) interesting and adaptable for present day living.

You'll share their enthusiasm for collecting the preserving Missouri's heritage when you visit

THE ANTIQUE TAYLORS' of
Peculiar, Missouri

N. B The chubby old lady and the little old man lived "happily ever after," but new 71 Highway construction will bring them within a half mile of the Peculiar exit. Remote? Quiet? Retired? Visit them and see for yourself.

"Once upon a time…" Karen Vogler of Excelsior Springs had just started collecting antiques in 1968 and was attracted to the "Antique Taylors" ads in the Kansas City Star antique column. As I have said elsewhere, Taylor and I were always a couple. It was no surprise when our ads in the K.C. Star related to the activities of "the chubby old lady and her little old husband." You'll get the picture! I'm hoping Karen will have an opportunity to see this manuscript, for I treasure her candid responses.

As I recall, Taylor had 22 church pews on this load.
They were all sold to one dealer and we took them strait to her furniture stripper.
Taylor got a ticket for going too slow. I wonder why?

Taylor with Mildred Hammond and her daughter.
The settle on which they are sitting was crafted by my son, Bill Brackman, from old barn
lumber. Bill had a great sense of design and proportion, just as many early craftsmen did.
I wish we had kept more of his "primitive" pieces.

LETTERS TO EDITOR

(Ed. Note: The following was submitted to us as a Letter to the Editor and an open letter to the residents of this area).

Dear Friends:

The kids have gone. The busses are pulling away. The building is almost deserted. All that remains is for me to pack up this typewriter and remove my blue willow coffee cup from the teachers lounge, except

Thank you Belton . . . . . for making it possible for me to spend 14 wonderful years with your children and grandchildren. Knowing them has made it possible for me to be a better grandmother. Certainly, they have kept me alive to all that is good and real in this world and have introduced me to "adventures" other grandmothers would find unbelievable. They've made me as curious about things as they are and instilled a mounting disrespect for what is phony. To them I owe what I hope will be a happy retirement and a "new beginning."

Thank you Peculiar . . . . . for letting me share the lives of two very interesting fifth grade classes at the advent of my teaching career. It was their insatiable appetite for local history that catapulted us into the worlds of Carrie Nation and Cole Younger and introduced us to the world of historical inquiry. Their unrelenting pursuit of what happened and where opened an entirely new Missouri to Taylor and me. Without them there would have been no "Peculiar Heritage" no restoration of McCredie, and there would have been no Taylors Landing . . . . .

To all of you we extend our heartfelt appreciation for all you have meant to us in the past . . . . and for making our future a most promising one.

With Love,
Betty and Bill Taylor

New Address:
Taylors Landing
Hermann, Mo. 65041

"Letter to Editor" Farewell letter to the Belton Community: 1977

Photo from Missouri Life magazine, with original caption
"Betty Taylor has dreamed of running a restaurant like the Calico Cupboard
since she was in high school." As my glasses slipped down my nose,
the photographer said, "Next time your glasses slip down, look at me."
The rest is history. This is my grandkids favorite picture of me.

Photo from <u>Missouri Life</u> magazine
At McCredie, we served pie from an old cook stove.

Photo from <u>Missouri Life</u> magazine
My Grandmother Jones' footed fruit bowl deserved this festive background.

Photo from <u>Missouri Life</u> magazine, with original caption "William Taylor, known to friends simply as "Taylor", performs many functions at the Calico Cupboard around McCredie, but none is more enjoyable than his job as his wife's number one taster."

Reader's Notes

Saturday morning pie making at Calico Cupboard
Photograph from Missouri Life article: Pie shells cooling "Tables crowded with pie shells
inspire a feeling of abundance and well-being, and as dinner time approaches, colorful dishes
blend with antique furnishings to create atmosphere perfect for a downhome feast."

Recipes

The original Calico Cupboard buffet was served from a quilt covered antique table alongside a "Callaway" cabinet. These were kitchen cabinets that included a flour bin, a sugar bin, a sliding bread board, and sometimes a retractable towel bar. Above the work area was a shelf cabinet that included spice drawers for bulk spices, including salt and pepper. These cabinets were made at the Fulton School for the Deaf. The earliest ones extended over the base far enough to allow a narrow sliding drawer for knives.

Most of our salads did not require refrigeration, for most bowls were refilled from refrigerated containers before each table's guests were invited to the buffet. The lettuce salads were served in a bowl of crushed ice. The bread was cut for each table from a bread board atop a flour bin. Taylor loved to cut the home style bread for each group, using the same saw-toothed bread knife that my family had used.

We always had coleslaw, potato salad, cottage cheese with caraway seed, marinated vegetables, and anything in season; such as sliced cucumbers and tomatoes. Local gardeners found an outlet for their surpluses in Calico Cupboard. One time, a resident brought us Jerusalem artichokes; a first for us. After cleaning in several rinses, we sliced them and put them in a sweet vinegar dressing that we used for Crock Salad. People thought we had found a way of preparing new potatoes.

Photograph from Missouri Life article: Betty seated at the table
"Mrs. Taylor describes her method of restaurant management as "cooking on paper.
" Every detail is carefully planned in advance. Thus, she spends as much time working
at the table in front of her calico cupboard as she does in the kitchen."

Corned Beef and Cabbage looked great in my Grandmother Jones' tea leaf ironstone.
The china was as sturdy as the food.

We were besieged with requests for recipes from the beginning of Calico Cupboard. These were selected based on their personal significance. As a consequence, they are not categorized as to desserts, casseroles, etc. We couldn't categorize the women whose recipes we were using, so please find your own method of indexing the ones that interest you.

Buttermilk Pie

During the "Great Depression," farm women from north of Champaign, Illinois (where I worked for the power and light company) arranged to come to a vacant building near this busy intersection and offer their home-made foods in a sort of buffet. Buffets weren't everywhere in those days. The mother of one little girl who worked with me was among those country women. She brought "sugar pie" and "buttermilk pie." Of course, every farm wife had a surplus of dairy products at her disposal. These are two of the recipes I took to the Calico Cupboard when it became a reality in McCredie and later in Hermann.

We always took a tea wagon of assorted pies or desserts to the table for our customers' selections. At the McCredie dining room, we displayed the whole pies on an old fashioned cook stove. <u>Missouri Life</u> magazine visited us one Saturday morning during baking time after we had prepared shells for the weekend. (See photo on page 120)

3 eggs (beaten)
1 C. sugar mixed with 1 T. flour
1/2 t. nutmeg
1/4 t. salt
1 1/2 C. buttermilk
1 1/2 T. melted butter
1 t. vanilla

In a prepared, unbaked shell; bake for 40 minutes at 375 degrees.

Sugar Pie

1 c. sugar mixed with 3 T. flour
1/2 t. salt
1 1/2 c. cream (or Carnation milk)
2 t. vanilla

Fill unbaked pie shell and bake for 10 minutes at 425 degrees (to seal crust), then continue baking at 325 degrees for 45 minutes.

Jeff Davis Pie

When we found ourselves at McCredie in Callaway County, we soaked up the southern influence that had dominated that area. In the local recipe books, a Mrs. H.W. Craig was always quoted; both as a cook and as a community leader. Her "Jeff Davis Pie" fit right into Calico Cupboard's purpose of bringing traditional foods to wherever we were.

2 c. sugar mixed with 3 T. flour
4 whole eggs (beaten)
1/2 c. Carnation milk (or cream)
1/2 c. melted butter
1/2 t. lemon extract

Bake for 10 minutes at 425 degrees, then continue to bake at 325 degrees for 25-30 minutes.

In the Jeff Davis Pie, and the following Lemon Sponge Pie, you will see traces of a much more affluent farm area. Of course, the "Depression" was long over by this time. You will notice that most of these recipes were for "pantry ingredients." No one had to put off making them to go to town for extra ingredients.

Lemon Sponge Pie

This is a dessert that has a slightly "southern" taste.

2 T. shortening creamed with a mixture of 1 c. sugar and 3 T. flour
1/2 t. salt
3 egg yolks (beaten)
1 c. milk
2 heaping T. lemon juice and lemon rind (Remove seeds and grind in a
blender. Excess may be saved in the refrigerator.)

Add the above mixture to 3 egg whites that have been beaten stiff.
Bake in raw shell for 10 minutes at 375 degrees, then continue baking at 350
degrees for 35 minutes.

Marinated Vegetables

This recipe is a welcome addition to a busy schedule.

2 cans Shellie beans (drained)
1 can red beans (rinsed)
1 can green limas (drained)
1 can wax beans (drained)
1 can whole kernel corn
1 can small mushroom pieces
1 two ounce jar chopped pimentos

Dressing preparation:
1 c. sugar
1 c. cider vinegar
1 t. celery seed
1/2 t. salt
1/2 t. paprika
1 t. mustard seed
1/2 c. salad oil

Heat the above ingredients to boiling point to dissolve sugar, then add:
2 c. chopped celery, onions and green peppers
This will be usable for a week to ten days if refrigerated.

Cole Slaw to Share

2 heads cabbage (shredded)

Heat the following mixture:

1 c. sugar
1 c. cider vinegar
1/2 c. salad oil
1 t. celery seed
1/2 t. salt

Add mixture to shredded cabbage and then add:

2 c. chopped celery
green peppers
red peppers
green onion

This will be usable for a week to ten days if refrigerated.

Cucumbers and Sour Cream

Growing up, I could not appreciate our "harvest" of fresh cucumbers. It just meant afternoons of washing jars in preparation for canning. And then that smelly vinegar bubbling on the stove! Grandma Goby always served fresh sliced cucumbers marinated in water, salt and vinegar with slices of fresh onion in it. If you prepared it early in the morning, the cucumber slices were ready for lunch and still crisp by the evening meal. But they held no "fresh from the garden" enthusiasm for me.

At Calico Cupboard, fresh cucumbers took on a whole new role. They were always in good supply and a "quick fix" if we needed to add to our salad bar. We could always go back to Grandma Goby's marinade but once we offered cucumbers in sour cream, we never went back.

Chop 2 or 3 cloves of garlic.
Add 1/4 t. salt and 2 T. vinegar for each cucumber you plan to use.

Slice cucumbers to medium thickness and sprinkle lightly with salt.
Add one 8 oz. tub of sour cream to garlic/vinegar mixture.
Sprinkle bowl or salad plate with chopped parsley.

Fred, my caretaker, serves a glass bowl of cucumbers and sour cream in the center of a dinner plate surrounded by sliced tomatoes and parsley sprigs. Guests serve their own salad plates, taking as much as they wish.

Serves from four to six people.

Glessie Eggers' Hot German Potato Salad
which became...
Calico Cupboard's Hot German Potato Salad

(You'll be able to share this recipe)
Boil, peel and slice 10 potatoes.
Fry 1 c. chopped bacon until crisp (save drippings).

Mix:
1 1/2 c. cider vinegar
1 1/2 c. water
2 c. sugar mixed with 3 T. flour
2 t. salt
1/2 t. pepper

Bring mixture to boil and keep stirred to prevent lumping.
Pour dressing over sliced potatoes and add crisp chopped bacon.

Add:
1/2 c. green onion
1 c. diced celery
1 t. chopped pimentos or 1/4 c. chopped red pepper
1/2 c. chopped green pepper
1 t. celery seed
Mix well. Reheat in quantities as needed.

Note:
I have also boiled chopped bacon in a skillet with 2 c. of water to render fat and then proceeded with the rest of the recipe in the same skillet, adding sliced potatoes to finish the sauce. (See photo on page 135)

Grape Salad

Because we never knew how many we would be serving on a weekend, we always had to be prepared to run out of some regular salads.

Grape salad became a welcome addition because it also served as a dessert.

3 lbs. White seedless grapes (removed form stems)
1 - 12 oz. tub sour cream
2 heaping T. brown sugar

Mix all ingredients.

Sprinkle with nutmeg until you can see it on brown sugar.

Let stand.

Peas and Dumplings

My grandmother had a way of finding enough vegetables in her garden to spice up a regular meat and potatoes meal. With a half cup of peas, just shelled in her apron, she would make peas and dumplings. As she boiled the peas in a limited amount of water to cook them, she mixed the dumplings in another bowl. When the peas were done, she added milk and a dollop of butter with a couple of shakes of salt to the pan in which the peas cooked. As the milk came to a slow boil, she dropped the dumplings into the pan using a tablespoon. The milk would thicken as the dumplings cooked. When done, the dumplings would be studded with green peas and a luscious sweet pea gravy. She also did the same thing with sweet baby carrots, which she thinned out of her garden carrots.

To satisfy my requests when I came home, my mother used Green Giant Peas to accomplish the same result for our larger family.

1 can Green Giant Peas (un-drained)
1 can milk
1/4 stick oleo
1/4 t. salt
Let contents boil and add dumplings made from Bisquick or Jiffy Mix recipe.

Short Ribs and Poppy Seed Noodles

Boil 3 lbs. Short ribs of beef until meat leaves bones easily.
Bring broth up to half way in the container by adding water and bring to a slow boil.
Add 1 package of Kluski Noodles and cook slowly until done.
Remove meat from bones and place in the kettle with noodles.
Add one 12oz. tub of sour cream. Sprinkle sour cream with 1/2 to 1 t. poppy seeds and mix well.
The heat of the meat and noodles converts the sour cream into a sufficient amount of gravy to serve with potatoes and other vegetables.
This is a welcome casserole dish that requires little preparation time.

Do not try this recipe with regular noodles.

Homemade Noodles

Because we always had eggs and milk on hand, angel food cakes were regular fare. But a by-product of angel food was egg yolks; a natural reason for making noodles. The Kluski Noodles we get today most nearly match the homemade noodles, for they were thicker and always covered with dry flour.

Combine:
1 egg (beaten)
2 T. milk
1/2 t. salt
1 c. flour

Roll very thin. Allow to stand at least 20 minutes.
Dust flattened dough with flour. Roll up loosely and slice 1/4 inch wide.
Spread out sliced noodles and allow to dry for 2 hours.

My mother always made noodles with the egg yolks that remained after making an angel food cake. When you see these dried noodles, they will remind you of Kluski noodles that you see in the grocery store shelves. But they are much thicker than rolled out homemade noodles.

My grandmother would cook noodles, drain them, and then fry them in 2 T. butter, 1 T. bacon fat and 1/2 c. bread crumbs. Sometimes, she mixed the cooked noodles with bread cubes she had fried in left-over bacon fryings. Grandmother never wasted anything!

In 1943, when I was newly married to Hugo Brackman, my mother wrote me about this wonderful new product she had found in the grocery store. It was called "Bisquick." At that stage, I was using a recipe for biscuits that had been given to me by a co-worker whose mid-Missouri family had depended on it for years. It required buttermilk and, of course, baking soda.

Calico Cupboard's Buttermilk Biscuits

Combine:
2 c. flour
1/2 t. salt
4 t. baking powder
1/2 t. baking soda
5 T. shortening

Add: 1 c. buttermilk and stir with a fork
Bake at 450 degrees for 12-15 minutes.

When the National Food Editors & Writers Association visited us in 1981, we served hot biscuits. At the close of the luncheon, they began with a question and answer period. The first question, which brought up countless hands, was asking how we made the biscuits. As a result, we found Calico Cupboard in Food Sections from St. Paul, Minnesota to Mobile, Alabama. They wrote not of our down-home German food, but of our home style biscuits.

Years later, Mother sent me a recipe for making a quantity of biscuit mix for ready use, much like Bisquick; a "have-on-hand" recipe.
12 c. sifted flour
6 T. baking powder
2 T. salt
1 1/2 c. shortening

For 12 biscuits, mother used:
3 c. dry mix
1 c. milk
Mix with a fork and knead ten times
(For buttermilk biscuits, add 1 c. buttermilk and 1/2 t. soda)
Pat out to 1/2 inch thickness and cut in rounds
Bake at 450 degrees for 12-15 minutes

For Short Cake:
Add 3 T. sugar to mix
1 c. thin cream instead of milk
Knead as above, form into loaf or biscuits, brush with melted butter
Bake at 450 degrees for 25-30 minutes

Holly Horton's Bran Muffins

Holly Horton Tyree is one of my "Missouri Daughters." She was a terrific hostess at Calico Cupboard in the evenings and she preferred to host and serve without other help. We've kept in touch even though she married and moved to St. Louis County.

5 T. baking soda dissolved in 1 quart of buttermilk
5 c. flour
3 c. sugar
1 - 15oz. package Raisin Bran
2 t. salt
4 eggs (slightly beaten)
1 c. salad oil

Mix dry ingredients.

Add eggs, oil, and buttermilk mixture.

Stir just enough to mix.

Fill greased muffin pans 2/3 full.

Bake at 400 degrees for 18-20 minutes.

Refrigerate balance of mixture to use as needed for up to 6 weeks.
Makes 4 1/2 dozen.

(Photographs of Holly and her pie cart are elsewhere in the book.)

Calico Cupboard's Poppy Seed Dressing

Start saving empty salad dressing bottles because this recipe makes four quarts. If you have ten empty bottles, you'll be able to share with ten lucky friends. Everybody loved it. Frank Van Kamp almost figured out the recipe, but he hadn't figured on tarragon vinegar.

16 T. poppy seed
16 c. salad oil
1 c. grated onion
1 c. lemon juice
5 2/3 c. honey
4 c. tarragon vinegar
4 t. salt
12 t. dry mustard
8 c. sugar

For 1/4 recipe or roughly 2 quarts:

4 T. poppy seed
4 c. vegetable oil
1/4c. grated onion
1/4 c. lemon juice
1 1/2 c. honey
1 c. tarragon vinegar
1 t. salt
3 t. dry mustard
2 c. sugar

P.S. Twenty bottles will mean twenty happy friends. Everybody will enjoy it. On just plain leaf lettuce, it makes a "whole" salad.

Kraut Salad

1 large can sauerkraut
3/4 c sugar
1 c. diced celery
1 c. diced green pepper
1/4 c. diced onion
3 T. vinegar
1/2 t. salt
1/8 t. pepper
1 t. celery seed
3 T. diced pimento

Drain sauerkraut for 15 minutes.

Using kitchen scissors, cut into 1 inch pieces.

Add the rest of the ingredients, mix, and refrigerate for at least 24 hours.

Keeps indefinitely.

Ginny Lone's Crock Salad

Ginny Lone and John Lone graced our Blue Willow Room every Sunday and often with longtime friends. They never failed to ask me to join them near the end of their meal if I had time. They left a chair available to me near the door that would give me a small glimpse of what was going on in the big dining room, for ready access in case of an emergency. We shared happiness, we shared sorrows and concerns. As we parted, we also knew we shared a loving God.

I've misplaced the original crock salad recipe so I'll give you the recipe that I remember, for the taste I remember. It's been a part of every summer's garden goodies. You may not use a crock, but do plan to have enough for a couple of days because it is so simple and keeps well.

sliced tomatoes
sliced red onions
sliced green peppers
sliced red peppers
sliced cucumber

Make a marinade or dressing of:
1 c. cider vinegar
3/4 c. sugar
1/4 c. olive oil or good salad oil
1/4 t. celery seed

Glessie Eggers and her husband, Bud, were good friends of Calico Cupboard.
I had never appreciated Hot German Potato Salad but Glessie made a convert out
of me with this recipe and her happy manner.

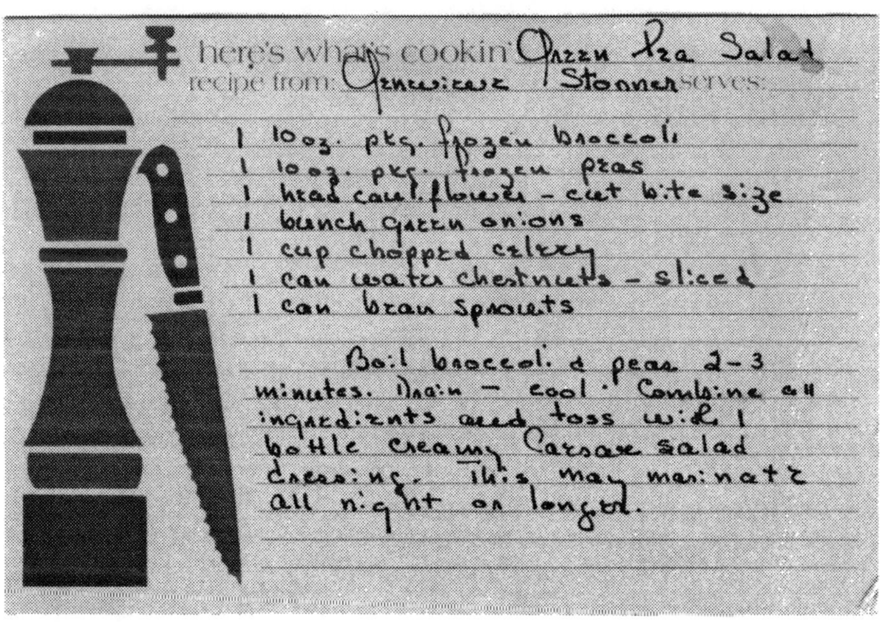

Original recipe card for Green Pea Salad

135

Genevieve Stonner's Green Pea Salad

Genevieve lived in the Berger area, south of Hermann. She always insisted on visiting on the occasions that brought her to Hermann. She was a delightful and interesting lady. We are reprinting her recipe as she gave it to us. Wouldn't you love to see her recipe box?

1 - 10oz. package frozen broccoli
1 - 10oz. package frozen peas
1 head cauliflower (cut to bite size)
1 bunch green onions
1 c. chopped celery
1 can water chestnuts
1 can bean sprouts

Boil broccoli and peas for 2-3 minutes, drain and cool.

Combine all ingredients and toss with one bottle creamy Caesar salad dressing.

Marinate over night or longer.

Crescent Rolls

These rolls have remained a stable part of our family's favorites. Louisanne Mamer introduced me to selling farm women on the idea of electric cookery during my REA months. No sooner had we organized my area when WW II's electrical needs wiped out REA's efforts.

The following recipe makes three dozen rolls.
1 c. milk
1/2 c. shortening
1.2 c. sugar
1 t. salt
1 cake compressed yeast
3 eggs (beaten)
4 1/2 c. flour

Heat milk to scalding and add shortening, sugar, and salt.
Cool to lukewarm.

Add yeast and stir to dissolve.

Add beaten eggs and flour.

Knead lightly on a floured surface.

Place dough in a greased bowl, cover, and let rise to double in bulk.

Divide dough into thirds.

Roll each third to the size of a pie pan.

Cut each circle into 12-16 wedges.

Roll each piece from wide edge to center.

Arrange on cookie sheet and brush lightly with melted butter.

Let rise until very light.

Bake at 400 degrees for 15 minutes.

Lemon Bread Pudding

1 c. soft white bread cubes
2 T. freshly grated lemon peel
1/2 t. salt
2 c. milk
2/3 c. sugar
3 T. butter
4 eggs (separated)
5 T. lemon juice

Put bread cubes in a large bowl and sprinkle with lemon peel and salt.
In a sauce pan, heat milk and sugar to boiling.
Add butter.
Pour milk mixture over bread and let cool.
Beat egg yolks and add to the mixture.
Add lemon juice.
Beat egg whites stiff and fold into bread mixture.
Pour into large baking dish and sprinkle with powdered sugar.
Bake until light brown at 375 degrees.

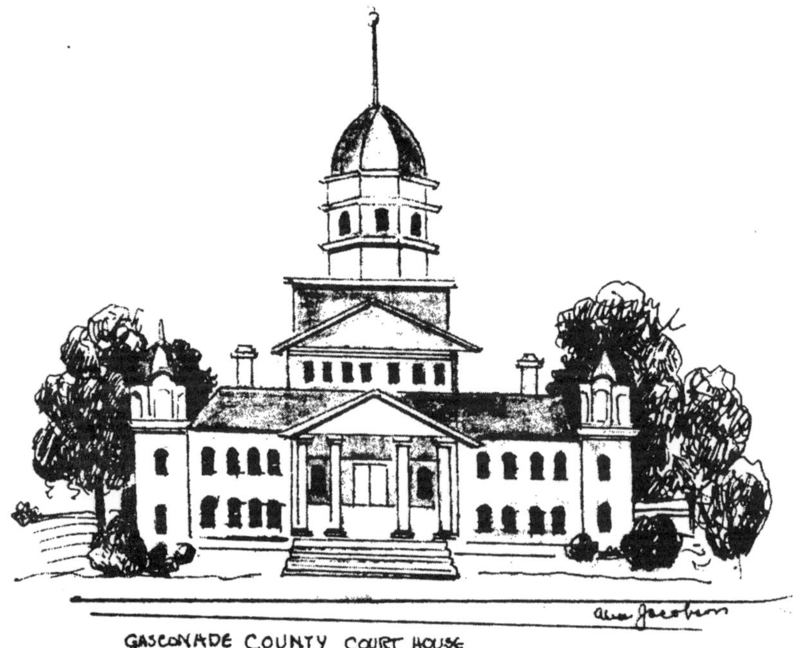

Sugar Cookies

My daughter-in-law, Joan, was a great cookie baker and she always had an eager audience in my grandchildren, Tim and DeAnn, and their friends. When <u>Ford Times</u> magazine asked us to submit recipes for their publication, this one made it into print, along with a beautiful painting of Calico Cupboard.

Mix the following ingredients thoroughly:
3/4 c. margarine (soft)
1 c. sugar
2 eggs
1/2 t. vanilla

Sift together:
2 1/2 c. flour
1 t. baking powder
1 t. salt

Mix sifted dry ingredients into butter-egg mixture and chill for at least one hour.
Roll out to 1/2 inch thickness and cut as desired.
Place on un-greased cookie sheet and sprinkle with sugar.
Bake at 400 degrees for 5-7 minutes, until golden.

Makes about 4 dozen 3 inch cookies.

This is the recipe that <u>Ford Times</u> used in its inclusion of Calico Cupboard among Ford Times' favorite eating places in 1980.

Favorite Recipes from Famous Restaurants
Nancy Kennedy

THE CALICO CUPBOARD
HERMANN, MISSOURI

When Betty Taylor retired from teaching, she and her husband, William, opened a charming waterfront hostelry in Hermann, Missouri, a historic town 60 miles west of St. Louis. It is housed in an 1870 building that once was a tavern and billiard parlor catering to the railroad and steam boat travelers at the busy wharf. Today it is a "gasthaus" furnished with antiques, offering food, lodging and quiet relaxation. German food is featured in a setting of Missouri primitives. Open Monday through Saturday for luncheon 11 a.m. to 2 p.m. and dinner from 5 p.m. to 8 p.m. On Sunday, a special Peasant Breakfast is served from 9 a.m. to 11:30 a.m., and a Farmers' Feast (a country food buffet) is served 11:30 a.m. to 6 p.m. Reservations advisable. During January and February, guests must call and make arrangements for meals or overnight accommodations. It is 14 miles south of I-70 on State Highway 19.

SUGAR COOKIES

¾ cup soft margarine
1 cup sugar
2 eggs, beaten
½ teaspoon lemon flavoring
2½ cups pastry flour
1 teaspoon baking powder
1 teaspoon salt

Combine margarine, sugar, eggs and flavoring. Mix thoroughly. Sift dry ingredients together and stir into the margarine mixture. Chill at least one hour. Roll out ¼ inch thick. Cut into desired shapes. Place on ungreased cookie sheet. Sprinkle with sugar. Bake in 400° oven for 5 to 7 minutes. Makes about 3 dozen 3-inch cookies.

Bonnie's Pie Crust

If I had known Bonnie's recipe for pie crust, that's what I would have used at Calico Cupboard.

This recipe makes 6 pie shells or three 2-crust pies.

Mix:
4 c. flour
2 c. Crisco
1/2t. salt

When ingredients are well mixed and granular, add 1 c. 7-Up (the carbonated beverage).
Knead thoroughly and form dough into 6 balls.
Use one for each crust. You may freeze pie crust balls for later use.

Note:
Bonnie is the grandmother of my youngest great granddaughter, Anne' Tharp.

Mom's Date Pudding

Every fall when I went home, I would ask my mother to make her Date Pudding. I always enjoyed it thoroughly, for it was my earliest recollection of fall recipes. The dates would arrive at the grocery store in wooden boxes from some far off land. The English walnuts could be easily cracked to recover the goodies inside, unlike our locally harvested black walnuts which tasted great but left everything tinged with their black interiors.

Now we have such seasonal foods available all of the time. If you want strawberries at Christmas, they are available frozen, whole or sliced. Another interesting thing about the pudding was that Mother made it in two bowls, one of which she poured hot water over to begin the soda's action with the other ingredients in the recipe, like this:

In one bowl:
1 c. chopped dates
1 t. baking soda
1/2c. butter
1/2 c. English walnuts
Pour 1 c. boiling water over this mixture and let cool.

In another bowl:
1 c. sugar
1 t. salt
1 1/2 c. flour
1 t. vanilla

Add this mixture to the first bowl.
Then add one beaten egg and mix.
Bake in 9x13 cake pan at 375 degrees for 25-30 minutes.
Serve warm or cold with a topping of vanilla sauce or cream.

Mother made a vanilla sauce with water, vanilla, sugar, and 1 t. cornstarch. I thought cream was the most appropriate topping.

Moloney Potatoes

Ginny and John Lone were our regular Sunday guests in the Blue Willow Room at Calico Cupboard. Most often, they had guests and they always invited me to join them at dessert time. We had many lively discussions, about a lot of things. Sometimes, I felt that Taylor thought I was shirking my hosting duties on a busy day. Their daughter, Linda, and her family often joined them and added a new dimension to our discussions.

Ginny brought me her daughter's recipe for "Make Ahead Potatoes" one day, but we've always thought of it as Moloney Potatoes.

6 potatoes (peeled and boiled)

Drain and mash them, then add:

8 oz. cream cheese
8 oz. sour cream
1 t. onion powder

Beat until fluffy.

Spread into a greased casserole dish.

Sprinkle with paprika and drizzle with melted butter at the time of baking.

Bake at 350 degrees for 1 hour.

Volney Hildreth's Salad Dressing

The Volney Hildreth's had been in the food business, but we met them as antique lovers. When they learned we were planning on a small restaurant in the double-wide trailer between the antique shop buildings, they came weekly on their way to St. Louis.

Finally, trying to spur us on during the lovely fall weather, they said they were going to be there in October (the 19th I think) and if we weren't ready to serve, they would help us get ready. It was just the encouragement we needed. They were our first customers at McCredie and again when we opened in Hermann.

18 oz. Wesson oil
18 oz. cider vinegar
2/3 pint honey
4 t. ground mustard
juice of 2 lemons

Mix well and put two cloves of garlic in the bottle.

Volney Hildreth

Potato Pancakes

6 large potatoes
2 eggs
1 t. grated onion
1 1/2 T. flour
1/4 t. baking powder
1 1/4 t. salt

Grate potatoes in small bowl, add small amount of water, then pour into a towel and wring towel to remove water.

There will be about 2 c. of potatoes.
Mix in eggs, onion, flour, baking powder, and salt.
Drop by the spoonful into 1/4 inch of hot grease in skillet.

Brown and serve.

Sweet Kosher Dill Pickles

At a friend's home years ago, I made a pig of myself with the sweet dill pickles that accompanied our luncheon. They were baby pickles and when I bought them at the grocery store, I was surprised at the price. Remembering how good they were, I began sweetening regular dill pickles. You'll agree that they are a welcome change.

Open a jar of your favorite brand of Kosher dill pickles.
Pour out about 1/4 c. of the pickle vinegar.
Add 3/4 c. of sugar slowly until the brine absorbs it.
Reseal the jar and turn it upside down.
Let stand for 2-3 hours and then turn right side up.
Repeat this for a 24 hour period and refrigerate.

You'll be pleasantly surprised.

Sweet and Sour Red Cabbage

Red cabbage was a natural compliment to our bratwurst and German potato salad, both in taste and texture.

Shred one medium size head of red cabbage.

Cook with 1 c. water at a low temperature until wilted.

Add:
1 apple (cored and sliced thin)
2 T. cider vinegar
2 T. butter
1 t. salt

Add 1/2 c. concord grape jelly and mix well.

This recipe re-heats easily. Serves 6-8.

Caraway Seed is VERSATILE.

Caraway seed and parsley were my Grandmother Jones' signature.

She served luscious food and she presented it beautifully.

With sauerkraut, she added a heaping teaspoon of caraway seed to a large can of kraut and cooked it slowly.

With cottage cheese, she added 1 teaspoon to what now would be a small carton of cottage cheese.

Of course, she used quantities of this flavorful seed when she made springerlie at holiday time.

Gingered Carrots

Peel 1 lb. Garden size carrots and cut into 2 inch segments.
Barely cover with water and bring to a slow boil.
Cook until crisp tender and drain.

Add:
1/2 c. sweet orange marmalade
2 T. butter
1/4 t. powdered ginger

Strawberry Bread

As I recall, Glessie Eggers introduced us to strawberry bread.
3 c. flour
2 c. sugar
1 t. baking soda
1 t. cinnamon
1 t. salt
2 - 10 oz. packages frozen strawberries (thawed and drained)
1 c. oil
4 eggs (well beaten)

Mix dry ingredients thoroughly.
In a well in the center, add drained strawberries, oil, and beaten eggs.
Mix well.
Bake in 2 greased loaf pans at 350 degrees for 1 hour.
Remove and allow to cool.
To make tea sandwiches:

Mix:
1 - 8 oz. package cream cheese (softened)
1/2 c. strawberry preserves (or orange marmalade)
Slice cooled bread thinly and spread with cheese/preserve mixture and create
sandwiches. Cut them into thirds. Ideal with a fruit plate.

Torte Henrietta

1 prepared sponge cake (12-16 oz.)
1 small package instant vanilla pudding
2 c. milk
1/2 c. red raspberry spread
1/4 c. chopped pecans or toasted coconut
1 - 8 oz. package whipped topping

Prepare vanilla pudding according to directions and let set.
Split pound cake into four layers, placing bottom layer on a large paper doily
on a serving plate.
Spread bottom layer with vanilla pudding.
Place next layer on top and spread this with red raspberry preserves.
Add the next layer and spread with vanilla pudding.
Place final layer on top and spread the top with raspberry preserves.
Ice the entire assembled cake with whipped topping and sprinkle with chopped
pecans or coconut.
Allow to set at least I hour before serving.
Serves 6-8 people.

Dutch Apple Cream Pie

This apple pie is slightly different. German cooks often hid bits of fresh fruit
in their custard pies, but this carries the idea a little further.

12 apples (quartered and cored, blemishes removed)
1 1/2 c. sugar blended with:
4 T. flour
1/2 t. cinnamon

Mix 1 c. evaporated milk with:
1 stick melted margarine
1 t. lemon juice

Fill unbaked pie shell with apple wedges until even with edge.
Pour liquid mixture over apples.
Bake at 375 degrees for about 50 minutes, until lightly brown on top.
Don't peel the apples!

Hopping John

Assured good luck for the New Year with these black-eyed peas.

3 c. black-eyed peas (soaked over night and drained)
1/2 lb. Salt pork or ham bone cooked in 4 c. water for 30 minutes

Add soaked peas to pork broth and add:

1 whole onion (studded with 3 whole cloves)
1 bay leaf
1 pinch red pepper

Cook for one hour, then add:
1 c. uncooked rice.
Adjust water, salt, and pepper to taste.

Red Cross Canteen Slaw

When a quantity of slaw is needed for a group of people, this recipe can be multiplied with good results and many compliments.

Shred one head of cabbage.
Chop two or three medium size onions.
Layer cabbage alternately with chopped onion.
Then sprinkle 3/4 c. sugar over last layer.

Mix and boil:
1 T. sugar
2 t. dry mustard
1 t. celery seed
1 1/2 t. salt
1 c. cider vinegar

Then add 1 c. oil and bring to a boil again.
Let simmer for 2 minutes.
Pour mixture over cabbage, do not stir.
Cover tightly and let set for 24 hours.
Stir when ready to serve.

Aunt Amy Dale's Butterscotch Pie

You've met the Purcells elsewhere in the book. Now you will meet Mary Lou Purcell's loving aunt.

Combine:
1 1/2 c. brown sugar (or a mix of brown and white)
5 T. margarine

Bring sugar and margarine to a slow boil over medium heat.

Mix:
3 egg yolks (beaten)
2 T. flour
1 1/2 c. milk

Pour mixture into bubbling sugar, stirring constantly,
until it reaches a glossy stage.
Pour into a baked pie shell.
Beat egg whites with 2 T. sugar until mixture peaks.
Spread completely over filled pie shell, sealing all edges.
Bake at 325 degrees until lightly browned, about 12 minutes.

Cauliflower Salad

1 head cauliflower (separated and sliced thin)
1 c. sliced red radishes
1/4 c. diced green onion
1/2 c. chopped parsley
4 t. poppy seed

Mix:
1 c. mayonnaise
1 c. sour cream
1 package cheese and garlic dressing mix (Good Seasons)

Combine vegetables with dressing and allow to refrigerate 24 hours before serving.

Broccoli Flowers

When you need a green vegetable with some character to set off the rest of your meal, this works well.

Separate florets from one bunch of broccoli and place them in a skillet with 2 T. oil.
Cook slowly on low heat until tender.

Add:
3 T. red wine
1/4 t. salt
1/4 c. chopped green pepper
1 t. butter

Arrange around steak or pork chops.

Coconut Bread Pudding

This recipe adds a new dimension to bread pudding.

Beat:
1/4 c. sugar
1 egg
1 t. salt
1 t. vanilla
1 T. butter

Add this mixture to 2 c. scalded milk.

Add:
1 c. bread torn into small pieces
1/2 c. coconut

Bake at 350 degrees for about 30 minutes. Serve with whipped cream.

Strawberry Glaze Pie

Mix:
1 c. sugar
1/2 c. water
1/2 c. crushed strawberries
3 T. cornstarch

Cook until thick and clear.
Add 1 T. butter and red food coloring as needed.
Fill pie shell with whole berries and pour glaze over them.
Refrigerate until serving and garnish with whipped cream.

Kraut Burgers

Brown 1/4 lb. Sausage and drain.
Add 1 lb. Ground beef and cook until done.
Drain 1 no. 2 can of sauerkraut and chop

Add:
1/2 t. oregano
2 T. onion soup mix

Make up hot roll mix and cut into 4 inch squares.
Put kraut mixture in the center of each square, fold over, and seal edge.
Place on cookie sheet and bake at 350 degrees for 30 minutes.

Quick Hollandaise Sauce

Whisk together:
1 c. mayonnaise
2 eggs
3 T. lemon juice
1/2 t, salt
1/2 t. dry mustard

Cook over medium heat until mixture thickens.
For Eggs Benedict, serve over poached eggs and English muffin half.
This sauce is also appropriate for serving over vegetables or seafood.

Hot Spiced Fruit

This was a recipe I did on Diane's TV Show in Columbia, Missouri. It is really a fall or wintertime addition to a festive meal.

Melt together:
1/3 c. butter
3/4 c. brown sugar
2 T. curry powder

Drain:
1 large can of peach halves
1 large can of pear halves
1 can pineapple chunks
10 maraschino cherries

Arrange fruit in a glass baking dish and pour butter mixture over the fruit.
Bake at 325 degrees for about 1 hour.

Cucumber and Potato Soup

Don't turn the page! Its really good.

Peel and dice 4 potatoes
Cook in 2 c. cold water until soft

Stir in:
1 c. half and half
1/4 t. white pepper
1/2 c. milk
1/4 c. chopped green onion

Add 1 cucumber that has been peeled, seeded, and diced.
Simmer until cucumber is soft.
 Serve hot, topped with sour cream to which dill has been added.
Sprinkle soup bowl with fresh chopped dill.

Stuffing Mix

12 c. toasted bread cubes
1/3 c. snipped parsley
1/3 c. chopped onion
1 t. ground sage
1 t. thyme
1 t. crushed rosemary

Moisten with chicken broth, hot water, or left over fried chicken gravy.

My grandmother used this stuffing for poultry, but often as a base for a beef chuck roast.

Kraut Salad to Share

1 no.10 can of sauerkraut
2 large onions (chopped)
2 green peppers (chopped)
1 small can chopped pimentos
1 1/2 c. sugar
1 c. salad oil
3 c. chopped celery
1 c. cider vinegar
1 t. celery seed

or

1 no. 2 can sauerkraut
1/2 c. vinegar
1 c. sugar
1/2 c. celery (chopped)
1/2 c. green pepper (chopped)
1/2 c. onion (chopped)

Mix ingredients well and let stand for several hours.
Then refrigerate.
Good for 2 weeks with refrigeration.

Green Tomato Mincemeat

When we began Calico Cupboard at McCredie, a neighbor lady offered to make a supply of this mincemeat for use in our desserts.

1 1/2 pints apples (peeled and chopped)
1 pint green tomatoes (chopped fine)
2 t. cinnamon
1 t. salt
1 t. allspice
1 t. cloves
3 c. sugar
1 lb. Raisins
1/4 c. cider vinegar
1 c. suet (beef fat)

Mix all ingredients.
Simmer until thick.
Pour into sterilized jars (pint size) and seal.
You may also freeze the mixture in pint size containers.
 A pint is adequate for a two-crust pie.

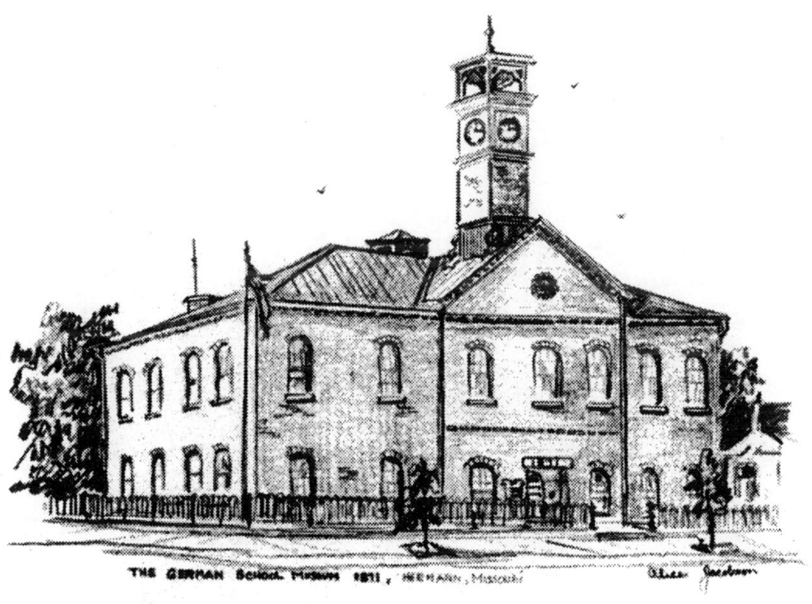

Crullers

Grandmother Jones called her doughnuts "crullers."
I wish her recipe had been in ink so that I could have used it, but the lead pencil was very faint.

1/4 c. butter (softened)
1 c. sugar
3 eggs (beaten until light)
1 1/2 - 2 c. flour
1 t. nutmeg

Mix flour and nutmeg together.
Gradually add sugar and softened butter to beaten eggs.
Gradually add flour/nutmeg mixture.
Turn out onto a freshly floured dough board.
Add enough flour to handle dough easily.
Pat dough into 1/3 inch thickness and cut into shapes with a knife or cookie cutter.
Fry in oil that has been pre-heated to 375 degrees.
Fry until brown, remove from oil, and roll in dry sugar.
Serve warm.

Herb Fried Potatoes

Peel, slice and fry potatoes in quantity you plan to use.
In the last five minutes of cooking time, add:

1/2 t. oregano
2 T. chopped celery
2 T. chopped parsley
2 T. onion
salt and pepper to taste

Spinach

Cook 1 - 10oz. Package frozen chopped spinach

Add:
2 T. butter
1/4 c. light cream
2 T. horseradish
1/2 t. salt
dash of pepper

Heat thoroughly.

Apricot Jam

As my mother's pantry of jellies, jams, and butters disappeared each winter, she reached for this simple jam made of dried apricots.

1 lb. dried apricots
2 - 2 1/2 cans crushed pineapple
1/2 c. sugar for each cup of fruit and juice

Soak dried apricots for 24 hours.

Chop soaked apricots into small pieces.
Add crushed pineapple.
Mix well and measure to add 1/2 c. sugar for each cup of fruit mixture.
Cook until thick and place in pint size jars.
Makes about 5 pints or 10 half pints.

Pickled Peaches

I'm sure my Dad's orchard never came from a nursery. In fact, the only source of plants we knew was the Henry Field Seed Catalog. If you wanted a tree to plant, you made a cutting of a full grown tree and nurtured it well. For a peach tree, you planted a peach seed.

Sometimes, nature planted the seeds and when a baby tree appeared, you simply thanked God and put stakes around it for protection. We had such a tree, a peach tree just outside the confines of our orchard. It bore fruit with a delicious flavor, but it was a "cling." In other words, the flesh of the peaches did not leave the seed. Freestone peaches yielded their fruit readily to the housewife.

With cling peaches, you made peach pickles. Without a cling peach tree, you made them like this:

1 large can peach halves in juice (or syrup)

Drain the juice from the peaches into a sauce pan and add the following to the juice:

1/2 c. vinegar
1/2 c. brown sugar
1 cinnamon stick
1 t. whole cloves
1 t. whole allspice

Boil the above for 5 minutes at a high heat.

Add the peach halves and simmer for about 5 minutes over reduced heat. Do not discard spices.

Cover and refrigerate.

At Calico Cupboard, we used #10 cans of peach slices because they were so popular. We increased spices accordingly.

Serve in a pretty glass bowl so the cinnamon sticks and whole cloves can be seen.

Molasses Pie

As I have told you before, molasses and corn syrup were in every pantry. Molasses was made each fall somewhere in the neighborhood, usually "over West," and you put your order in ahead of time. You might also arrange to take a barrel along to replace the one you were going to get.

My dad's sister, Aunt Frances, made a special molasses pie as follows:

3 egg yolks (beaten until stiff)
Add 1 1/2 c. molasses and 2 T. butter

Combine:
3/4 c. brown sugar
1/2 t. nutmeg
1/2 t. cinnamon
1/2 t. salt
1 T. flour
1 T. cornstarch

Add the above combination to the egg mixture and fold in 3 stiffly beaten egg whites.
Pour mixture into unbaked pie shell.

Bake for 15 minutes at 375 degrees.

Then reduce heat to 325 degrees and bake until a knife inserted into the pie comes out clean.

Pecan Pie

No sorghum molasses? Use Karo Syrup from the grocer.

Combine:
1 c. Karo
3 eggs
1/8 t. salt
1 t. vanilla
1 c. sugar
1 T. margarine (melted)
1 c. pecan pieces

Mix all ingredients together and pour into unbaked pie shell.

Bake at 400 degrees for 15 minutes, then reduce heat to 350 degrees and bake another 30-35 minutes.

Strawberry Rhubarb Pie

This is a two crust pie. The second crust may be cut into strips to make a lattice topping.

1 lb. rhubarb (trimmed and cut in 1 inch pieces)
1 lb. strawberries (whole or halves)

Combine rhubarb and strawberries in a mixing bowl and add:

1 1/4 c. sugar
5 T. flour
1/4 t. nutmeg

Place in an unbaked pie shell and dot with 2 T. margarine.

Put top pastry in place, sealing edges by moistening the places where the top crust touches the bottom crust.

Bake at 400 degrees until crust is golden brown and juices are bubbling.

Jack Carney's Black Bean Soup

In one of our newsletters, you'll read about Jack Carney's bean soup. Jack was one of St. Louis' best known radio personalities. He had a farm near Hermann that he visited every weekend. One Saturday night, we had added black beans to what was left of our navy bean soup in order to have plenty for the evening. We had chopped red onions in cider vinegar near the crock pot that contained the soup and another bowl of sour cream. It was a hit that night with Jack Carney and he told his listeners about how he looked forward to having it again. The first time was an accident, but the next time would take some planning. This is the result. This takes a large kettle. You can freeze the excess. And thank Jack Carney!

Place a ham bone in a large kettle and cover it with water.

Cook slowly for 30 minutes.

Add 1 lb. Great Northern White Beans and 1 large onion, chopped or sliced.

Cook until beans are tender, adding water as needed.

If salt from ham bone is not sufficient, add salt to taste.

Add at least 1 can of black beans (rinsed).

The bowl of chopped red onion in vinegar was always a favorite of many of our bean soup customers. We actually began using that for all our black bean soup. For that, we used chopped white sweet onions because they made such a pretty contrast with the black beans.

Jack was a great fan of Calico Cupboard and he never missed an opportunity to include us in his daily radio broadcasts. Thank you, Jack.

Grandma Bracky's Graham Bread

If we gave Hugo's mother ample notice that we were coming to Concordia, she always had Graham Bread. It always tasted good and seemed to me a truly down-to-earth accomplishment. Of course, she was always laden with grape jelly from her abundant grape arbor.

Pour 1c. scalded milk over:
1 T. sugar
1 t. salt
1 T. butter

Soften 1 package yeast (or 1/2 c. cake yeast) in 1/4 c. lukewarm water and add to the above mixture.
Gradually add 1 1/2 c. flour to make a ball.
Gradually add 1 1/2 to 2 1/2 c. sifted graham flour, until the dough is stiff enough to be handled and not stick to the dough board or your hands.
Place in a greased bowl and brush the top with oil.
Let it rise in a warm place until double in bulk.
Knead lightly, shape into a loaf, and let rise again to double in bulk.
Bake for 50-60 minutes at 400 degrees.
Remove from pan and put on rack to cool.

Taylor's Poverty Hash

This isn't just a name. Taylor knew personally what "poverty" was all about. It just makes the name more authentic.

Dice 1/2 lb. of sliced bacon into 1/2 inch pieces.
Place pieces in a skillet in about 1 inch of water.
Boil to extract fat and flavor from the bacon.

Add:
6 potatoes (peeled and diced)
1 onion (chopped)
salt and pepper to taste
Cook until potatoes are done. This makes a great aroma in your home.

When I had late classes at the University, Taylor occasionally surprised me with this luscious hash. I knew before I opened the door because the windows would all be frosted up. Taylor was a dear. We had 27 beautiful years together.

Mayonnaise Cake

In the 1950's, mayonnaise cakes were very popular. The best ones, I think, were made with cocoa which produced a lovely moist chocolate cake. They were so good, they didn't get a chance to dry out. They went out of style because cake mixes came on the market and simplified cake baking.
Below are two recipes for chocolate mayonnaise cake.

Sift together three times:
1 c. sugar
2 c. flour
2 T. cocoa
1 t. baking soda
pinch of salt

Add:
3/4 c. mayonnaise
1 c. hot water
1 t. vanilla

Mix well. Bake in a greased pan at 350 degrees for 30-35 minutes.
Spread with frosting of your choice.

Alternate recipe:

Grease two 9 inch cake pans and line with waxed paper.
Preheat oven to 350 degrees.

Mix:
3 c. flour
1 1/2 c. sugar
1/3 c. cocoa
2 1/4 t. baking powder
1 1/2 t. baking soda

Add:
1 1/2 c. mayonnaise
1 1/2 c. water
1 1/2 t. vanilla

Pour batter into prepared pans and bake for 30 minutes.
Cool for 10 minutes before removing cake from pans.
Frost as desired when completely cool.

Harvest Home Chicken Croquettes

For as long as I can remember, our Presbyterian Church in Raymond, Illinois prepared a fall dinner of home cooked food for the community. It was a sort of homecoming for people who has once been a part of the community. At noon time; fried chicken, mashed potatoes and gravy was the entree. This was accompanied by an assortment of vegetables, salads and desserts prepared by the ladies of the church.

At supper time, the entree was chicken croquettes and my mother was responsible for preparing them. As a farm wife, she could not help with the noon meal. But in the evening, she prepared the croquettes from chicken that had been cooked earlier in the day.

White sauce was added to the ground chicken meat with salt and pepper. After the croquettes were shaped, they were dipped in beaten egg and rolled in bread crumbs. They were fried in deep fat just long enough to brown them because the meat was already cooked.

These were the proportions she listed in her recipe box:

1 qt. or 2 lbs. chopped or ground chicken
1 c. thick white sauce
3 beaten eggs

Use no crumbs in croquette mixture unless necessary to thicken.

Mrs. Klinger's German Coffee Cake

In the 1970's, when I was researching Hermann's history and William Klinger's beautiful Victorian home on Second Street, I became acquainted with their granddaughter. She was interested in my offering the Klinger home to the public as a bed and breakfast inn. Mr. Klinger was a successful flour miller, but we had little information about his wife. The granddaughter, Margaret Jackson, sent a copy of her grandmother's handwritten recipe. I have adapted it below:

Dissolve 1 yeast cake in 1/4 c. of water.
Heat:
1 c. milk
1/3 c. butter or shortening
1/2 c. sugar
3/4 t. salt

When mixture reaches a lukewarm temperature, add:
dissolved yeast mixed with 1 t. sugar
1 egg (beaten)
1 1/2 c. flour

Beat for a few minutes and add balance of flour.

Form into a ball and place in greased bowl.
Allow it to rise until double in bulk.
When double, remove from bowl and roll out to a half inch thickness.
Place in a greased baking pan.

Cover the dough with a mixture of:
3 T. melted butter
1/3 c. sugar
1 t. cinnamon

Let dough rise again.

When double in bulk, sprinkle with crumbs from the following mixture:
1/2 stick butter
2/3 c. flour
1/4 t. cinnamon

Bake at 375 degrees for 35 minutes.

Sweet Potatoes with Apples

There's much of "thanksgiving" in all country cooking. There's thanksgiving for homes, thanksgiving for nature's bounty, and thanksgiving for healthy appetites around the kitchen table. We always grew sweet potatoes where the early garden lettuce had been. Apples of some kind were always available. You'll find this recipe welcome at home or for a carry-in.

Cook 6 to 8 medium size sweet potatoes (or use 2 large cans from the grocer)

Peel and slice sweet potatoes.

Slice three un-peeled apples and mix with:
1/3 c. chopped pecans
1/2 c. brown sugar (packed)
1/2 t. cinnamon

Alternate layers in a 9x13 cake pan.

Dot with margarine.

Cover with foil and bake at 350 degrees for 35-40 minutes.

Remove foil, sprinkle with miniature marshmallows and broil lightly until browned.

Scalloped Oysters

Winter holidays allowed us to enjoy foods that had to be used immediately. We had no refrigeration and no freezers, and were fortunate to have a screened in porch to accommodate perishable items for an over-night. My dad loved oysters and they were only available temporarily at Litchfield, about ten miles from home. From Thanksgiving to Christmas, we enjoyed oyster stew, fried oysters, or scalloped oysters.

I remember my mother preparing fried oysters for a group of neighbors that had helped Dad with butchering. It seemed like she spent all afternoon breading them so that they would fry quickly in the huge shallow skillet reserved for doughnuts and oysters. She used her big roll pan that held 36 hot rolls to keep the fried oysters warm in the oven until serving time. It looked like she had enough to feed an army, but they would all be gone quickly after our guests arrived.

Scalloped oysters were a simple preparation and they continue to be a favorite with my family. My grandson, Tim, thinks I should experiment with canned oysters from the grocery store, but that seems like infamy to me for I cannot separate oysters from my recollections of home.

Grease a two quart baking dish with butter.

Layer broken soda crackers on the bottom, about 1/2 inch deep.

Cover with a layer of oysters and 1/2 c. of oyster juice.

Repeat until baking dish is full with a layer of broken crackers on top.

Dot with 6-8 pats of butter.

Pour milk over layers until it is barely visible around the edges.

Sprinkle with black pepper and a little salt. The soda crackers add salt on their own.

Let stand for about an hour or longer if you have refrigerated the casserole.

An hour before serving time, place in a 350 degree oven and bake until puffy and browned.

Luscious Leftovers

Grandmothers had few leftovers, for they cooked for large families using foods they had grown or preserved. But at Calico Cupboard, with a buffet, we always had leftovers; particularly of meats. We had more leftover fried chicken than anything else, usually the less popular pieces of chicken. There might also be leftover gravy.

For leftover chicken:
Place chicken pieces in a baking dish.
Mix the gravy with sour cream and chopped green and red peppers.
Bake at 300 degrees for one hour.

OR

Cover fried chicken with a can of mushroom soup mixed with an equal amount of sour cream.
Add chopped green and red peppers and bake as above.

For leftover pork chops:
Follow the same method but mix sour cream with a package of onion soup mix and spread over the chops.

For round steak:
Follow the same method for sour cream/mushroom soup mix and add 1/2 t. poppy seeds.

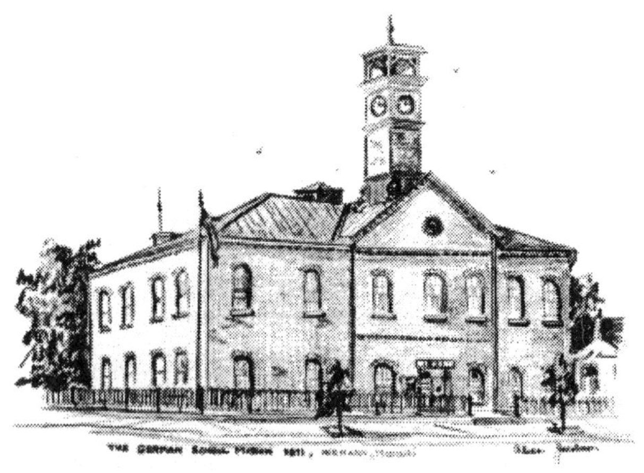

French Dressing

When Tim and DeAnn used to weekend with me in Peculiar, they had two favorite places to eat. "Goodie's" in Peculiar was known for their over sized tenderloin sandwiches. They also went to "Irene's" in Harrisonville to enjoy her pies, and I went to enjoy the French Dressing on her salads. My attraction was based on its decidedly onion flavor. Goodie's is not Goodie's anymore and Irene's is not Irene's, but Irene and the atmosphere she created in her "Harvest House" live on. She was a perfect hostess!

The following recipe approximates what I enjoyed at Irene's.

Blend:
3 1/2 c. sugar
1/4 c dry mustard
1/4 c. paprika

Add:
1/4c. Worcestershire sauce
1 qt. cider vinegar
1 qt. salad oil
46 oz. can cream of tomato soup

After mixing, add 1 c. finely chopped onion. Mix well.
Makes 4 quarts, so you'll be able to share with friends of give as gifts.

This dressing is particularly good on plain head lettuce without any other vegetables. A teacher at Belton Junior High School gave me the following similar recipe. It tastes exactly like Irene's.

1 50 oz. Can Campbell's tomato soup
1 50 oz. Tomato soup can full of salad oil
2 c. sugar
2 c. vinegar
1 scant t. black pepper
2 T. celery seed
1 T. garlic powder
1/2 T. Accent seasoning
1/2 T. salt

Mix the ingredients in a small dishpan and blend a quart at a time.
Makes approximately 3 quarts.

Meatballs and Spaetzle

1 - 10 oz. can beef broth
1 - 3 oz. Can chopped mushrooms
1/2 c. chopped onion
1 c. sour cream
1 T. flour
1/2 t. - 1 t. caraway seed

Meatballs: (for 24 balls)

1 lb. ground beef
1 egg
1/4 c. bread crumbs
1/4 c. milk
1 T. parsley
1 t. salt
1/4 t. poultry seasoning
dash of pepper

Brown meatballs.
Add broth, mushrooms and onions.
Simmer 30 minutes.

Blend sour cream, flour and caraway seed and stir into broth.
Cook until thick.

Spaetzle:

2 c. flour
1 t. salt
2 eggs (slightly beaten)
3/4 c. milk

Force through colander into boiling salted water.
Cook for 5 minutes and drain.
Sprinkle with buttered bread crumbs that have been toasted.

Fran Parketon's Quiche Lorraine

Fran and Blake Parketon operated the old Central Hotel in Hermann at the same time Taylor and I were operating Calico Cupboard. They were on Hermann's main street, Market Street, and we were near the river front. Our paths seldom crossed because we were all busy. Now, coincidentally, we both live near the airport in Kansas City and we see each other frequently. Recently, they invited me for breakfast and Fran's quiche was delicious. It serves six but not six Betty Yeddises!

4 eggs (slightly beaten)
1 1/2 c. whole milk
1/4 t. salt
dash of pepper
2 c. or 8 oz. Cracker Barrel cheddar cheese (shredded)
3/4 c. diced and cooked ham
1 - 9 inch pie shell (unbaked)

Combine ingredients and mix well.

Pour into pie shell and bake at 350 degrees for 40-45 minutes.

Allow quiche to cool slightly before cutting in wedges to serve.

First Street - Hermann, Missouri

Adele Yeddis' Chopped Chicken Livers

My Grandmother Jones always made chopped chicken livers as she remembered them from the year she lived with the Blooms in St. Louis. She was twelve and her mother worried that life on the Illinois prairie denied her insight into the real world. So she arranged with her Jewish friends in St. Louis for my grandmother to attend a better school.

My grandmother also made blintzes regularly and I learned to love both foods, not knowing that they were traditional in Jewish households.

Morris' cousin, Rose Londi, served appetizers of chopped chicken livers one afternoon when we visited her with cousin Jennie Gershenson in St. Louis. This was shortly after Morris and I had been married. The appetizers brought back recollections of what Grandmother Jones had served. I remember my mother's stories about how Grandmother Jones always talked about her year with the Blooms.

1 lb. chicken livers
3 hard boiled eggs
1 large red onion (diced)
salt and pepper
rendered chicken fat

Fry diced onion in chicken fat.
Fry livers.
Combine all ingredients and grind together.
If mixture is too dry, add a touch of water or broth.
Place in a container that will serve as a mold for serving, or serve in a shallow bowl.

Yummy Sauce for Waffles

1/2 c. butter
1/2c. brown sugar (packed)
1 t. vanilla
1 egg yolk beaten with:
4 T. milk
1 c. heavy cream

Beat mixture until it holds shape.
Refrigerate.
Serve on waffles in walnut size spoonfuls.

Applesauce and Sour Cream

Doesn't it sound terrible?

This was a favorite at Calico Cupboard for people who wanted a dessert lighter than our delicious pies.

Fix individual servings of chunky apple sauce. Footed ice cream sundae dishes are perfect for this recipe.

On top of each serving, place a dollop of sour cream that has been mixed with brown sugar to a sweetness that suits you.

Sprinkle generously with nutmeg.

This recipe can also be presented in a glass serving bowl and with interesting results. As you dip the applesauce out, the spoon carries the sweetened sour cream and nutmeg down into the bowl so that by the time you come to the bottom, it is truly delicious.

Alphabetical List of Recipes

Check your favorites for later reference.

____ Adele Yeddis' Chopped Chicken Livers
____ Applesauce and Sour Cream
____ Apricot Jam
____ Aunt Amy Dale's Butterscotch Pie
____ Bonnie's Pie Crust
____ Broccoli Flowers
____ Buttermilk Pie
____ Calico Cupboard's Buttermilk Biscuits
____ Calico Cupboard's Hot German Potato Salad
____ Calico Cupboard's Poppy Seed Dressing
____ Caraway Seed
____ Cauliflower Salad
____ Coconut Bread Pudding
____ Cole Slaw to Share
____ Crescent Rolls
____ Crullers
____ Cucumber and Potato Soup
____ Cucumbers and Sour Cream
____ Dutch Apple Cream Pie
____ Fran Parketon's Quiche Lorraine
____ French Dressing
____ Genevieve Stonner's Green Pea Salad
____ Gingered Carrots
____ Ginny Lone's Crock Salad
____ Grandma Bracky's Graham Bread
____ Grape Salad
____ Green Tomato Mincemeat
____ Harvest Home Chicken Croquettes
____ Herb Fried Potatoes
____ Holly Horton's Bran Muffins
____ Homemade Noodles
____ Hopping John

_____ Hot Spiced Fruit
_____ Jack Carney's Black Bean Soup
_____ Jeff Davis Pie
_____ Kraut Burgers
_____ Kraut Salad
_____ Kraut Salad to Share
_____ Lemon Bread Pudding
_____ Lemon Sponge Pie
_____ Luscious Leftovers
_____ Marinated Vegetables
_____ Mayonnaise Cake
_____ Meatballs and Spaetzle
_____ Molasses Pie
_____ Moloney Potatoes
_____ Mom's Date Pudding
_____ Mrs. Klinger's German Coffee cake
_____ Peas and Dumplings
_____ Pecan Pie
_____ Pickled Peaches
_____ Potato Pancakes
_____ Quick Hollandaise Sauce
_____ Red Cross Canteen Slaw
_____ Scalloped Oysters
_____ Short Ribs and Poppy Seed Noodles
_____ Spinach
_____ Strawberry Bread
_____ Strawberry Glaze Pie
_____ Strawberry Rhubarb Pie
_____ Stuffing Mix
_____ Sugar Cookies
_____ Sugar Pie
_____ Sweet and Sour Red Cabbage
_____ Sweet Kosher Dill Pickles
_____ Sweet Potatoes with Apples
_____ Taylor's Poverty Hash
_____ Torte Henrietta
_____ Volney Hildreth's Salad Dressing
_____ Yummy Sauce for Waffles

Reader's Notes

"A tea room to offer my grandmother's
Pennsylvania style food to an
appreciative public."....

CALICO COUNTRY ANTIQUES

. . . a village of unusual shops and studios
Open daily 10 a.m. — 5 p.m.

On CALICO LANE . . . .

The Little Shop	The Strawberry Pincushion
Bilyeu's	Oak Ridge Antiques
Howell's Antiques	The Neighbor Lady
La Petite Gallerie	The Cabbage Patch
	Country Oak

In the old bank . . . . The Grandmothers Shoppe

In the General Store . . . . Frank & Marie McCully, Managers

In the Calico Cottage . . . .

The Calico Cupboard (Weekend and Reservation Dining)
Sunday - Smorgasbord - 12 noon-3 p.m. (or later)
Saturday - Buffet - Salad Bar - 6-8 p.m.

Reservations - or special arrangements for groups
314–642-4325

The *CALICO CUPBOARD* . . . . .

Country dining in a "Home Comfort" atmosphere . . . with
seven sweets and seven sours . . . . . and much, much more.

CALICO COUNTRY ANTIQUE VILLAGE

On 54 Hwy 1 mi. N of I-70
Kingdom City, Missouri
Reservations: 314–642-4325

Wm. M. & Betty Taylor
The Antique Taylors
Peculiar, Missouri 64078

Calico Country Antique Village: McCredie (Kingdom City) Mo.
as prepared and sketched by Betty Taylor, later Yeddis.

Tea Room Dream

As I grew older and my mother and I found opportunities to get away from her responsibilities on the farm, we made it a point to enjoy cute, inviting places that we found along the way. Mother and I were both intrigued by the inviting exteriors and beautifully decorated interiors. We admired the darling window treatments, the crystal, the china, and the cozy atmosphere. Our dreams always included Grandmother Jones' Pennsylvania style food.

The White Cottage in Raymond, my hometown, came nearest to my mother's dream. She and my dad enjoyed dining there and, in their later years, that was frequent. Mother never lived to see The Calico Cupboard, but her earlier energies and ideas were very much a part of it.

Calico Country Antiques: Kingdom City, Missouri (envelope/letterhead) This sketch was a "dream" doodle as we were deciding to do Calico Country Antique Village. I actually drew it on muslin, embroidered it and signed it; but it disappeared from its spot by the front door.

Blue Willow table setting with Calico Country Antique Village card displayed

Taylor assists a guest at our original Calico Cupboard
where we served pie from an old cook stove.

Writings from <u>The Calico Cupboard Scrapbook</u>:

From my introduction to Ada Foster's Home Economics class in Raymond (Illinois) Community High School in 1926, I longed for and planned to some-day have a Tea Room. Ada was also my Sunday school teacher and whatever she said, I believed. In Home Economics, we had electric cook plates at our work stations, but for baking we used a coal-fired cook stove. It was my job to leave study hall during the early part of the hour to have adequate oven temperature by class time. Hildegarde Haarstick (whose last name later became Folkerts) was my partner at my work station. She was an "A" student but I know I got an "A" because I was a good fire builder. Ada and I planned decorations, china, flower arrangements, and furnishings for my dream Tea Room and made lists with costs to go with them. Ada had graduated from a nearby woman's college and she knew what she was talking about. I had never been near a tea room , but that didn't matter. I was seeing things through Ada's eyes.

As far as actually cooking, my experience had been with our family at home - five people with one or more hired men. My mother usually got dinner (at noon) and it was always from scratch, of course. It was my job to get supper. I would have it ready at 6:00 p.m. for the hired men but my Dad might not come in from the field until an hour later. I've always felt that a lot of the weight I've carried all my life was due to successive tastings to be sure the food was hot when Dad actually came to the table.

Very candidly, I never thought my mother was a very good cook. She was too practical and times were too tough to buy "store bought" ingredients when we had so many things on hand from the farm that needed to be used. Mother made delicious breads, cookies, and pies but her cakes never compared to Aunt Flora's. My mother taught me planning, organization and processes. I think she learned this from Grandmother Jones, who never discussed ingredi-ents but emphasized the importance of using the right kettle, the right lid, and the right amount of heat. In other words, she taught me what went on under the lid. Grandmother Jones dumplinged and noodled everything. That was her way of coping with the hard times and raising a large family on a blacksmith's earnings.

So in 1973, I talked Taylor into letting me try to serve my Grandmother's style food in McCredie. It was a little out-of-way town of twelve people a mile away from Kingdom City, Missouri, the intersection of 54 Highway and I-70. We adapted a double-wide mobile home specifically for this purpose. It was an immediate success and with in the first year, we had great reviews and great

Debbie Daro graced our first Calico Cupboard in McCredie. It was a new experience
for her just as it was for Taylor and me. She tossed her blue jeans, donned our frilly pinafore
and became a part of our dream. She also became one of my "Missouri Daughters."

Debbie Daro Craighead in 1998 with her husband, Mark, and Patrick, Amanda & Dori

customers. We could serve twenty-five people at a time. We served on Saturday night and Sunday by reservation. Monday through Friday, I was still Junior High Librarian in Belton, Missouri. Taylor brought in the staple groceries and I arrived each Friday night with fresh produce and meat from Kansas City. We were so out-of-the-way that we could not get any deliveries. When the customers from Hermann kept asking us to come to Hermann with our food, we listened. The Kallmeyers offered us their building if we would give them two years to vacate. We accepted and took possession in December, 1976. I was planning to retire in 1977.

What followed were the most creative years of our lives. Taylor was a perfect host and me, I cooked and cooked and cooked. The two-story part of the Kallmeyer building was originally the St. Charles Halle, which offered wine, beer and billiards for the railroad passengers. The railroad was built in 1855 and it replaced the river boat traffic at that intersection. Pine lumber and iron-ore had been shipped on the river. The lumber was floated down the Gasconade River to the Missouri and the iron had been carted from the St. James, Missouri area.

Hermann had been established in 1836 and by 1977, there were 108 of its original German style buildings in a historic district which was on the National Registry of Historic Sites. After World War II, a Kaiser-Fraser showroom was added to the original St. Charles Halle. There were always residents in the second floor quarters, after it was no longer used for the first Hermann High School. Lee Kolterman copied an original section of gingerbread from the front porch of a house in Prairie City, Missouri. We erected the porch across what had been an ordinary auto sales room exterior. Our dining room overlooked the Missouri River and the intermittent train delighted the youngsters who came. We decorated with antiques from the Hermann area that we had accumulated at the Kallmeyer-Schroff auction, never knowing we would be a part of this delightful village in Missouri's "Rhine" country.

Hermann was beautiful any time, but it was delightful in the snow. It looked like a Grandma Moses painting. You could see the Court House dome and part of the Court House just beyond our building. Sometimes, school would be out for days and days because the buses couldn't navigate the seven icy hills surrounding the town. We were fortunate to have access to a parking lot just across the street. In the summer, Taylor kept petunia barrels blooming full and vibrant by watering them and picking off dead blossoms. Dorothy Rae Lewis called Taylor a little "leprechaun" as he was quietly engaged somewhere in Calico Cupboard or the Inn every day.

Bed and Breakfast - Missouri Style

We frequently heard from Calico customers with ideas that had reminded them of the Taylors. We worked most of them into our atmosphere or our service. But when they sent tear-outs about a bed and breakfast, we read them over and over. They had thought that our second floor rooms overlooking the Missouri River were a natural, and they were. They also tempted us to buy Wilford Kallmeyer's beautiful Victorian home on Second Street.

These farmer hens' nests added excitement to our assortment of jellies, jams and relishes.
If we didn't sell them, we served them.

It was a natural for public enjoyment. It had been built by William Klinger, the town's successful flour miller. As we explored the possibilities, we found the beautiful dining room mantle in the attic, above the third floor ballroom. But we did need additional baths and plumbing. While these problems were solved by local contractors, I researched the newspapers of the 1870's when the house was built. I wanted to name the rooms for local people so there would be some history in each; like Mrs. Silber who had been a local dress-maker with a street front business. The ballroom became three guest rooms with their own bath and a multi-purpose area that would make a wonderful display area for our old needlework collection.

Everything went together with the help of Paul Viola and Lee Kolterman who, by this time, knew what to expect from the Antique Taylors. Our regular publicity outlets continued their great cooperation and we were accepted by <u>Back Roads and Country Inns</u>. People continued to offer us properties and we finally bought two of Hermann's oldest houses facing Third Street, and across what we personally called Hollyhock Alley. We asked Joan Keiser's permission to use the name "Hollyhock House" for another two-story frame house nearby. She had called her rural home Hollyhock House. With the Garden Club's help, we attempted to get the city to let us name the town's beautiful alleys for easily grown summer flowers like marigolds, petunias, and chrysanthemums; but without success. As we were leaving Hermann a few months ago, my attention was called to a large "Hollyhock Alley" sign on Market Street; a sort of monument to an idea that did not find acceptance. Few towns in America could match Hermann's beautiful and well cared for alleys.

Now Bed and Breakfast is everywhere in Hermann. Der Klingerbau was the beginning, but it is now called "Angels in the Attic." The needlework I planned to display on its third floor is packed and stored in my attic in Kansas City, hoping someone will someday find it interesting. See next page.

The laundry room never escaped decoration; displaying our collection of wash boards, soap boxes, and a variety of early day clothespins. See clothespin collection.

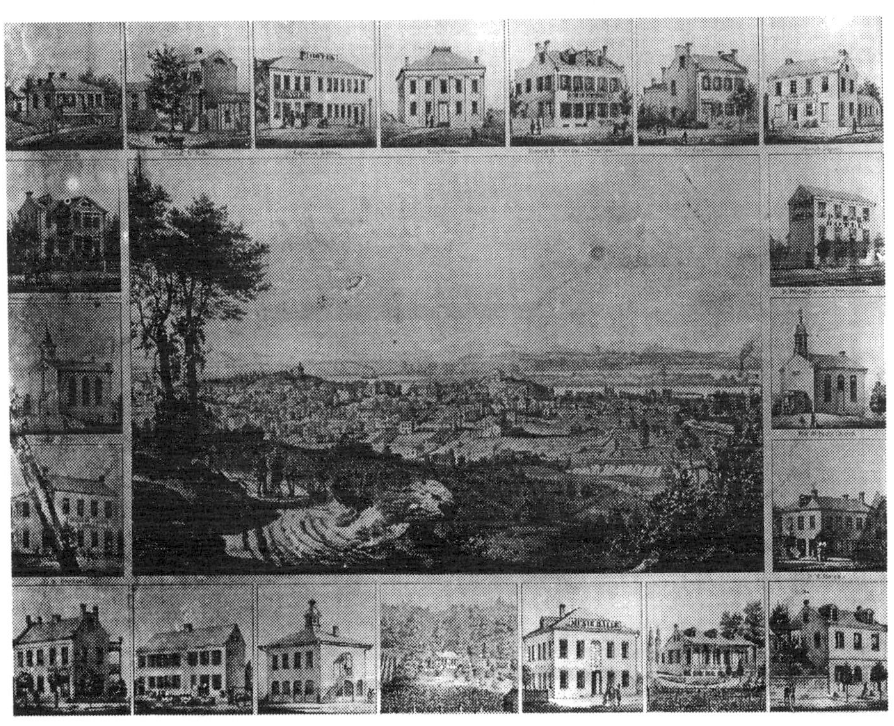

Early sketch of Hermann, Missouri: 1859-1860
(Credit the State Historical Society of Missouri)

Joan Keiser Bredehoeft prepared this card for us while I finished teaching at Belton. The "caution" side was a quotation from me and Taylor. It was our first effort to build tourism in Hermann. It worked. And as I find excuses to get back to Hermann every few months, I know why. Hermann IS habit forming.

Storefront photograph of Calico Cupboard Taylor and I had saved a section of gingerbread from Prairie City, Missouri only because it was too pretty to abandon. Twenty-four hours after we showed it to Lee Kolterman, the porch was being added to the front of the former Kaiser Frazer showroom to protect guests from the weather. The original St. Charles Halle stood alongside and the two buildings became Calico Cupboard's Country Dining and Antiques.

Hermann, Missouri

THE CALICO CUPBOARD

4 Schiller Street, Hermann, MO 65041. 314-486-2030. *Innkeepers:* William and Betty Taylor. Open March through December.

The Calico Cupboard is a dream come true in at least three ways. It has everyone's fantasy of an endearing country restaurant, it is a very special place to stay, and it is the realization of a lifelong dream for innkeeper Betty Taylor. Betty spent her spare time while she was a teacher in planning the inn she would open someday, and just after her retirement, a few years ago, she and her husband, Bill, purchased the old St. Charles Halle in Hermann.

Called by many the "Rhine Country of Missouri," the region is an important center of German culture. Twenty blocks of Hermann's downtown area and the renowned Stone Hill Winery are listed in the National Register of Historic Places. St. Charles Halle, itself, offered wine, beer, and billiards for the steamboat and railroad traffic that converged at a wharf on the Missouri River in the last quarter of the nineteenth century. Into this waterfront building, the Taylors tucked six dining rooms ranging in size from the intimate Blue Willow Room, with its oaken drop-leaf table, 1890s chairs, and china cabinet filled with the Taylors' blue-willow collection, to the roomy main dining room, whose walls are decorated with primitives purchased in the surrounding countryside.

As for the food, Betty Taylor has designed her menu to pay tribute to the German heritage of the region. Dishes such as bratwurst, eintopf (a casserole), and chicken grandmother style typify the selections. On Sundays a *Bauernschmaus,* or farmer's feast, is offered, featuring seven meats and a bountiful supply of vegetables, salads, and desserts.

The suites have spacious, high-ceilinged rooms overlooking the Missouri River. They are furnished and decorated entirely from the 1879–90 period, with one suite having a Victorian theme and the other more of a "country" feeling.

Bill and Betty recently bought four more historic homes in Hermann; so now guests can chose from a variety of "Old World"-style houses. Der Klingerbau Inn, built in 1878 by a local flour miller, is furnished with Victorian antiques suitable to its age. It is here that all the guests of the Taylors' places gather for breakfasts of German pastries and coffee served by a dining-room fireside. The Von Arx House and the 1840 Haus are next door to each other, and both reflect the early-German architecture of this river town. The 1840 Haus is the only one of the houses suitable for children and pets and is furnished with them in mind. It has a spacious lawn. The fourth house is an old 1870 salt-box style. All of the houses are furnished with antiques, and each has a sitting room with a bar.

Accommodations: 16 rooms and some 2-room suites, all private bath. *Driving Instructions:* The Calico Cupboard is 14 miles south of I-70 on Routes 19 and 100.

Article from <u>Inns, Lodges, and Historic Hotels</u>: 1984-85
We were very proud to be included in this directory.

Sketch of the Third Street houses

Photograph of my grandson, Tim, and my son, Bill The hammer and the paint represent the first stages of transforming a century old home into a bed and breakfast inn. My son, Bill Brackman, and his son, Tim, were always agreeable to reclaiming an aging building. This was also the first stage in my grandson's plan to become "The Man Around the House" in Kansas City. Fourteen years later, he has a well established home and commercial maintenance business, but it found its origin with the Von Arks and Loehnig houses in Hermann.

Tim's first business card.
His ad in the Jewish Chronicle has been running for over ten years.

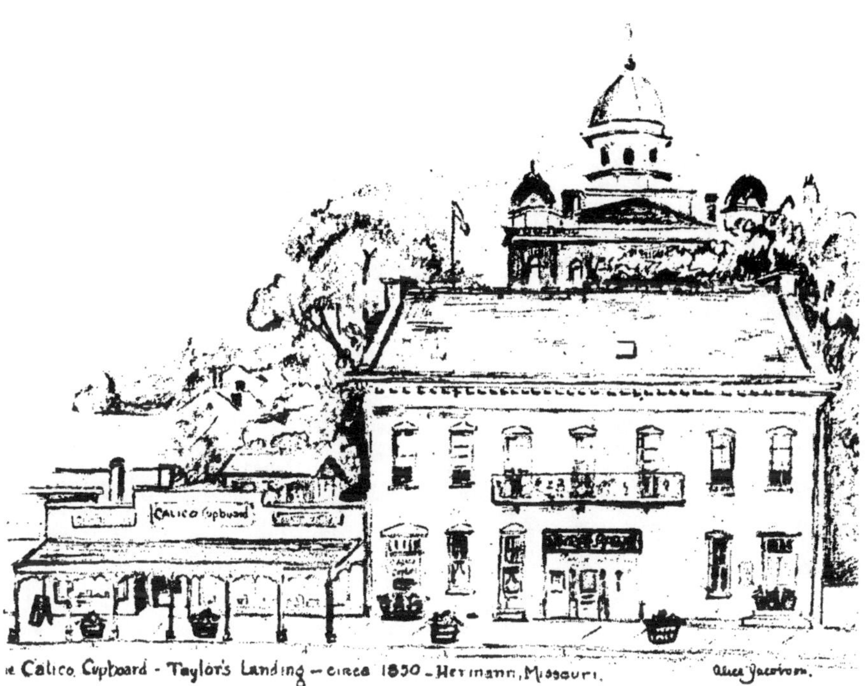

Sketch of the Calico Cupboard - Taylor's Landing We had barely landed in Hermann when Alice Jacobson introduced the Calico Cupboard into her historic Hermann note paper series. She caught the feeling of what Taylor and I were trying to do and we made sure Calico Cupboard's appearance measured up to the image she had created.

Actually, this picture at the bottom of the twenty-six steps to Calico Cupboard's second floor disguises a heavy double door that once led from the street to Hermann's high school in St. Charles Halle. We blocked the door rather than break up the front of the building by trying to fashion a new door.

The Volney Hildreth family: Our first customers at McCredie.
Our first customers at Hermann. You'll find Volney Hildreth's salad dressing in the
Recipe section. We were fortunate to have enjoyed their confidence in our undertaking.

The Boyce's had been every Sunday guests at Calico Cupboard at McCredie. By the time
we got to Hermann, Gabriel had joined them. They left Missouri a short time later.

Anita, Marcella, and Gertrude in the Calico Cupboard kitchen.
Anita personally filled her salad bar bowls in preparation for luncheon guests.
You can see that even the kitchen displayed antique trivets and muffin pans.
Gertrude was our first cook and Marcella joined as our needs grew.

Lee Kolterman was always a happy guest. We were fortunate that he chose to be
in Hermann those years. There were never problems for Lee, just solutions.
He was very active in Hermann organizations while he and Roberta lived there.

Robert and Georgene Weigel were both journalists in the Washington, Missouri (Marthasville) area. Robert wrote about Calico Cupboard often. His heart felt reflections on Calico Cupboard and Hermann always reassured us that our efforts and planning were in character with this little bit of "old country" in Missouri. Robert passed away two years ago.When I remarked about the name "Georgene," she said that after five sons and no daughters, an early father said, "I'll just name you Georgene." Three generations later, there are six Georgene's in the family. Notice the collection of hand-forged hinges decorating the wall where they are seated at Calico Cupboard.

Lois Pierce, Roberta Kolterman, and Raygene Meyers

Hermann's "Mr. Music" was Doc Schmidt,
shown here dancing with Betty.

Raymond friend Jimmy Bowsher and, if my memory is up to par, I
think he has his cousin, Dorothy McCammon, with him.

In 1979, we introduced Dinner Dancing to Calico Cupboard guests
as often as B.A. Wagner was available to us. This picture shows the
B.A. Wagner Orchestra with Mimi Schmidt at piano.

Raygene and Glenn Meyer

Marvin Bruens dances with Irene Schweerkoetting

At Calico Cupboard, our assortment of pies was presented on a tea cart at the end of our customer's meals. The sight of it being wheeled to other tables ruined a lot of diets.

Holly Horton.
Everybody should have
a daughter like Holly.
She was a jewel.

Inside of card from
Holly Horton Tyree: July 24, 1995
Holly Horton Tyree hosted the
Calico Cupboard in its earliest years.
She is one of my "Missouri Daughters."

July - 24, 95

Betty,
thank you so much for
keeping me up on your add
I think of you often and
I sure would not want to
loose track of you! — Just
the other day my Dad
asked me to make him
some " Betty Taylor Cole Slaw"
I grew so much at Calico
Cupboard —! I would not
trade those years & memories
for anything in the world!
You were a _perfect_ role
model for a young girl
growing up in Hermann!
I hope this card finds
you well! Please keep in
touch!
With love,
Holly

Taylor enjoyed being photographed. The Calico Cupboard customers loved him.
And he loved our customers. And he loved me! Without him, there would have been no
Brookwood, no <u>Peculiar Heritage</u>, and no Calico Cupboard. At 88, he was a perfect host
in a 110 year old inn. He gave Der Klingerbau reality rather than atmosphere.

The Calico Cupboard - Taylor's Landing — circa 1890 — Hermann, Missouri,

Alice Jacobson.

Letters

Our newsletters, The Grapevine, really did reveal our happiness in Hermann and our enthusiasm for Missouri tourism efforts. Unfortunately, only a few of these letters remain because our notebook collection of them was lost when Bill Nunn died suddenly. He had asked if he could submit them to a client and we were glad to comply. His family made a thorough search after his death, but they probably were in the hands of someone with whom he had planned to collaborate - just as he had done with our calendar.

Bill Nunn found us engaging and energetic and he always had ideas for us. Gibson Greeting Cards distributed 43,000 of the Just Country Cookin' calendar. People tell us they still have them. Bill Nunn introduced us to Missouri Life's publisher and assured Calico Cupboard's success in Hermann. He kept us dreaming. So we'll include the newsletters we do have and portions of the Missouri Life article with its great photography. To his family and to The Nunn Group, we are greatly indebted for our happy retirement and offer our continuing appreciation for Bill's role in our efforts to make Missouri and Hermann "don't miss destinations."

First Street - Hermann, Missouri

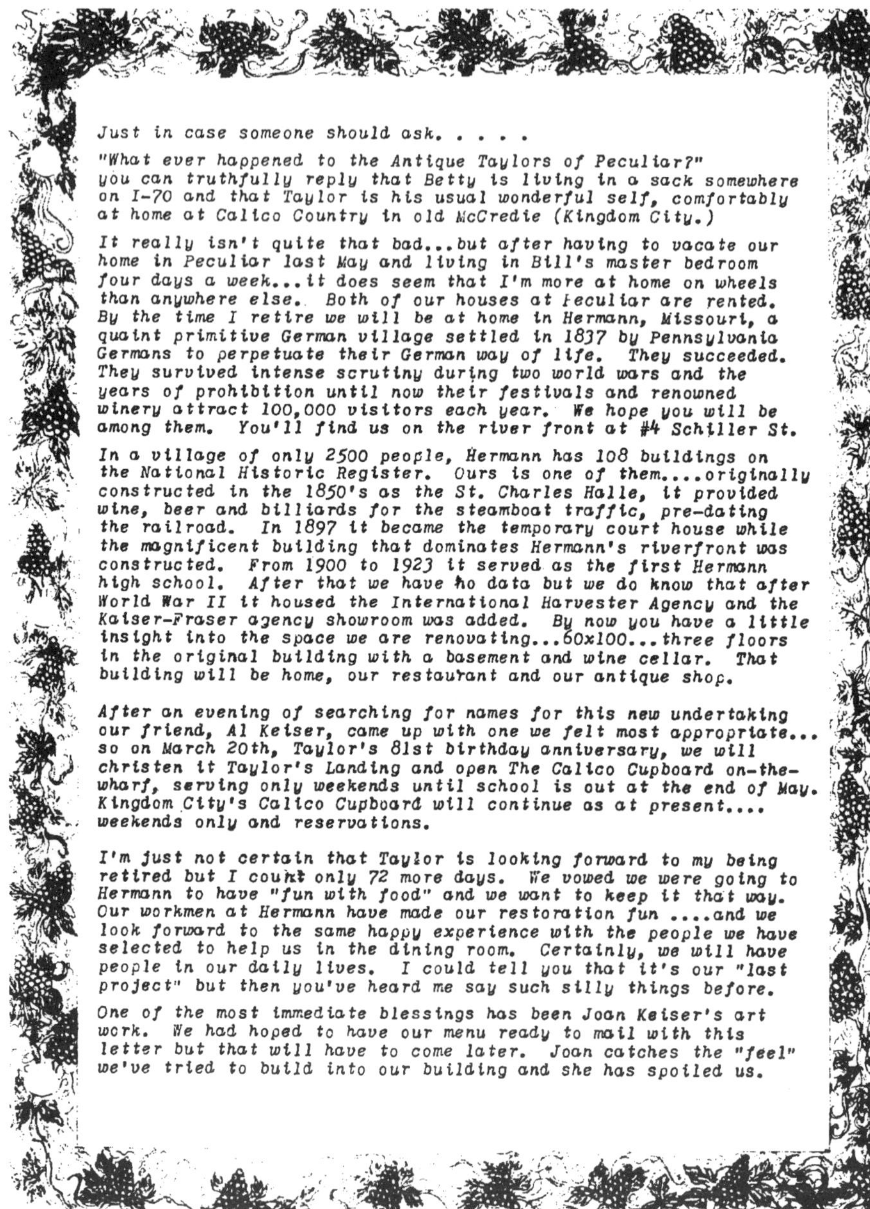

Just in case someone should ask. . . . . .

"What ever happened to the Antique Taylors of Peculiar?"
you can truthfully reply that Betty is living in a sack somewhere
on I-70 and that Taylor is his usual wonderful self, comfortably
at home at Calico Country in old McCredie (Kingdom City.)

It really isn't quite that bad...but after having to vacate our
home in Peculiar last May and living in Bill's master bedroom
four days a week...it does seem that I'm more at home on wheels
than anywhere else. Both of our houses at Peculiar are rented.
By the time I retire we will be at home in Hermann, Missouri, a
quaint primitive German village settled in 1837 by Pennsylvania
Germans to perpetuate their German way of life. They succeeded.
They survived intense scrutiny during two world wars and the
years of prohibition until now their festivals and renowned
winery attract 100,000 visitors each year. We hope you will be
among them. You'll find us on the river front at #4 Schiller St.

In a village of only 2500 people, Hermann has 108 buildings on
the National Historic Register. Ours is one of them....originally
constructed in the 1850's as the St. Charles Halle, it provided
wine, beer and billiards for the steamboat traffic, pre-dating
the railroad. In 1897 it became the temporary court house while
the magnificent building that dominates Hermann's riverfront was
constructed. From 1900 to 1923 it served as the first Hermann
high school. After that we have no data but we do know that after
World War II it housed the International Harvester Agency and the
Kaiser-Fraser agency showroom was added. By now you have a little
insight into the space we are renovating...60x100...three floors
in the original building with a basement and wine cellar. That
building will be home, our restaurant and our antique shop.

After an evening of searching for names for this new undertaking
our friend, Al Keiser, came up with one we felt most appropriate...
so on March 20th, Taylor's 81st birthday anniversary, we will
christen it Taylor's Landing and open The Calico Cupboard on-the-
wharf, serving only weekends until school is out at the end of May.
Kingdom City's Calico Cupboard will continue as at present....
weekends only and reservations.

I'm just not certain that Taylor is looking forward to my being
retired but I count only 72 more days. We vowed we were going to
Hermann to have "fun with food" and we want to keep it that way.
Our workmen at Hermann have made our restoration fun ....and we
look forward to the same happy experience with the people we have
selected to help us in the dining room. Certainly, we will have
people in our daily lives. I could tell you that it's our "last
project" but then you've heard me say such silly things before.

One of the most immediate blessings has been Joan Keiser's art
work. We had hoped to have our menu ready to mail with this
letter but that will have to come later. Joan catches the "feel"
we've tried to build into our building and she has spoiled us.

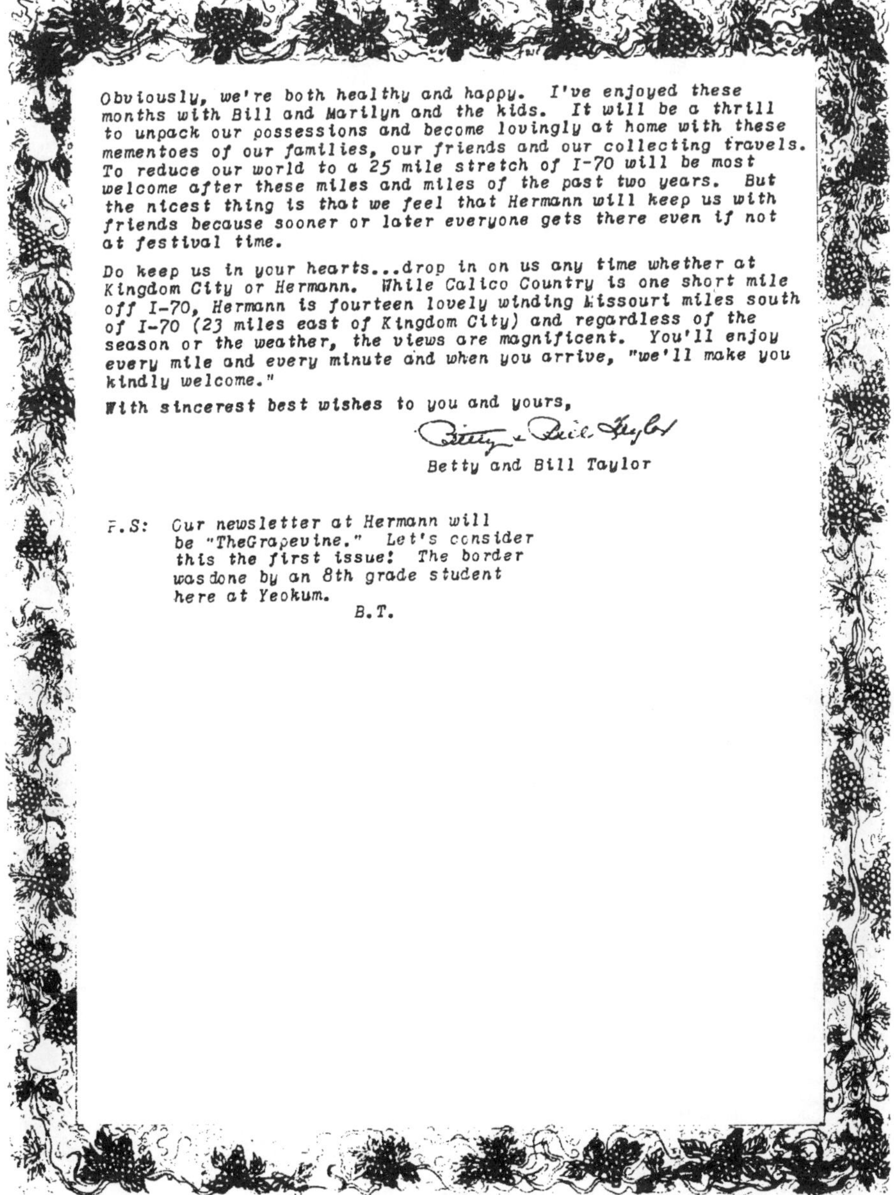

Obviously, we're both healthy and happy. I've enjoyed these
months with Bill and Marilyn and the kids. It will be a thrill
to unpack our possessions and become lovingly at home with these
mementoes of our families, our friends and our collecting travels.
To reduce our world to a 25 mile stretch of I-70 will be most
welcome after these miles and miles of the past two years. But
the nicest thing is that we feel that Hermann will keep us with
friends because sooner or later everyone gets there even if not
at festival time.

Do keep us in your hearts...drop in on us any time whether at
Kingdom City or Hermann. While Calico Country is one short mile
off I-70, Hermann is fourteen lovely winding Missouri miles south
of I-70 (23 miles east of Kingdom City) and regardless of the
season or the weather, the views are magnificent. You'll enjoy
every mile and every minute and when you arrive, "we'll make you
kindly welcome."

With sincerest best wishes to you and yours,

Betty and Bill Taylor

F.S: Our newsletter at Hermann will
      be "TheGrapevine." Let's consider
      this the first issue! The border
      wasdone by an 8th grade student
      here at Yeokum.
                  B.T.

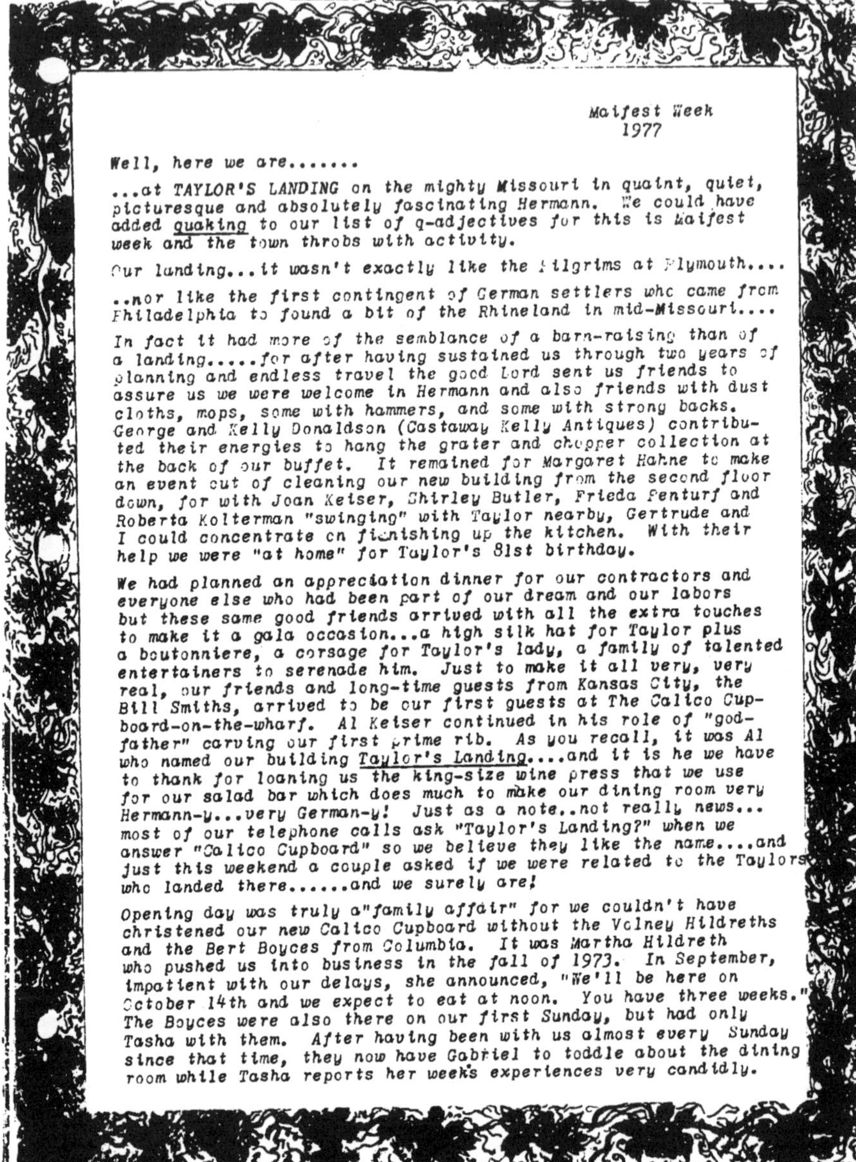

Maifest Week
1977

Well, here we are.......

...at *TAYLOR'S LANDING* on the mighty Missouri in quaint, quiet, picturesque and absolutely fascinating Hermann. We could have added <u>quaking</u> to our list of q-adjectives for this is Maifest week and the town throbs with activity.

Our landing...it wasn't exactly like the Pilgrims at Plymouth....

..nor like the first contingent of German settlers who came from Philadelphia to found a bit of the Rhineland in mid-Missouri....

In fact it had more of the semblance of a barn-raising than of a landing.....for after having sustained us through two years of planning and endless travel the good Lord sent us friends to assure us we were welcome in Hermann and also friends with dust cloths, mops, some with hammers, and some with strong backs. George and Kelly Donaldson (Castaway Kelly Antiques) contributed their energies to hang the grater and chopper collection at the back of our buffet. It remained for Margaret Hahne to make an event out of cleaning our new building from the second floor down, for with Joan Keiser, Shirley Butler, Frieda Fenturf and Roberta Kolterman "swinging" with Taylor nearby, Gertrude and I could concentrate on finishing up the kitchen. With their help we were "at home" for Taylor's 81st birthday.

We had planned an appreciation dinner for our contractors and everyone else who had been part of our dream and our labors but these same good friends arrived with all the extra touches to make it a gala occasion...a high silk hat for Taylor plus a boutonniere, a corsage for Taylor's lady, a family of talented entertainers to serenade him. Just to make it all very, very real, our friends and long-time guests from Kansas City, the Bill Smiths, arrived to be our first guests at The Calico Cupboard-on-the-wharf. Al Keiser continued in his role of "godfather" carving our first prime rib. As you recall, it was Al who named our building <u>Taylor's Landing</u>....and it is he we have to thank for loaning us the king-size wine press that we use for our salad bar which does much to make our dining room very Hermann-y...very German-y! Just as a note..not really news... most of our telephone calls ask "Taylor's Landing?" when we answer "Calico Cupboard" so we believe they like the name....and just this weekend a couple asked if we were related to the Taylors who landed there......and we surely are!

Opening day was truly a "family affair" for we couldn't have christened our new Calico Cupboard without the Volney Hildreths and the Bert Boyces from Columbia. It was Martha Hildreth who pushed us into business in the fall of 1973. In September, impatient with our delays, she announced, "We'll be here on October 14th and we expect to eat at noon. You have three weeks." The Boyces were also there on our first Sunday, but had only Tasha with them. After having been with us almost every Sunday since that time, they now have Gabriel to toddle about the dining room while Tasha reports her week's experiences very candidly.

At this point, we hope to find someone who would like to live at
our Kingdom City location for we know the possiblities at Hermann
are limitless and even now require all of our energies.

It's been seven weeks now since that first happy evening when
we literally christened Taylor's Landing with the Theissen's gift
of champagne. Business has far exceeded our expectations. Our
guests come from far and wide and the New Haven Leader found us
sufficiently interesting to feature us in a story. This week
brought reporters from Cape Girardeau doing an article about
the Maifest. Dorothy Roe Lewis (who put us in the K. C. Star
years ago) and her daughter, Judy Turner, were here with friends
to bless our undertaking. Somewhere in all the hub-bub of opening
we missed Peg Burris from Pennsylvania who has been back and forth
in connection with her work at Stephens College as well as her
granddaughter's wedding. Peg has been waiting for us to land
at Hermann. During Easter vacation I did have an opportunity to
do another "lazy" recipe on Diane Larkins's It's a Woman's World,
Channel 8, Columbia, and to talk about Taylors Landing and the
area Folk Craft Festival held in our exhibit hall April 16-17.
Channel 8 also covered the display of hook, needle and loom crafts
which was particularly well attended this year. As you see, we
continue to be blessed with publicity and we will work hard to
keep it "good."

Watch for our new placemats...another Joan Keiser special...
with a map listing a variety of antique shops from Columbia to
St. Charles, and mid-Missouri's wineries.

Nestled in the fabric of our dream for this new Herman undertaking
are two delightful and talented friends, Bill and Shirley Butler.
We regret that Bill's work has necessitated their moving to
Indiana but they will never cease to be an inspiration to us.

This morning I made my first trip back to school, leaving Hermann
at 2 a.m. Next week, I'll make the last. Fortunately, our
faculty at Yeokum Junior High School has provided me with a
balm for the emotional stress of leaving, surprising me last week
with a retirment party, the theme of which was "A New Beginning."
It is truly that. The real trauma will come when I receive my
last paycheck this week....and when I move out of Bill and Marilyn's
master bedroom. Few mothers have an opportunity to exchange dreams
as we have done these past two years. Hermann will be a catalyst
for all of them.

Our calendar at Hermann includes some exciting summer weekends....
and the fall months are already filling up. Our two guest suites
will be ready for occupancy after July 15th...if I hurry. So,
include us in your prayers....and include a happy Hermann weekend
in your summer. We'll be expecting you.

                    Love,

                                    No. 3
                                    The Grapevine

We've been here sixteen weeks......

Six of them full time, eleven to nine daily.....after ten weeks
while I finished teaching at Belton when we were only open
weekends and mostly by reservation.

On May 28th we closed the Calico Cupboard at Kingdom City and
rented it to a family for living quarters. I'll bet they have
company for dinner every Sunday! Fortunately when people phone
for reservations their calls are interrupted and the operator
tells them there is only one Calico Cupboard listed and that
is at Hermann.   That added phone service would not have been
possible during the old "information" days.

People say nice things about our food. We were apprehensive
lest we lose the chatty atmosphere at McCredie, but Saturday
night and Sunday finds people just as relaxed and happy as we'd
grown used to in the three years at Calico Country. Kids still
look down their noses when they find we have no hamburgers or
french fries, but all in all we have transplanted our original
"Calico Cupboard" feeling.

Taylor is stuck with me seven days a week now. I really think
he'd enjoyed those five days of being a bachelor but when things
close in around him, that little blue pick-up heads for Kingdom
City and Auxvasse. I know you won't believe this, but there
are weeks I never get in my car. My being retired should be a
major relief to the gas crisis if these first six weeks have
any influence on the future. Retirement may be great but right
now I'm at that stage when all the days run together and I have
to re-orient myself to be sure I'm ready for the weekends.
We have finally rearranged our personnel so that unless we are
expecting someone here, we can be away until 2:30 p.m. As it
stands now, I have retired from teaching but am looking forward
to retiring from moving....give me another two or three months
to get that done.

You've heard the old story about going home to eat "what the
neighbors have brought in." This has happened to us literally
during these weeks of heavy garden produce. Henry and Helen
Billingsley have kept us in squash and introduced us to the many
ways to use the sweet banana peppers. Joan Keiser and her family
have furnished us with cucumbers, plums, tomatoes, zucchini and
tucked in each sack is the inspiration that Joan always adds to
every visit. She's our artist, you know, one of our god-mothers
here at Calico Cupboard on-the-wharf and currently working on
our ice cream menu. She prepared a lovely "Be our guest" card
which is now at the printers and which our customers may use as a
gift certificate for anniversaries and special occasions.

(I really don't think too much has changed about my life. It
used to be that I couldn't write unless the kids were walking
to and fro in the Library. Now, since I started this newsletter,
Rosie has interrupted me to serve a party of ten, two couples with
six children who giggled their way through fried chicken, mashed
potatoes and green beans, a party of four from Washington, Missouri
and a couple now waiting for fried chicken which is in process
in the kitchen. So....back to the newsletter.)

When the party of ten left a few minutes ago, they reassured
us they would be back. Those are probably the most welcome
words we hear. People are not reluctant to say they enjoyed the
food, that it was delicious, or other complimentary remarks but
"We'll be back" makes it all worth while and keeps us working to
make Calico Cupboard a unique and enjoyable place in which to
dine.

Jackie Sicht and her mother dropped in last night on their
way back from Washington State via Michigan. We had hoped Jackie
would master-mind Calico Cupboard at Kingdom City at one time
but instead she'll be teaching clothing at Columbia College this
winter. Our new placemats in The Peasant Parlor, fashioned of
recycled jeans with the hip pocket holding the napkin, actually
grew out of Jackie selling us on the endless possibilities of
old jeans, and they are perfect in that particular dining room.

Gertrude's German Potato Salad and our newly discovered old
recipe for doing red cabbage with grape jelly have been a big
hit with our customers. We'll be doing the red cabbage dish on
Diane Larkin's show, <u>Its a Woman's World,</u> Channel 8, Columbia
this month. That's another one of our blessings since retirement...
the last Thursday of each month at 3:30 p.m. Jackie Slater,
Missouri Arts and Crafts at Columbia, introduced us to Diane and
fortunately Jackie has been on with us these last two months.
The apple dumplings have also been a big hit .....and every bit
as good and as big as those luscious ones those two brothers in
Lees Summit offer at their renowned orchard restaurant.

We're planning for Christmas, are you? December 6th is St. Nicholas
Day in the Germanic tradition, at which time children are given a
temporary evaluation of their behavior over the past year.....re-
ceiving a bundle of switches in their shoes if they have been bad,
and sweetmeats if their conduct has been exemplary. We'd like to
say that on December 6th or the weekend closest - and we haven't
looked at the calendar beyond October - that we'll be having our
first open house......not a grand opening....just "open house".
We'll also have switches and sweet meats!

Timmy has been here for a week and spent most of the time on the
river or talking to the old men who sit on the bench in the shade
and talk about the river. Reminds me of the "groves of Academe."
When I return him to Kansas City tomorrow, Deanne will return
with me, and perhaps Jaylene if her schedule permits. Hope I'm
equal to two girls!

Tomorrow is not only August 1st but the date on which I should
receive my first pension check. Heaven knows when my first
social security check will arrive. After reading all of the
news about impending crises in social security financing, I
would like to get started but as of June 15th they told me that
I"wasn't on the computer." You really can't expect much to happen
until you're on the cumputer these days, now can you? It's
a good thing the food doesn't flow around the Calico Cupboard
via computer.

Bill Butler was back from Mishawaka, Indiana this weekend and
shared the Blue Willow Room with Jackie Sicht and her mother
while we hosted the Herman High School Class of 1952 in our main
dining room. We did sneak in occasionally to catch up with the
Butler household and learned that Shirley had taken a job with
an insurance firm. What a bonanza for that agency!

Since our last issue of <u>The Grapevine,</u> we have accomplished a
few changes around the building. June was particularly productive
giving us a very attractive gingerbread porch across the front of
our 1950 building and contrasting it completely with the front of
the 1850 building. We also managed to change our produce room into
an office for the Calico Cupboard, and build a new produce room
that also houses our excess refrigeration and freezers. Nothing is
really excess, but equipment that we do not need in the actual
kitchen. Then just to make the month really great Lee Kolterman
fashioned two antique shops in our big room (St. Charles Halle).
Paul Viola has them almost in shape for us to decorate and furnish.
A few more weeks and we should have something for antique browsers
to enjoy.....but first of all, we're in the food business. Never
forget.....food prepared with love and seasoned with the tidbits
of experience and history collected over a combined total of 146
years, every one of which was most enjoyable.....and the gift of
a loving God.

People ask if we are using family recipes...particularly since
we now have my mothers, grandmothers and great-grandmothers (forgive
those three missing apostrophes) pictures hanging in our dining
room. We have no recipes.....but we remember well their methods...
the utensils they used.....the few simple gadgets...and most of all
we remember that they were not "chintzy" cooks. Our sauces are
rich because that was the way I was taught to prepare them....and
because we always had a wealth of ingredients on hand from which
to prepare them. At Calico Cupboard we cut no corners...if anything, we're inclined to embellish everything a bit. My mother
did not have a grocery store at her finger-tips and shopping was
weekly if that frequently. At times she was inclined to combine
things that should never have been seen together.....but she was
the first one to realize it. Reminiscing, I sometimes think she
could have been the Rona Barrett of the kitchen for she always knew
what should be seen together....or if there was a new combination
that caught her attention, what new love affairs were current in
her culinary world.

Save this newsletter for sometime when you're waiting for your
kids to get out of the pool or finish dancing lessons. It's
already three pages long and it's Monday....and I could write
for hours. Hang in!

Taylor and I used to say (at Peculiar) if we could just sort
and clean three square feet a day, we'd have it made. Three square
feet a day here has been reduced to "if we can just unpack two
or three boxes today" we'll eventually get through this mountain
of things. (Personally, I'd almost invite the trash man to back
up to the door so that I could once again see bare floor space
and begin getting ideas again!) A few minutes ago I toured the
basement of old St. Charles Halle with a super-critical eye as to
how it could serve our space needs. One room has a concrete floor
in it (where the old stoker used to be), one room is rock just as
it protrudes from the hillside in a terrace like formation with
each level eight or ten inches above the other.....and then there's
the wine cellar with its vaulted brick roof (ceiling). The only
obstacles to making it all open to the public is the variation in
floor levels in the room with the original rock floor. We think
our customers might like to see not only the wine cellar but
just how they supported a building like St. Charles Halle in the
1840's. If you would like for us to open this area to the public,
tell us the next time you're in. We'll work a little harder if
you're interested in touring this area after dinner.

Hope your summer has been as happy as ours.....and thank you
all for making these first four months of Calico Cupboard great!

Love from both of us,

Bill & Betty Taylor

211

It's October 14th. . . . .

four hundred and eighty-five years since Columbus did his
thing and discovered America..in the process....and

four wonderful years since Taylor and I discovered how much
fun we could have with antiques and food and the people who
love them both.

I've been trying to get to this issue of _The Grapevine_
for days but, as I've told you, I can't write unless there
are a dozen things going on. If this one is mediocre, it's
because I can only count about nine things that need my
attention. In fact, we're knee-deep in serving dinner and
Taylor has just handed me the mail...it's been that kind of
a day.

We're also knee deep in Oktoberfest and the weather is coopera-
ting beautifully. First it was the Art Fair on October's
first weekend. Last week Margaret Hahne outdid all her records
with a wonderful antique show, and the winery began its three-
week long celebration. In contrast with last spring's Maifest
when nobody knew we had arrived in Hermann, this past weekend
found us turning away almost as many as we fed. (Do take time
to make a reservation if you're here for a festival....even if
it's just an hour's notice.) This week will no doubt continue
very active business if the weather holds out. There's still
another weekend to go in the winefest plus one more October
weekend that will bring more tourists through these winding
Missouri miles to see the gorgeous colors of the hillsides.
The white of the sycamores and the limestone bluffs are just
the right contrast. How do you suppose God accomplished all
that without an executive committee or a board of directors?

Last issue when I was bragging about our apple dumplings I
failed to mention the apple dumplings at Lola's, a nice quiet
restaurant that serves only dinner, located at the south end of
Butler, Missouri on old 71-Hwy. Lola used to serve luncheon also
but since losing her husband several years ago she serves only
dinner, beginning at 5 p.m. Her apple dumplings are"out-of-this-
world." They are available daily and are served snuggled in a
rich, chunky apple. The best anywhere!

While I'm talking about other places to eat, we want to acknowledge
Mrs. Lorene Nagel who cooks in a restaurant in Middletown, Mo.
where she says they try to prepare home style food for their
customers. Neither she nor her employer are long in the restaurant business...just long in the kitchen ...and now are having
fun serving the public. We're going to try to get there. Hope
you do, too, if you're in that area.

December 3, 1978

It's been one full year since our last newsletter!

We didn't plan it that way for we thought we'd get about six letters
out throughout the year. I don't know about you, but I have to be really
"moved" to come up with a newsletter. There were plenty of times when
I was "moved" but I made the mistake of giving my grandson, Timmy, my old
typewriter last Christmas which also included his December 22nd birthday.
Then I told myself it would be selfish for me to indulge myself in a new
super typewriter during our first winter at Calico Cupboard. Winter for a
new restaurant in Hermann is akin to winter at Valley Forge as reported
by the historians. But we survived with the help of a lot of friends
and here we are, twelve months later after a great year that kept us going
so fast we sometimes questioned our judgment in attempting this lifestyle
at our age.

But the Lord must have wanted us in Hermann or we wouldn't have made it
and we're gratefully accepting the energy and health He puts at our
disposal to carry on.

We scarcely had time to become depressed about last year's long winter
when our St. Louis customers found us an interesting place to visit.
As a host restaurant with the Carriage Trade Dinner Club, we made about
400 new contacts every month. If you haven't heard of Carriage Trade or
become a member, it provides a great opportunity to enjoy new and interesting
places to dine at a very nominal price. With your $15.00 membership card
you are entitled to two meals for the price of one at about 60 well selected
dining rooms throughout St. Louis. They will soon open in the Kansas City
area and we'll be included in that group, too. Several cities throughout
the United States have had clubs much longer than St. Louis but St. Louis
has grown rapidly. For us, it's been like having our own public relations
firm in St. Louis and it continues our experience of having the nicest kind
of customers.

When we bought this building, we felt that it would give us an opportunity
to adapt the space to our needs as they developed and would give us an
outlet for the different things we like to do. After all, we are staying
in one place these days. Some weeks go by without my ever getting behind
a wheel. I know that Mobil and Amoco must think we died. So....the latter
part of the summer we began to redo the wine cellar in the original St.
Charles Hall. Our customers tell us that when Ochsners had the garage here
it was more fun to buy a fan belt here because they always got to visit
the wine cellar. Paul Viola (without whom we could not do!) cleaned the
old brick and hosed down the vaulted walls the first week of renovation
and came back later in the week to pick up the garden hose he had used.
When he went to the basement he found about two inches of gasoline in the
wine cellar. Obviously some tank at the filling station next door had
begun leaking. The new sump pump carried the gas into the sewer, plus
the water and detergent we were flushing it down with, and finally after
a long, long weekend they found the leak and corrected it. Had we not been
redoing the cellar, it might have accumulated to a tragic state before we
ever happened to go to the basement.

Anyway, the wine cellar is done. The furniture is in place, and we're
looking forward to adding it to the tour of the building this weekend
during our Kris Kringle Festival and Open House. We don't think it will
be interesting to everyone but it will make a great hospitality area
for groups that are supple enough to navigate the "original" stairs
which we designed for more rugged souls.

Taylor is absolutely great! He still does things his way, at his pace,
with his sense of humor, and while he still maintains that I just think
I'm having fun and he's not going to be the one to set me straight, he
loves this version of retirement as much as I do. One of the nicest
blessings of 1978 was our acquaintance with Paul Warner of WIL and his
referring John Auble to us. John came in September and featured us on
Newsbeat on Channel 5 just about the time the October foliage crowd began
to come. This October will be a hard act to follow! Renee Stovsky and
Karen Hader who edit the Globe Democrat's Guide section used our material
mid-way in October and the following weekend our local paper reported
5000 people in town that weekend. I know we turned away as many as we
fed and we're going to try to correct that situation by the next festival
weekend....the first of which is Maifest....May 19th...in the original
Maifest tradition but with a few crowd controls added.

We have sold our home at Peculiar to Pete Erickson with whom I taught
for several years. We have sold Calico Cupboard at Kingdom City with the
exception of the Community Hall and the Bank Building. We almost have
the first apartment completed in the Community Hall, and there is space
for a second. The bank will become an apartment later if our energies
and resources continue.

What was our own antique shop here has been converted into a farm-style
dining room, complete with cookstove in full operation, blue and white
checked tablecloths, kerosene lamps on the tables, and ironstone dishes
Now if we can just come up with a napkin ring that is appropriate,
plus the wooden handled forks and knives we'll have it as I remember my
Grandmother Goby's. (Actually, the napkin ring is Grandmother Jones'
idea.) We have the cedar water bucket and dipper but even I would frown
on using that. Would make a great ice bucket, though.

We're still doing It's a Woman's World with Diane Larkin on Channel 8
at Columbia each month. As I understand we're going back to a live
telecast, which will take some early rising in Hermann to make Columbia
by 8:30 a.m. Taylor says he's going with me so we'll see if we can get
him on camera.

Here I am typing and I have a list three pages long of things that must
be done 'ere nightfall. Do keep in touch! Taylor and I hope that your
year has been blessed as abundantly as ours has been. We couldn't be
happier!

Love to you all,

Bill & Betty Taylor

It was such a l-o-o-o-n-n-n-g winter!

The vacation Taylor and I planned in Ft. Lauderdale was pre-empted by
Mother Nature with a flu bug descending on both of us January 9th. It was
very evident the Lord did not plan for us to leave for Florida on the 15th
as we'd planned. But had we gotten to the sunny South we'd have missed
the fun of mopping our roof after each snow storm....or breaking up the
ice in the gutters so they'd drain. Taylor spent most of the sunny hours
each day on the roof.   But we weren't alone.....and now we know we should
never plan a January-February vacation.

Some of our friends are watching for the first robins and geese in flight
to reassure them spring is around the corner........but we want to see
the Scharnhorsts, Mim Schmidt, Glessie and Bud Eggers, Laura and Katie,
Janice Greene, the Bassman's.....then we'll know spring is here and we can
turn our energies to something more creative than mere survival.

The summer brochure of Hermann's activities is "a birthing" and there
will be a Maifest this year. The Calico Cupboard is sponsoring "The Wurst
Festival in Missouri" on March 10th and 11th. During the bitterest cold
weather we put together a cookbook, <u>The Best of the Wurst</u>, which give us
an opportunity to research sausage-making and also old Hermann history.
It was fun to include the old advertising from the Hermann German newspaper
in 1894 and know that the descendants of these early merchants are among
our most cherished customers. The papers were a gift of Bill and Maureen
Coe at the very outset of our planning to bring The Calico Cupboard to
Hermann.

The Wurst Festival is a real tribute to the cooperative spirit in Hermann.
We've had unbelievable help from the local sausage makers and the other
restaurants. Today we received a copy of Missouri's Tourism Department
press release covering the Wurst Festival which was an unexpected blessing.
The Missouri Pork Council also gave us a nod of approval. Don't look for
our ads anywhere else this season for we've shot our advertising budget
and more. We have Diane Larkin's <u>Womans World</u> on Channel 8 at Columbia
to thank for the great reception of our cookbook. Taylor keeps making
excuses but someday don't be surprised to see him cooking up something on
Diane's show.

As soon as the roads were open Jackie Slater from Missouri Arts and Crafts
at Columbia spent the day with us and we dreamed....and we dreamed....and
we dreamed. Melva Beeler (who carves the cute Calico signs) introduced us
to Jackie years ago....Jackie introduced us to Diane ....and Honest Charlie.
We don't know if Honest Charlie is really honest but as long as it says so
on his truck, we keep enjoying our visits with him and Mary Elizabeth (or is
it Mary Margaret). At least we know it's always fun to stop there and you can
never tell what you'll find. We start looking for chairs but then we usually
stumble into another goodie or two.

Honest Charlie is bringing us a piano for Howard Wood to entertain Saturday
night of The Wurst Festival. Howard is an art teacher at Troy and a most
mellow fellow. Paul and Michael Warner (WIL-St. Louis) will host for us
that weekend so that we can keep our attention on the food service. Gertrude
made all of the sausages listed in the cookbook and with the local sausages
available, we plan to have at least 25 kinds of wurst to serve during
Saturday and Sunday.

Have you ever tried a cinnamon stick in your coffee. One of our guests,
a Mr. Darnell from St. Louis, asked for a cinnamon stick instead of dessert.
It is a most welcome change ....and makes that last cup of coffee a
mini-dessert.

Since mid-February we've been sponsoring a radio program on Montgomery
City's KCVM called "Antique Country." Jack Morris hosts this Saturday
afternoon program with information about antiques and collectibles. From
what our customers tell us, it appears to be of general interest, if only
for getting tentative appraisals on family heirlooms.

A few days ago a group of young veterans were our guests. They had just
come from meeting here in Hermann in an effort to organize Vietnam veterans
and to find solutions for some of their problems. One of the things they
hope to accomplish is a Vietnam Era Veterans Memorial in the State Capitol.
It's strange how we seem to turn our back on that war.........but if the
opportunity comes your way, we hope you will support their groups activities
and goals. One chapter of Missouri Veterans Council is located at 4900
N. Hanley Road in St. Louis (63134). There is also a chapter at Columbia
and one at Eureka, Missouri.

We're getting homesick to get back to the Belton area. We know the forsythia
and the pussy willows are beginning to bloom on our home place at Peculiar
but this year the Erickson's can enjoy them. We finally begged Dr. Schmidt
to bring us some from the Schroeder place so that we could enjoy these first
wisps of spring.

It will be a fast track from now until November in Hermann's wine country.
Unless gas becomes unavailable or out-of-sight Hermann should enjoy one of
the best tourist seasons ever. Hope you're part of it! Bring your guests
when you have company from out of state. They'll never forget!

                    Love to you all,

                    Betty & Taylor

P.S: Just have to tell you that
       Taylor will celebrate his
       83rd birthday on March 18th!
       He's the greatest!

                    Betty

THE GRAPEVINE

July 1, 1979

Just never thought retirement could be this interesting.........

or this much fun..........

or this much work!

When I was junior high librarian at Belton, I got to read the Sunday paper
each Monday because we were never home weekends to have the Star thrown in
our driveway. Now....that I'm retired....and we have the Sunday paper
delivered to our door.....I seldom get to read more than the headlines
until Tuesday. But we're not complaining ....just comparing...and
realizing that these truly are the "golden years."

Sometimes we get so busy that our guest book isn't circulated the way
we'd like for it to move from guest to guest. We do hope it gets to your
table before you leave. It even makes good reading when you see how many
faraway places are represented by our guests. Speaking of "good reading"
one afternoon a gentleman read the book to his lady guest while she applauded
her favorite geographic names. In the event you get carried away and
would like to duplicate this act, just ask. We'll find a private dining
room just for you!

We had not planned on another typewritten issue of <u>The Grapevine.</u> If
our dreams are healthy .....and the gasoline crisis doesn't exhaust our
source of customers....we'll have a printed newsletter next time. We're
seeking a little professional help to smooth out the details. To tell
the truth, we're just getting old and not accomplishing nearly as much as
we did in past years. As a matter of fact, this year Taylor and I represent
150 years.....and we'd like to think it represents an 150 year accumulation
of enthusiasm and ideas and appreciation for all the blessings the Lord
has brought our way.....and we'd also like to think we'd earned a few of
them.

This year's Maifest brought a much smaller crowd but definitely the nicest
kind of visitor. We feel that once again we have a basis for a truly
traditional German festival apart from the carnival-like atmosphere of the
past few years. Somewhere in our research before coming here I read that
the Maifest represents or was in celebration of the final cultivation of
the vineyards and that the number of sunny days from then until the grape
harvest was an index to the quality of wine to be produced that year....
with 120 sunny days being the optimum for superior wines.

Calico Cupboard will sponsor the Wurst Festival again next year and some
of our cooperators have already told us of their plans. We're never going
to be so fortunate as to have another 70 degree weekend in mid-March like
this year.

217

Belatedly we'd like to pay tribute to Joe Kruegel, whose antique shop on
Second and Schiller was a popular place to visit on Hermann trips. Joe
passed away this spring. He was the excuse for our first visit to Hermann
and our first breath-taking view of this quaint town from the Missouri
River bridge. Doone Jackson, Auxvasse, had told us to contact Joe if
we were really interested in finding true German primitives and craftsman-
ship and as a source of unlimited knowledge in this area. He was a most
talented man and pointed out the clues to fine furniture construction.
He also gave us our first taste of Hermann wine. Many of the primitives
we still display came from his collection but more than that, the warm
spot he kindled for Hermann eventually grew into The Calico Cupboard.

The river continues to fascinate us and our customers. Our front tables
overlooking the river are the most popular. On World Environment Day
we had 165 canoe people for a breakfast buffet prior to their putting
in the Missouri for a float trip down to New Haven. Another group floated
from Arrow Rock to Hermann this week.

Our son Bill and his family are looking forward to having an acreage of
woods and water in this area. Tim, our grandson, spent three weeks with
us during June and divided his time beween the restaurant and the River.
Not every grandson can have his own private river at his side door.
Tim grows more helpful each visit and this summer he just plain spoiled
us. DeAnn and Jayleen will come before the summer ends but their world
centers around the Library, the Museum and the Pool.

One of the brightest spots in our world recently was the visit of my
1928 classmates from Raymond, Illinois for our 51st anniversary. Twelve
of us got together on June 2nd and from the acknowledgments I've had
from them over the past few weeks, it was a refreshing experience for
all of us. It was an absolute thrill for me.

Another high-light was a visit with my Goby cousins in Rochester, Illinois.
Tim accompanied me on a two day safari that included my first (and last)
Rock Concert at Mississippi River Festival in Edwardsville.....Lincoln
Land including New Salem and a lovely evening with the Jack Gobys.

Taylor continues to amaze me with his energy.....much more agile than
I am....but he's faithful about taking time out to rest a couple of times
a day. He loves browsing through the building with guests when he's not
carving ham at our buffet. He still prepares the baked ham and the
green beans plus most of the local marketing. Most of our decorations
are truly old morsels of the past.........and so are some of Taylors jokes!

Be sure to sign our guest book and be sure to leave your business card.
A special thanks goes to Marti Kardinal who arranged World Environment Day
canoe-in...to Joan Keeser who brought the Wally Byram Air Stream Caravan....
Alice Jacobson who hosted James Scott's water color workshop...to the Tampa, Fla.
AARP group and Miss Winter, their leader....and to Mrs. Wehmueller and the
St. Francis Hospital Auxiliary. All of you make our efforts most rewarding.
We're glad we came to Hermann. Hope you are, too. Take an extra newsletter
for a special friend......and spread the word. We'll try to make it even
more interesting on your next visit.

Love,

Bill and Betty Taylor

Group photograph of the Missouri Restaurant Association including (from left to right): Max Koerner, Fran and Blake Parketon of Hermann's Central Hotel, Debbie and Gary Buckler, Betty, and John Foster who was president of the association at the time (now president of the Waids restaurant chain). The picture was taken in 1979 at a Missouri Restaurant Association meeting at Stone Hill's Vintage Restaurant.

Photograph: Bill Nunn of <u>Missouri Life</u> magazine arranged to publish a calendar of Calico Cupboard interiors with recipes in cooperation with Gibson Greeting Cards. Here, the photographer is arranging final details and checking lighting. See the final photo in the Recipe section of this book.

The Grapevine

Christmas, 1979

Hope you can see the holly berries and mistletoe
woven into this "Grapevine." If not....just use your imagination
for we sincerely wish you not only a merry but an inspiring
Christmas season.

Nobody is more dependent on friends than the Taylors and The
Calico Cupboard. It's a real treat to look back over our guest
book at the end of the day and see the geographic area from
which you all come. We want to always be worth the trip!

It was fun for Taylor and me to be 150 years old in 1979 but I
can't get too ecstatic about being 152 in 1980. It started out
mighty slow in January and February with wall-to-wall ice and
snow....but our first Wurst Festival in March was a great success
and every month has been building since then. In September we
started Dinner Theatre with the Columbia Entertainment Company
and are booked now through next September with them. This weekend
we have Dinner Dancing for the first time with B. A. Wagner's
orchestra and he's Mr. Music in Hermann.

So much happened in Hermann this year.......

The Maifest was held in May after a year without this traditional
celebration. It was without incident and will provide a new
foundation for this festival without the carnival atmosphere that
brought our problems. Jim and Betty Held did a great promotion
job for their Grape Stomping in August at the beginning of the
grape harvest. The year Tom Cabot spent in planning the Volksmarch
was reflected in the number of people who arrived from all over
Missouri for this "first" in
Missouri as well as in
Hermann.

The Calico Cupboard
4 Schiller Street

Hermann, Mo. 65041
(314) 486-2030

Speaking of the Cabots, Julaine organized the Volksplatz during the Maifest and it was another well received "first."

Hermannhof Winery opened in May and by next season will have restored - really recreated - the old stables of Herr Kropp's brewery to make it a most interesting addition to Hermann. They are fortunate in being located at the site of the original landing of the first 17 people who came to Hermann in 1837. We hope they will join us in the Kris Kringle Festival in 1980 for these first German immigrants landed on St. Nicholas Day (December 6th) and that has always been our reason for sponsoring this activity the first week in December.

Our new placemat by Joan Keiser showing all of Missouri's wineries has been very well received. We want to take this opportunity to express our thanks to Missouri's Department of Tourism for distributing them and to Dr. Arneson (Peaceful Bend Vineyards, Steeleville) for his encouraging letter.

Over the years I've belonged to a lot of professional and trade associations but I never felt so "represented" as I do with the Missouri Restaurant Association. They truly want to help you be a better and more responsive restaurant operator. The MRA magazine and <u>Briefing</u> from American Express get my attention the same day they arrive for each one of them charges my battery and nudges me into action. MRA has been most helpful to their members in Hermann and have initiated a closer look at tourism in this quaint village by all segments of the community. Tourism is the No. 3 business in Missouri (next to auto manufacture and agriculture) but it is the No. 1 retail business in the state. There has been a great increase in intra-state tourism since the increase in gasoline prices, however, Missouri is within one day's driving time from one-third of the population of the United States. (Taylor threatens to get me a soap box if I keep on talking about Missouri tourism.)

One of the great blessings of 1979 was to renew acquaintance with so many friends from my home town in Raymond, Illinois. In My my graduating class of 1928 celebrated our 51st anniversary here. Since that time we've seen many old friends even though I missed some of them by not being here that particular day. (I still do a segment on Diane Larkin's Womans World - Channel 8 in Columbia, third Thursday of each month and usually take advantage of the occasion to do what shopping I need to do while in Columbia.)

I really planned that this would simply be the Christmas edition of <u>The Grapevine</u> but during this season, looking back becomes great fun. I share an old friend's outlook......"That's what makes these the Golden Years." Make your 1980 a "golden year."

Love to you all,

Betty and Taylor

I know I promised newsletters ago that there would never be another
three-page newsletter, but from where I'm perched on Cloud 9 I just
have to tell you what a great success our first dinner dance last night
turned out to be......thanks to the wonderful people who celebrated
Lee Kolterman's birthday party and friends from Owensville, Cuba,
Montgomery City, New Haven and the other hills surrounding Hermann.

Before the evening was too far along it truly became a gathering
of friends.......and B.A.'s music left me dewy-eyed with remembering
evenings at the Muehlebach's Terrace Grill, the Southern Mansion and
long-ago Saturday nights. We've asked B.A. to play for a Valentine's
Dance on February 10th and again in May when I'll celebrate my
birthday!   In the meantime, Mim Schmidt has spoiled us and we can't
wait until she presents An Evening of Ragtime in Old Hermann.....but
first we have to get her back from Florida. Mim reminds me of those
talented gals that used to accompany silent movies .....she is so
versatile and so talented.

Wish you could be here for New Year's Day Brunch........but if you
can't we appreciate your visits in 1979 which nurture our enthusiasm.
Again, our best wishes for 1980.

                                        Betty

April, 1980

The gestation period of a calendar is............

slightly longer than that of Homo sapiens....and considerably shorter than
that of an elephant, but..........

None-the-less traumatic. The surprise...the feelings...the uneasiness...the
burden....the environmental accommodation are very similar......even to the
day "the doctor comes" to deliver your "brainchild" and you quietly and privately
determine that it is complete with all appendages and vital parts!

It was in March of 1979 that Bill Nunn stopped by one evening and, in my absence,
told Taylor that Missouri Life would like to do a calendar at The Calico Cupboard.
Bill has been a part of our Calico Cupboard family ever since he found us at
McCredie and put us in print in 1974. Of course, we were flattered. Thinking
it was just a page or two featuring German food, I phoned him to learn the
details....only to find that all the photography would be done here....with
our interiors....our antiques ....with recipes from our kitchen....and that
Chuck Dresner (also responsible for the 1974 article) would again be the
photographer.

While still on the phone, my mind was coming up "black-eyed peas for January"...
"cast iron cookery in February"...."a birthday cake decorated with violets in
May"....and finally, I simply told Bill to call me back in a couple of days for
I just had to start dreaming on paper.

During April we met twice with Bill's daughter, Jeannie, planning and pin-point-
ing the actual backgrounds, china, table linen, menu themes, and recipes.
Chuck dropped by to see just what was involved and we readied our staff to
spend May 3rd doing nothing but bring up freshly prepared food hour-by-hour as
the photographer requested.

It was in the produce department of the Kroger store that the idea "quickened"
and I became fully aware that what we were actually creating was a series of
twelve collages.....and I continued selecting just the right colored apples to
enhance an aged dough bowl. In Schnucks (Columbia) the shapes and textures
of the bread would be perfect for the wine cellar shot that could include a
very primitive bread knife and a most interesting cutting board.

As in every pregnancy, there are some bleek, forbidding moments. Just when
we had every corner filled with accumulations for March or September
or May, Chuck Dresner phoned to say his company was sending him
out of town and we would have to delay his coming to
The Calico Cupboard. The next weekend was
Mother's Day and the next one, The Maifest. We
settled on Memorial Day weekend when he would
just vacation with us and his camera.

The Calico Cupboard • 4 Schiller Street • Hermann, Mo. 65041 • (314) 486-2030

It was mid-May when Bill Nunn phoned to say that because of editorial changes
at _Missouri Life_, the calendar would probably be postponed. Subsequently, we
received a copy of their letter to the publisher that the idea was being
abandoned.

A little bit of Betty Taylor died that moment. Taylor was just as disappointed
as I because we had delighted in bringing everything together to make each
picture as authentic as we could remember. Faced with the prospect of returning
every piece of polished silver to its cupboard as well as stacks of linen and
china, I phoned the publisher, Bob Hennkens, saying simply: "I'm Betty Taylor
of The Calico Cupboard. A little bit of me died when _Missouri Life_ cancelled
the calendar." He replied, "Are you the lady looking at me over her glasses
from the corner of my desk." With that I knew the magazine article was still at
hand and that the idea might survive.

On June 26th Bob and his party came for dinner. As they arrived and while still
introducing ourselves, Bob told us "the calendar is 'go'." Over coffee we reviewed
all the planning we'd done with Bill Nunn and Jeannie and arranged for Chuck to
come for two crowded days of photography.

The settings were photographed to accommodate the kitchen and not in calendar
order. Everything fell into place beautifully and Chuck's fascination with
what he was seeing through the camera lens only lent more enthusiasm for the
next shot. Only after we photographed the "strawberry party" theme with the
white tablecloth and crystal dishes did Chuck express disappointment in the
lack of contrast, but it had been a long, hot day and we were half way through.
It was then I suggested a 13th shot to be sure Chuck would not have to come back...
but where would it be...what would it be...and what food would we feature for June?

The next morning I picked up a red and white quilt, headed for the front dining
room window overlooking our mighty Missouri River and thought....catfish!
The quilt would be a perfect setting for Christian Gohl's handmade blue and
white stoneware. This setting is the gift of a loving God! It was a perfect
finale for two strenuous days of absolutely exhilarating composition and
photography. In fact, we likened it to "two days in the labor room." The
calendar was real.....in film.

We really thought Crosswinds was teasing when they asked us for the text, but
in November we submitted our suggestions, reliving the country cooking story
from season to season as we remembered it from our childhood.

It is April, 1980. The calendar is alive and well in Crosswinds warehouse.
Bob Hennkens is delighted and the Taylors are extremely proud. We are so
fortunate to be able to spend our retirement actively in association with
the lovely people that find their way to The Calico Cupboard. We hope we will
always merit your attention.

In the meantime, _Just Country Cookin'_ provides a perfect opportunity for
Taylor and me to share our combined 150 years of love and enthusiasm for remembering our families most fondly. Please share our dreams, as well as our recollections of old friends...old times....and old things.

Most gratefully,

Betty Taylor

The Calico Cupboard • 4 Schiller Street • Hermann, Mo. 65041 • (314) 486-2030

The Grapevine

It's half-past 1980.........

Do you know what happened to your dreams for a bright new year
that appeared full of promise and exciting plans?

We think ours are stranded somewhere between election-year politics
and a chaotic economy..........but we are here ....watching with
interest our third....or is it the 4th....recession, knowing that the
American people will survive and accommodate themselves to things
as they are.

We're glad we're not situated on a high-rent corner somewhere in
a metropolitan area with excessive overhead. Our customers are the
type that always managed well and will continue to visit us periodically. All we have to do is continue providing great country fare at a
reasonable price. It just happens that's where we get our greatest
satisfaction. We both enjoy every moment of this venture!

The publisher has just told us that the 1981 Just Country Cookin'
calendar photographed here last summer has sold out the first
20,000 copies and is into a reprinting. Hope you take time to look
it over while you're here.   We can take orders until September 1
for any quantities you might want for gifts.

The publisher also told us that the photographer would come during
August to photograph Yesterday's Kitchens. Instead of complete
meals this calendar will feature early kitchen furniture and accesso-
ries with one food in the process of preparation. It, too, will have
a recipe section. We presume it will be for 1982 which seems a
long way away just now. It's such a delight to work with Chuck
Dresner, the photographer, that we look forward to his coming in
spite of all the work involved.

The Calico Cupboard
4 Schiller Street

Hermann, Mo. 65041
(314) 486-2030

One of the joys of the "golden years" is renewing old friendships.
We wouldn't have seen anyone had we stayed in Peculiar but here
at Calico Cupboard there's a bright spot in every day either through
renewing old acquaintances or catching up with old friends through
other people.

Jimmy Bowsher and Dorothy McCammon Bay visited us a week ago. They
both grew up in Raymond (Ill.) but were younger than I. Wayne
McCammon and his wife came on an earlier visit. This weekend we
are expecting Hildegarde Haarstick Folkerts for her birthday party.
She w as in my class in high school and patiently shared a work area
with me in Home Ec. class. Last year my class held its 51st reunion
here. My cousins, Jack and June Goby from Rochester, Ill. stopped
by en route to Arkansas. Jack shares my interest in the Goby geneal-
ogy and I had copies of some early pictures to share with him.
My nieces, LaRue Brackman Welch and Von Cile Brackman Heerman,
came last week. It had been 10 years since we had seen them and then
had not had an opportunity to visit. La Rue is in charge of the
government book store in Houston, Texas and Von Cile is in an office
at St. Paul's college in Concordia. We continue to have guests from
Waterloo who always bring greetings from Roberta Hotz, a distant
cousin. She and I search for family data on the Doerr side of the
family. I'm hoping she'll find it possible to accompany me to
Wiesbaden in the spring.

Another happy contact was to renew contact with Wilbur Zink of
Appleton City. He is the most knowledgable resource person on the
Younger family and in 1967, together, we hosted the Younger family
reunion. It was very successful and we've chosen July 27, 1981
for the next reunion. Carrie Nation and the Youngers....really
just Cole....were Taylor's and my first efforts in historical
research.

The Wurst Fest for 1981 is in the planning stage. Bill Nunn and
his daughter, Jeannie, who now are The Nunn Group, have taken
over the publicity for this event.

We enjoyed having DeAnn here for two weeks. Timmy has a job this
summer and can't spend time with us. Jayleen is baby-sitting
regularly, and we're glad they're all constructively occupied
during these vacation months.

We were fortunate in locating a talented young woodworker in the
Rolla area recently. We hope you'll enjoy the "peasant" chairs
he's building for us. We've only carried the pattern around for
15 years hoping to eventually find someone sensitive to our
needs. He far exceeds our expectations and we'll be glad to refer
you to him. They do a beautiful job copying old mouldings and
millwork so we may even be able to get new front doors made for
St. Charles Halle.

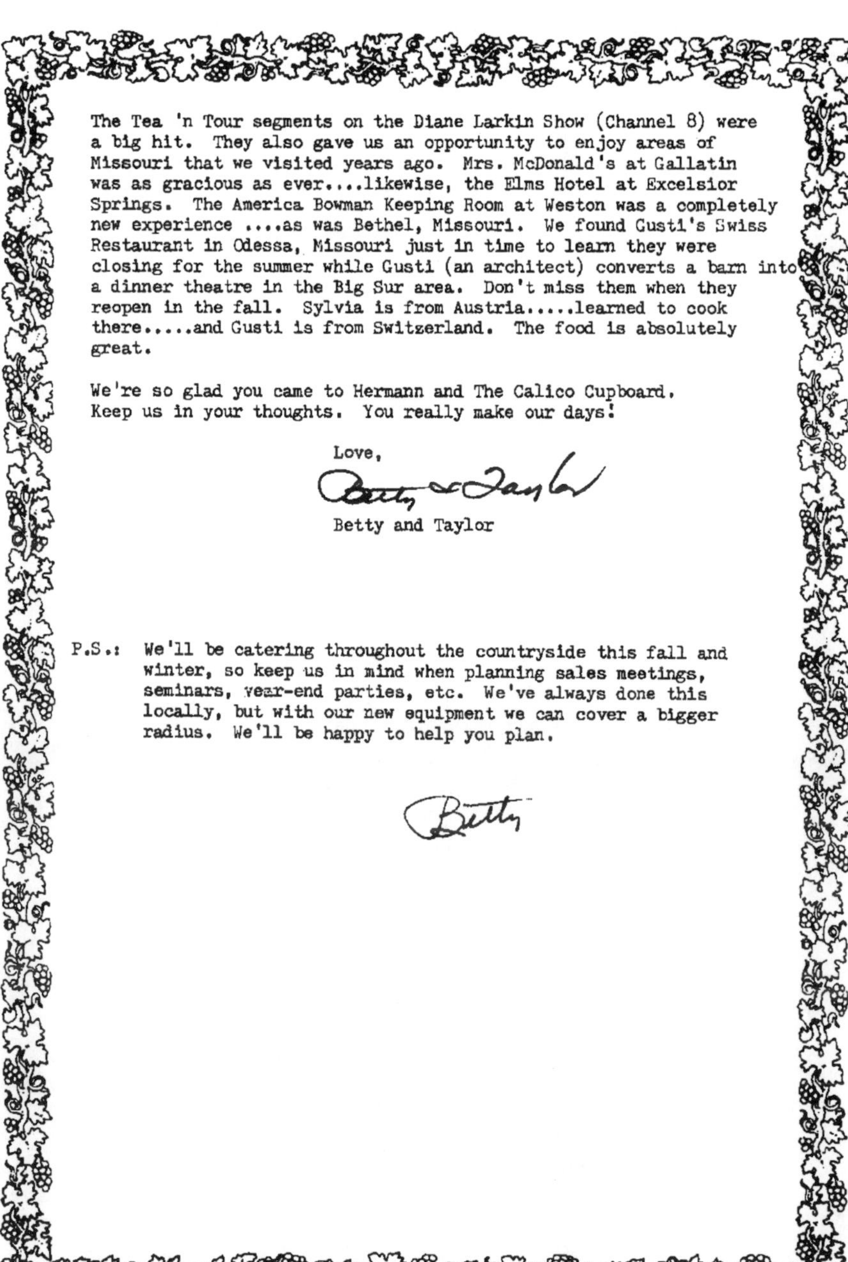

The Tea 'n Tour segments on the Diane Larkin Show (Channel 8) were
a big hit. They also gave us an opportunity to enjoy areas of
Missouri that we visited years ago. Mrs. McDonald's at Gallatin
was as gracious as ever....likewise, the Elms Hotel at Excelsior
Springs. The America Bowman Keeping Room at Weston was a completely
new experience ....as was Bethel, Missouri. We found Gusti's Swiss
Restaurant in Odessa, Missouri just in time to learn they were
closing for the summer while Gusti (an architect) converts a barn into
a dinner theatre in the Big Sur area. Don't miss them when they
reopen in the fall. Sylvia is from Austria.....learned to cook
there.....and Gusti is from Switzerland. The food is absolutely
great.

We're so glad you came to Hermann and The Calico Cupboard.
Keep us in your thoughts. You really make our days!

                    Love,

                    Betty and Taylor

P.S.: We'll be catering throughout the countryside this fall and
       winter, so keep us in mind when planning sales meetings,
       seminars, year-end parties, etc. We've always done this
       locally, but with our new equipment we can cover a bigger
       radius. We'll be happy to help you plan.

November 15, 1980

The cottonwoods on the riverfront are bare .....

The wind is brisk and piercing off the river, and the barges
ply the water with the end of the Missouri harvestheaded for
some foreign country that is currently in good favor with the
powers that be. For the remaining open months they will have
no competition from boaters....only the few hardy fishermen
who brave the wintry weeks.

When the cottonwoods are bare it's time to reminisce about
what did happen in 1980. The most spectacular month was
October when thousands of visitors found their way to Hermann.
Every writer predicted a dull October because of the summer
drought, but   the hills were aflame and the reds were later
but even more intense, it seemed.   October was very reassuring
after the dull summer weeks. Autumn has a way of summarizing
the previous nine months ....almost like a pat on the back when
your world's in disarray. Just when we thought we couldn't
stand another political commercial, Tom Warden's editorial
reassured us that there'd still be autumn next year and then
a candidate-free extravaganza produced by Mother Nature....
producer, director and star!

Last time we told you about the 1981 calendar that was photographed
here. There are a few remaining but they won't last long. We
hope we make some progress soon on the 1982 calendar. We're
simply awaiting the photographer for all the planning is complete.
Hope you get some of our new literature while you're here for
we're so proud of what Bill Nunn and his daughter, Jeannie, have
put together for us. By the way, we'd like to welcome the new
Mrs. Nunn, the former Becky Pearl   to the Calico Cupboard
family. Becky is also a writer   ....guess I should
have said "is a writer, also."

The Calico Cupboard
4 Schiller Street

Hermann, Mo. 65041
(314) 486-2030

<u>Candlelight, Kuchen and Christmas</u> is the theme for this years Kris Kringle
Festival which begins Friday night, November 28th. It will involve the
merchant community, some of the restaurants, a few historic sites, and give
an up-beat beginning to the retail shopping promotion that continues through
December. Native trees are being located on utility poles in the downtown
area to be decorated by organizations and businesses. There are some awards
involved plus voting for the most popular tree.

Our peasant chairs - <u>Bauernstuhle</u> - are finally in producation but we
have not been able to keep too many of them in stock. Take time to look
them over for they are very sturdily built. They were designed to be
painted in the Bavarian manner but they look good stained and varnished as
well.

We are delighted to have a small part of the National Tour Brokers Association
enjoying Missouri this week. One bus load will be our guests at luncheon
this weekend. We hope they find Missouri as exciting as we do. It's always
a pleasure to work with Missouri Tourism in any effort but this past year's
efforts have been more successful because of their whole-hearted cooperation.
Later this month they host the Missouri Tourism Conference and if it is anything
like last year's you come away loaded with good ideas and great "intentions."

Old friends make these years truly "golden" and long-ago associations
take on even greater meaning than when you were young. We were blessed
this fall with a visit from the Roy McLeans of Cedar Rapids. The McLeans
lived next door to my grandmother in Raymond. Earlier this year Lois
McLean Ross had visited us. We have only to hear from Helen now. We each
had such vivid recollections of those years but each remembered totally
different things. Jim Bowsher of Godfrey (formerly Raymond) has also been
here on several occasions, two of which included his cousins, Wayne and
Dorothy McCammon. If we had retired in Peculiar and rocked away our days
we would never have been blessed by these old friends or the new ones that
find their way to the Calico Cupboard.

While I'm writing, our kids are airborne for Hawaii. The travel posters for
Hawaii don't impress me one bit, but I can't wait to get to Germany...and
I'm planning that for the last of March. Taylor says he's seen all of Europe
he wants to see!

During the next few weeks, we'll simply tie the ribbon around 1980 and put
it under the Christmas Tree. It has been a great gift to the Taylors. Strangely,
1981 looks good, too! March brings the Wurstfest, May two additional weeks of
traditional German activity preceding the Maifest, etc. Hermann's calendar
continues to grow but some months are still not punctuated by any specific
activities.....but everybody's making an effort or researching traditional
German celebrations that would   be appropriate. We'd like to have
your suggestions too!

Have a happy Holiday with your family and remember us in 1981. We plan to
close in January and February and I plan to talk Taylor into taking a vacation
with me.......somewhere.....further than 50 miles from Hermann!

Love from us both,

Bill & Betty Taylor

Bill and Betty Taylor

The Grapevine

September, 1981

For a few months.....

we wondered if there would ever be another <u>Grapevine</u>. It wasn't
that there was nothing to write. In fact we've produced more
material this year than any other since we came to Hermann.......
but it took a different form. There was <u>The Wurst News</u> in March
for the Wurstfest. Then we published <u>The Rhine Country of Missouri</u>
and the copy to cover that. In May we finished the section of
Shifra Stein's DAYTRIPS that we had agreed to write.......and just
about the time we thought we were free of deadlines, Marcella
suffered a compound fracture of her leg. From that moment on,
I turned cook instead of public relations manager.

So it's almost October.......

Marcella is back and getting more mobile each day. We've had
a fantastic summer and we look forward to a productive winter
but also some quiet times.

In June the food editors visited the Rhine Country and had
breakfast with us here at
Calico Cupboard. We've
enjoyed the clippings
our customers have
brought with

The Calico Cupboard
4 Schiller Street

Hermann, Mo. 65041
(314) 486-2030

230

them. We learned quickly that people believe and expect everything a
food editor writes so we've done our best to live up to their articles
about us. We felt they treated us most graciously and really caught
the feel that we strive for here at Calico.

Ford Times and the St. Louis Post Dispatch gave our lodging its first
public notice and we enjoyed everyone that chose to overnight with us
during their visit to Hermann.

This summer we also added the Peasant Breakfast Buffet on weekends
and have it down to a routine now. "Best country breakfast," St. Louis
Magazine reported.

Taylor and I are the two happiest old-timers in Missouri. Maybe it's
just because we spend so much time with Calico Cupboard that we don't see
what's going on elsewhere. This is the first summer without grandchildren
to visit but all of them were busy working this summer.

I know you heard us say in 1977 that Calico Cupboard was our last project
but if you know us well, you know differently. Right now we're awaiting
possession of the beautiful Victorian Kallmeyer house on Second Street
(a block away) which we plan to turn into an inn before Spring. We'll
be part of several Bed and Breakfast arrangements as well as serve our
own customers and we'll live there! We've got a lot more up our sleeves
but you'll just have to come back again and see for yourself what we're
up to! You'll be surprised!

Have a happy Hermann visit.

Love,

Betty Taylor

P.S: Sylvia and Gusti Spoerri
are back from California and
reopening in Odessa. What a
treat you have in store!

Betty and Taylor

The Grapevine

January, 1985

We really didn't plan it this way, but.........

When we leased Calico Cupboard out in March of last year, we really thought we had retired completely. Guess it just wasn't supposed to be for here we are again, just as enthusiastic as ever about this interesting town and the "Rhine Country of Missouri" with all it has to offer visitors and guests. Just as _Ford Times_ wrote in 1981, we do have a "gasthaus atmosphere" and by February 1st we'll have the lodging here on Calico Cupboard's second floor ready for guests who enjoy its spacious rooms overlooking the Missouri River.

Last year before leasing the restaurant we remodeled to include a tiny dance floor, bar and another dining room overlooking the river. Recently our guests have enjoyed Bob Bigelow's music and his gracious response to the requests of their favorite tunes.

Without any further delay we must remember Jack Carney's contribution to the success of Calico Cupboard, both as a regular customer and for the very nice things he said about our food and atmosphere over the air. We'll always remember his delight in our bean soup which was a pure accident. He happened by one Saturday night when we had added dark beans to the white beans because our supply was limited. The next week numerous people told us they heard him talk about Calico Cupboard's bean soup and started asking for Jack Carney Bean Soup. We're glad we took time to tell him how much we appreciated him while he was here.

The Calico Cupboard
4 Schiller Street

Hermann, Mo. 65041
(314) 486-2030

Hermann has some "grape" plans in progress. The mills are grinding out
a sesquicentennial celebration for 1986. This spring National Geographic
should carry an article about Hermann in its Traveler magazine. We were
sorry to lose Peddler's Fare on Schiller Street but wish them success
on Market Street. The Blue Goose has also moved to Market Street.
Molly C's gift shop is well established on Third Street and a new shop
is scheduled to open across the street from her. It's good to have
the Bill Sloans on First Street as Hermann Fleisch Markt. They have
served the area as Swiss Processing for years and have always cooperated
with us in the Wurst Fest.

The Wurst Fest this year will be March 2nd and 3rd. This is the beginning
of Hermann's seasonal calendar and acknowledges the contribution of
seven sausage makers to the area as well as the importance of sausage
in the German cuisine.

Our grandson, Tim Brackman, has joined us in the operation of the
Inn and the restaurant since Taylor's health becomes more precarious
with each day. He still has a good sense of humor when he has the
energy to respond. He assures us he is in no pain but he never was one
to complain so we wonder. At 89, you anticipate health changes and
we were fortunate to enjoy twenty-six productive years together.

You've probably noticed our inset menu. If you want limited portions
of food, do not hesitate to ask. Our Sunday brunch has been well
received and will be even nicer as the new fruits come into season.

Our bed and breakfast Inn continues to lure honeymooners since Ozark
Airlines called us a "romantic hideaway." We enjoy serving our guests
fireside at Klingerbau but on Sunday we think they deserve to enjoy
Calico Cupboard's brunch, particularly during these wintry months.

Keep us in your hearts as we seek to maintain Calico Cupboard's
traditional quality in country dining.

       Sincerely,

       Bill and Betty Taylor

Photograph of Der Kingerbau Inn sign

Sketched business card for "Der Klingerbau Inn und Gasthauses" Der Kingerbau Inn was Hermann's first Bed and Breakfast. The concept of Bed and Breakfast was a natural for Hermann. In a short time, we were offered other authentic buildings in the Historic District to adapt to Bed and Breakfasts. The ones on Third Street were truly historic and we furnished them austerely but comfortably. We encouraged Michaela Warner to do River Country Bed and Breakfast as a reservation service. Now, after twenty years, she's only one of Missouri's Bed and Breakfast services.
Many communities offer their own referral and reservation agencies.

Photograph of Der Kingerbau Bed and Breakfast Inn
The former home of flour miller, William Klinger, and most recently the home of the
Wilford Kallmeyers, is now furnished with Victorian pieces appropriate
for the years in which the house was built.

Photographs from *News Tribune*, Jefferson City, Missouri: Sunday, April 10, 1983
"Owner Betty Taylor on the main staircase of Der Klingerbau Inn in Hermann"
and "Stately Inn: The stately Klingerbau Inn in Hermann was built in 1880 and
owner Betty Taylor says that everything in it is original except the light fixtures.
She has decorated the inn, including the bedrooms, with patchwork quilts
and furniture contemporary with that time to keep the atmosphere alive.

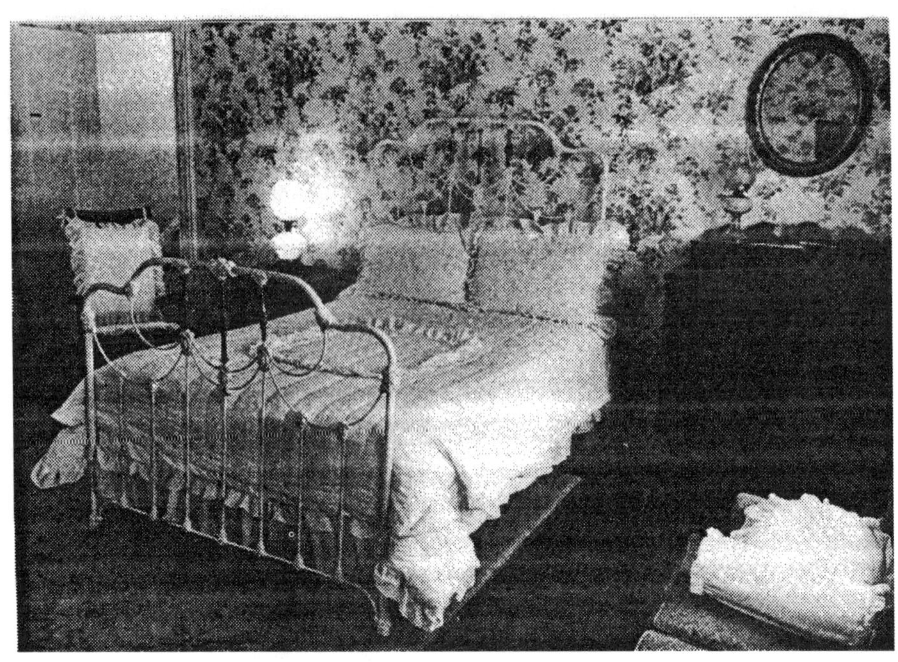

Upstairs at the Calico Cupboard - Bed and Breakfast suite overlooking the Missouri River

The Ochsner family once owned the Calico Cupboard building for their automobile dealership and lived upstairs. Their grown son told me he learned his alphabet on the twenty-six steps to the second floor.

Betty with a Mark Twain look-alike entertainer. Sorry I don't recall his name.

Wilford & Joy Kallmeyer
Our benefators in so many ways during the Hermann years and the antique years.

Hometown III - Hermann, Missouri

Again, the Kallmeyers played a major role in our personal lives. As they built their new building at the edge of Hermann, we had great success at McCredie with antiques and food, and telling everyone about the Calico Cupboard that would overlook the Missouri River in Hermann. It was no effort to love Hermann because it matched the history of my Doerr and Jones families' experiences on the Illinois prairie. Great Grandfather Doerr had been a brick mason in Germany and St. Louis before going to the prairie.

At this time, the Hermann Maifest was the only festival to expose this beautiful village to the public. In 1979, the Calico Cupboard invited Hermann's restaurants and grocery stores to join them in a Wurst Fest. In 1980, encouraged by our customers, we offered a bed and breakfast to the public. Of course, wine making had been an attraction in Hermann for years. With its 100 year old buildings, Hermann became a "don't miss" destination for Missouri's tourists.

With Taylor's final illness, we offered all of our buildings for sale, fully furnished with our great antiques, in appreciation for Hermann's support during the busy years in which we made our dreams come true. We would return to Kansas City simply "retired." Raymond had nourished our ideas of what a hometown should be, but Peculiar and Hermann occasionally will recall that Bill and Betty Taylor once lived there.

1984 photograph of Betty and Taylor
We truly are the "Antique Taylors" in this photo in front of the Calico Cupboard.
Taylor has lost his happy smile and outlook. I am concerned about our future
and the future of Calico Cupboard. Taylor is 88 and I am 72.
We've had 26 creative and wonderful years together.
We've dreamed dreams and we've seen many of them come true.
No one could have been more devoted than Taylor.

IN MEMORIAM

We sorrowfully mark the passing of

WILLIAM MATTHEW TAYLOR

May 2, 1985

We rejoice in recalling his quiet and gentle manner, his perennial sense of humor and his simplistic approach to the problems of daily life. We are grateful we could share twenty-seven of his 89 years and thank you most sincerely for the happiness your friendship brought to his long life.

Betty Brackman Taylor

William A. Brackman

108 E. Second Street

Hermann, Missouri 65041   314-486-2030

In Memoriam card for Taylor: May 2, 1985

Article from Hermann Advertiser-Courier: Wednesday, March 25, 1998
It had been 19 years since the first Wurst Fest. This year, the Advertiser-Courier asked if I
remembered the first one. I have many happy memories of Hermann. I was a "newcomer"
in 1979 but when I stop there now, and I stop as often as I can, I'm from "years ago." That
only shows how important it is to be all you can be wherever you are and whenever you are.
Hermann became our Hometown No. 3.

Betty Taylor-Yeddis remembers the first Wurstfest like it was yesterday

By Nancy Fagerness

Betty Taylor-Yeddis of Kansas City, Mo., visited Hermann recently. Many remember her as the owner of The Calico Cupboard (now, The Landing Restaurant), but some may not recall that she and her husband started the Hermann Wurst Festival 19 years ago.

She said she remembers the circumstances leading up to the first Wurstfest as if it were yesterday, and offered to share her story with our readers.

"I was driving over to Loutre Market to get bratwurst for the weekend. I didn't need much because it was January--in 1979--and tourists didn't hurry to Hermann so soon after Christmas. It occurred to me that I was extremely fortunate for in the Hermann area I could choose from seven sausage makers. This is the wurst town, I thought. Wurst town! A Wurst festival!

"With bratwurst for my weekend's need I hurried back to tell Taylor (Betty's late husband) what I thought was a great idea. Taylor agreed, but he knew we couldn't expect any cooperation for a midwinter activity. Therefore, we had to be prepared to sponsor it ourselves.

"This is the Wurst Press Release!" is what Betty called the document she wrote to inform the public about the event. She said, "We had immediate response from our friends at Missouri Tourism. Mid-winter activities in Missouri were scarce.

"One by one the area sausage makers were told of our plans, but only Bob Johnson at Loutre Market seemed to grasp the potential of this effort.

Photo by Wilding Studio

Bill and Betty Taylor started the Wurst Festival in 1979. The above photo was taken in the early 1980s

"Jack Carney had us on the air immediately. I was cooking every Friday on KOMU TV with Diane Larkin's show so the word spread over mid-Missouri. The Historical Society decided to have a kitchen tour of some of their most nostalgic kitchens. The Missouri Restaurant Association thought it was a great way to extend Missouri's tourism calendar.

"By the first of February, the mock-up of a sausage cookbook was ready for the printer. It contained 15 sausage recipes identified with the communities surrounding Hermann, and Bob Johnson had agreed to make a limited amount of each recipe for me to serve the weekend of the Wurst Festival.

"People came from everywhere," she remembered. "It was a beautiful March weekend. The town was alive! But, there was no sausage--except at Loutre Market where the TV cameras found them busily making sausage all afternoon...and on Sunday!"

Betty recalled, "One grocer told Taylor, 'We just thought Betty was rattling her chains.'"

In retrospect, Betty said, "Our years in Hermann with The Calico Cupboard were full of ideas and opportunities. Our customers from afar kept writing us to try bed and breakfast. We accepted their encouragement knowing they were seasoned travelers, first with the second floor of The Calico Cupboard and later adding the houses on Second and Third streets."

About her short stay in January Betty said, "I was so proud of Hermann when I visited there. Every street was spotless and every street mirrored the dedication of the Hermann people to its tourism goals. You have an illustrious past to share with the world. I'm so glad that Taylor and I could be part of it."

245

It's a Beautiful May Day!

May days always stir memories of Grandmother Jones' back yard. She with her full skirts swishing in and out of the back door, the cherry trees in full leaf with teensy weensy green cherries where cherry blossoms were a few weeks before. Only the birds looked forward with more anticipation to the fully ripened fruit. Grandmother could reach the lower branches for the first cherry pies of the season, but Aunt Florence and Aunt Elizabeth would be home from college in time to do the ladder picking as well as the canning, jelly making and cherry preserves. Cherry Sunshine, they called it, for they set it in the sunniest window and waited for it to thicken into syrupy preserves before canning.

Since Grandmother Jones lived in town, she always let me visit her on May Day and helped me make bouquets to hang on Mrs. Dill's and Mrs. Carter's doors. Usually the baskets were actually cornucopias made of wallpaper from an old wallpaper sample book. You don't believe me, do you? Wallpaper sample book? Sears Roebuck and Montgomery Ward provided them on request in these years, but Seymour's Drug Store was my source, if I begged. But back to the cherries. I never really appreciated all the goodies they contributed to, probably because seeding cherries was one of the first chores I was allowed to help with and the juice ran down my arms. They were the first of the summer's harvests and who could predict if there would be a peach crop or blackberries or raspberries or grapes to carry the family through the winter. My aunts were always glad to see the cellar shelves filling up because they knew that once they were back at college, Grandad would pack a wooden box of assorted goodies and wheel it down to the freight depot two or three times a year en route to Urbana.

This is a beautiful May Day, made only more so by these memories. But this is a special May Day - not because it's a Friday, in fact a Friday the 13th - but because it's my birthday marking 82 years since I became my parents' first child and the Jones' family's first grandchild. I share my friends' belief that these 82 years have witnessed almost unbelievable changes in all aspects of our lives. Dr. Kenton and Nurse White brought me to my mother at home in 1912. There was only telegraph to advise the world of the Titanic disaster and

Beatrix Potter had just introduced the juvenile world to Peter Rabbit, with violent content limited to what damage Peter could do to Mr. McGregor's cabbage plants. Not exactly violent but definitely naughty, naughty.

So join me as I reminisce about what we did and how we did it… about who I loved and who loved me… about the dreams I dreamed, the people who shared them and the few that came true.

Betty Taylor-Yeddis
May 13, 1994 (Age 82)

To My Dear Children:

It is May 13, 1996… the 84th anniversary of my birth and the day after Mother's Day.

You have all made it a glorious occasion, reminding me that parenting has great rewards; material, physical, and emotional. I remember my mother telling me that Doctor Kenton, our local family doctor and great friend, had pondered my tendency to carry too much weight and ventured that my life would not exceed 50 years. Every year after fifty, I thought would be my last. Eventually, I quit worrying about his prognosis. By that time, he was long gone and would not be embarrassed by underestimating my life span.

I have now outlived my mother, who died just weeks before her 80th birthday; my father, who lived almost 82 years; and Aunt Flora, who died at 83 (I think). Both of my Jones grandparents died in their 70's. The Goby grandparents were slightly heartier but Uncle Tone and Aunt Alice lived into their 90's.

It was so nice enjoying a quiet dinner tonight without the interruption of a single pager. You keep telling me that you are not embarrassed by my limited mobility, and I have no reason to think that you are less than sincere. Tomorrow, Salina will be here and the day is always a little more productive with her added energies and great understanding.

Thank you all for your beautiful cards, the flowers that brighten the living room, and this very comfortable "task" chair that moves about so easily. Now I must get to the many tasks that I put off during Morris' long illness.

Thank you all again for reminding me just how great it is to be a mother, a grandmother, and a great-grandmother.

Note: Dr. Kenton also said I'd never have any children! Having Bill was the greatest thrill of my life and I hadn't even dreamed about that possibility.

What a wonderful birthday!

It could not have been more exciting; first the E-mail, then the posies(including some pansies), then lots and lots of cards and lovely notes. We printed 103 cards, mailed out 92, and had 73 responses.

You all liked the "pansy" theme and I must tell you that "pansies are for remembrance" is a quotation of my dear mother, who always had pansies in the porch boxes by our driveway entrance.

Of course there would have been no card if it hadn't been for Fred and Bonnie who took the idea and never let it stop. DeAnn, my granddaughter, blessed the text. I tried to learn the whereabouts of old friends and succeeded except in the case of my high school graduating class of 1928. However, they celebrated our 52nd anniversary at the Calico Cupboard in Hermann.

Looking back, it really was more of a birthday month rather than a day. Thank you for the cards, notes, recollections and good wishes. I hope all your days are filled with loving memories. I find them very healthful. Thank you again for a wonderful 85th Birthday celebration.

Love, Betty Taylor-Yeddis

It's "pansy time" in mid-America and every little "face" recalls

Loving parents, grandparents - aunts,
uncles & cousins too, who still
bring a warm glow to long ago memories

Dear freinds from childhood, from college
and from the busy decades that followed in
Kansas City, Peculiar and Hermann

Dedicated teachers whose "Teaching" never
seems to go out of style

Enthusiastic students - and some of their parents-
to whom I almost feel related now

Encouraging employers sincerely interested in my personal growth

Business associates who responded to my personal
needs with constructive advice

Faithful employees equal to any emergency
and there were many

Caregivers who cared tirelessly for my loved ones
-----and who now care for me

My heartfelt appreciation to all of you for
bringing inspiration, purpose and promise
to my long life. Please join me in celebrating
the 85th anniversary of my birth on
May 13, 1997

        Fondly
        Betty Taylor-Yeddis

I am healthy according to last reports---however, crippled with arthritis and walk with a cane---on bad days, with a walker.

I'm comfortable in a lovely home in Kansas City just 3 miles from KCI airport.

I still enjoy driving.

I'm happily occupied remembering and recording people, places, events and recipes that filled these long years.

       The Goby years in Illinois (1912-1942)
          In Raymond, the "Village" that raised
          me.

       The Brachman years (1943-1951)
          My son, Bill, his children and
          grandchildren and their dreams.

       The "Taylor-ed" years in K.C., Peculiar &
          Hermann (1958-1985)

       The Yeddis years---a "Fairy Tale" finale to 75 years
          with loving friends, relatives and enchanting
          activities (1986-1996)

I hope I am a firm but loving grandmother - I had two wonderful role models.

Thank God for every moment, every recollection--I treasure them all.

I'd love to hear that you are well and busy. May God bless you as he has blessed me.

                              With warm regards
                              Betty

The Reporters Wrote:

"tenacious"

"the eternal grandmother"

"loving but firm"

"a spark plug"

"the newcomer"

"has an ethnic touch"

"best country breakfast" award
<u>St. Louis Magazine</u>

"eccentric"

"full-fledged Hermannites"
Sandy Barks

"a purist… ample"
Dorothy Roe Lewis
University of MO School of Journalism

"history buff"

"historian"
Greg Holzhauer in <u>Ozark</u>

"legendary"
John Heidenry in <u>Travel Holiday</u>

"Hermann's most energetic couple"
Mimi Schmidt

About the Artists:

<u>Alice Katherine Andrews-Jacobson</u>

Hermann was lucky when Leo Jacobson's toy factory decided to locate in Hermann. Hermann and toys go together, but no more than Hermann and Alice Jacobson. Her talent enhanced everything about the quaint German village, even though it became more sophisticated by the hour. Alice's education and travel is that of a seasoned professional and her paintings add immeasurably to Hermann's old world atmosphere. She wrote the following letter to help me describe her accurately in this book:

I was born in St. Louis 87 years ago! Is it possible I've lived so long and experienced so much? I was born to an engineer father and an artistic and loving mother, the youngest of five children. We lived in a large comfortable 14 room house with servants to care for it.

My father's business took him to far away places to direct his extensive engineering projects. Sometimes the whole family would travel with him, so my traveling began at an early age. I've continued enjoying traveling and with an understanding and supportive husband, I was able to paint on my travels which included the United States, Canada, Mexico, England, Scotland, Ireland, Switzerland, and Austria.

I am a member of the Hermann United Methodist Church where I've been Worship Chairman for a number of years. I've always been a church "goer". My father was a trustee and treasurer of our church. I taught Sunday School for fifty years.

I am a water colorist, acrylic painter, oil painter, muralist, illustrator, and weaver. With another woman I started the Weaver's Guild in Hermann, MO. I was an art teacher in the public schools, as well as privately, and art supervisor and a craft shop director. After I received a AB degree in English in 1932 I went, in succeeding years, to several universities so that I now have an equivalent of a Master's Degree in Art.

I married Leo V. Jacobson in 1939. We had a wonderful life together for almost 50 years. He was an engineer, inventor, salesman and spent many years in the toy industry. He died, at age 79 in 1989. Leo and I raised two children. Jane, an artist too, married a Canadian and lives on Vancouver Island off the west coast of Canada. Her three boys, my grandsons, are now grown university graduates and are engrossed in interesting jobs. David, our second child, was a brilliant scholar. After returning from Germany and Vietnam, he married June Booher, a nurse anesthetist. He went to Missouri Law School where he graduated with highest honors. The day after graduation, he went into the hospital with cancer and died nine months later. June and David had only 3 short years together but they were happy ones. I've kept close to June and her family and see them regularly.

I have always been interested in history and so was overjoyed to find Hermann when the toy company moved there. Hermann, the little historic town, surrounded by hills, packed with early 1800 houses and many people still speaking German. Its location on the mighty Missouri River and part of the Lewis & Clark Trail added to its charm. When we first moved to Hermann we bought 90 acres overlooking the town from the East. A 1840 stone house with a wine cellar was our home. The stone, for our house, was quarried from our property. Yes, we did try to make wine from cherries that had been brought from Germany. It was very effervescent and would explode without warning.

In the early 1970's, because of Leo's deteriorating health, we moved to the heart of the historic district of Hermann to our present home. It is another 1840 building but constructed of native brick. Located on the Missouri River it is a building with a colorful past. It was the first store in Hermann. It was built by Charles Eitzen, an early philanthropist store owner who was prominent in early Hermann history. He contributed ground and money for various public buildings. After Eitzen's death the building was given to the Masons for a Masonic Hall. Later, it was a warehouse for river boats. I live here today, at 206 Wharf where I have an apartment, rent out a third floor apartment, and have a Bed & Breakfast on my first floor containing a gallery of my pictures.

I have illustrated several historic books and other publications. I have a 35 foot mural of historic significance at the First Missouri Bank and am presently working with two other artists on a mural for the 100 year old Gasconade County Court House. I designed a number of Botanical Quilts that were sold to supply money for scholarships given by the Hermann Garden Club. I headed the Wharf Street Artists, an art group that painted together and had art shows over the years. I have exhibited in various competitions and won a number of prizes. I was chairman of the Maifest Craft Shop for many years and had the first craft shop in Hermann where I conducted tours and taught numerous classes and enlisted the help of many volunteers and other Art teachers. I've been a Board Member of Historic Hermann since the 1960's and I still volunteer in the Museum at the German School.

I'm the last of my immediate family. I have a busy and productive life. I'm still painting and enjoying the many interesting people who patronize my Bed & Breakfast. I have a host of friends near and far. I still don't have time to do many things I would like to.

<u>Joan Keiser-Bredehoeft</u>

When we first considered taking the Calico Cupboard to Hermann, Margaret Hahne made arrangements for me to meet Al and Joan Keiser who lived in a lovely old stone house in the Hermann countryside that they called "Hollyhock House." In fact, she arranged to bring them and their young family to the original Calico Cupboard in McCredie for dinner. As I became familiar with Joan's art work, I asked her to make me a bumper sticker saying "Caution, Hermann can be habit forming." (It was and it is!)

It was her husband, Al, who suggested the name "Taylor's Landing" for our building. He also suggested that an original wooden wine press he had might be adapted to be a salad bar. With a custom made stainless steel pan it worked very well and was photographed by many of our customers and several writers. The Keiser children were always along and were welcome guests. From promotional material to newspaper ads to place mats and menus, her art work caught the feel of Calico Cupboard and helped Calico catch the feel of Hermann. I had only to dream and tell Joan and it was a reality. Provincial, yes, but "Joan Keiser provincial." During Taylor's illness, I had no need for new things but I treasured what I had. I was not aware that Joan and Al had separated or that she had left Hermann.

After Morris' death, as I undertook to breathe life into <u>Recipes, Recollections and Reflections</u>, local artists were most accommodating but I was spoiled and I began to search for Joan again. Frank Van Kamp made a special effort and finally Fred took me to Hermann so that I'd feel I was really trying. Ginny Lone told me about Donna McEachern's Philosopher's Coffee Shop and how I would enjoy it, she also might know how to reach Joan. With Donna's help, I was able to locate Frieda Penturf who had been a close friend of Joan's. Frieda's daughter had seen Joan at a shopping mall in St. Louis and we were able to zero in for "the kill." I was finally able to reach her. With access to Joan's lettering, I could finish the book... and that's where I am now. Her lettering continues the Hermann feel. Her lovely well-behaved children are now adults, all engaged in interesting work. Joan had no reluctance when I told her how I had looked for her and how important she was to this story of my life. I know that you will agree that her lettering and sketches are important to every page just like Alice Jacobson's sketches almost reek with mustiness from the century old brick buildings in Hermann.

When Joan and I met in Hermann on the 31st day of August, I asked John Wilding to join us with his camera to record our re-acquaintance. My caregiver, Fred Besch, had driven me to Hermann and shared my enthusiasm for Joan's role. I was so euphoric about the future of the book. Only my wish to stop at Carol and Bob Johnson's Loutre Market before we left town kept my feet on the ground. Now I could complete <u>Recipes, Recollections and Reflections</u> in Hermann style; or at least in Betty Taylor-Yeddis Hermann style.

Forty-eight hours later, however, I was in the hospital with little recollection of my project. The following week, when Fred took me to the doctor for a check-up, I was immediately admitted. This second visit did not leave me comatose so I resigned myself to spend those hours finalizing my recollections of what I had left on the dining room table. Without a computer, a typewriter or even a pen; I concentrated on the people in my life whom I had loved and why I had loved them. I even dared to wonder why they had loved me. Fred visited me daily at the hospital with the day's mail and to assure me that Joe and Casey (my cats) were well cared for.

When I was released a few days later, Joan was well-along with the art work and I couldn't wait to complete the manuscript and meet with the publisher. By this time, the first three Dreams were complete, as was the recipe section. It remained for me to finish Dream IV about my life with Morris. As I lay in the hospital, I realized that Sarah and Jacob Yeddis had profoundly influenced my life even though I never got to know them. It was then that I decided Pop and she should share the dedication with Morris who loved them dearly. Now Dream IV is complete.

Photograph of Joan Keiser Bredehoeft, Betty and Fred Besch (her caregiver)

<u>Recipes, Recollections and Reflections</u> was intended to record the simple down-to-earth foods of Grandma Goby and Grandmother Jones that her customers enjoyed at the Calico Cupboard in Hermann, Missouri. Her guests had no doubt of her dedication to the past, for the past was all around them in Hermann and in Calico Cupboard. With each visit, guests became more sensitive to the energy and love that found its way into what she and Taylor planned; her cooking, her decorating ideas, everything she did and everything she dreamed for Hermann, for herself and for Taylor. But she never provided us with any insight into the dreams she had put aside for a variety of reasons. I never realized that with two loving husbands and three hometowns, my grandmother was in a constant state of "becoming" until…

And that's where <u>Recipes, Recollections and Reflections</u> becomes a love story. Not "boy meets girl" stuff, but an unbelievable, fairy tale, made-in-heaven, romantic love story. What she called her "scrapbook years" found meaning, reality and purpose. As a fourth generation *magna cum laude* dreamer, she was alert to every incipient opportunity she found nestled in between life's predicaments. She still is. My brother, Tim, and I are so happy she decided to include Jacob and Sarah Yeddis in her dedication of the book. Their story is such an inspiration. They were the in-laws she never had.

DeAnn Warren and Tim Brackman

Reader's Notes

To share my life with Morris Yeddis,
to share his dreams and to realize
my own with the loving support
of our families—

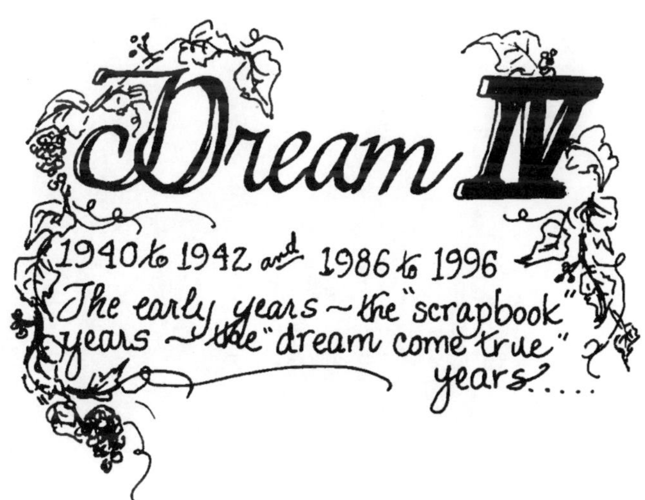

The way we were - Morris Yeddis (1942) and Grace Elizabeth Goby (1940)

The "Dream Come True" Years

Morris Yeddis and I were sweethearts in 1941 and 1942. I met him at the home of Sammy Kaplan, who lived across Armour Boulevard from me and with whom I had been associated in construction at Fort Riley. I had stopped at Sammy's to tell him and his wife that I was leaving for a short term construction job in Louisiana, Missouri. Before I interrupted them, they had been playing cards following dinner when Morris had been their guest.

"Louisiana, Missouri?" Morris interrupted. "That's like going to Kamchatka, Alaska."

"Kamchatka, Alaska?" I said. "Sammy, where did you get this man who thinks that Kamchatka is in Alaska?'

Then Morris replied, "Where did you get this girl who knows where Kamchatka is?"

About thirty minutes later, Morris left Sammy's apartment with me and my girlfriend. His car was parked on the street beside my apartment building and we talked for hours. The next morning, he phoned to tell me that he didn't want me to leave. I assured him that I would keep in touch and that I'd be back in Kansas City frequently. As an office manager on these jobs, I had to hire employees and I was in Kansas City occasionally interviewing. I always saw Morris.

As the construction job wound down, I knew I would return to Kansas City to seek regular work. By that time, Morris had become part of my life. He took great pride in his family and lived with his parents near Central High School. His deferment was extended because the contractor for whom he worked was engaged in government contracts. His brother, Al, was already in the Service. During our courtship, his other brother, Abe, had married his high school sweetheart. Back in Kansas City, I began work as a court reporter with an independent reporting firm that took assignments all over the Midwest.

We finally had to face up to the fact that Morris' parents would not allow him to marry a non-Jewish girl. As a first born son, and as Morris Yeddis, he would not do anything to displease his mother or father. It was also Sammy Kaplan who told them that Morris was seeing me.

During Yom Kippur in 1942, a Jewish mother introduced him to her daughter. I know what a conflict he endured knowing that he would soon be going into the Service and wanting to please his parents. He was candid with me from the beginning. He also knew I was heartbroken. My Jewish friends tried to console me by saying things like, "It never works out." He was married in February, 1943 and it was not too long before he went into the Service.

On the first floor of my office building, Brecklein's Pharmacy and its fountain were a vital part of 9th and Grand. The pharmacists knew everybody. One of them, Hugo Brackman, asked me to refer him to an attorney nearby who would handle a divorce for him. His ten year old son, Richard, spent weekends with him and I had gotten to know him for he delivered prescriptions to Doctor Owens' office nearby. One day he asked me if I would go to the show with him. I told him I could not take time that week but I promised him I would go another time. I was really flattered after having been a single woman for so many years that Richard thought he would enjoy my company. Weeks later, and after we had gone to the movie a couple of times, Richard asked me, "Why don't you marry my dad so I can live with you?"

My first reaction was that at ten years old, Richard had no idea of what he was suggesting or its consequences. I was an old maid; out of touch with the thinking of young boys (if I had ever known). At thirty-one I was reliving the same situation my Grandmother Jones faced when she, as a school teacher, met my Grandfather Jones and his six year old son, George. I wondered if Richard's father knew what he had suggested. He did. On Richard's next visit, he insisted that I join them for dinner. But there was only a slight refer-ence to Richard's idea. Each time I came into the drug store, someone behind the counter would jokingly remind me that they had heard. I was becoming more attached to Richard each week and enjoyed his stopping in the office. The Hoover sisters managed Brecklein's and, as mature single women, they tried to convince me that they would have jumped at the chance in their thir-ties, especially with such a nice young son as Richard.

But I was not Betty Hoover. I was Betty Goby and I had been in love with Morris Yeddis and that conditioned all my thinking. Even with Morris mar-ried for six months, I wondered what he would think of my decision. He, as well as I, knew what a rough and tumble world faced a single girl in these war years. By the first of October, after more movies and weekend visits from Richard, my questions increased. Was Richard the child that Doctor Kenton said I'd never have? Would it limit my future or was this my future? Should people marry when they aren't in love? Hugo was an honor graduate pharma-cist and that should please my folks! I was talking to myself! Finally, we decided to marry and, for my mother's sake, we chose the Park College Chapel which was being built when she was a student there in 1903.

Within days after we moved into a home in the Redemptorist area, I noticed Morris' mother's death in the newspaper. Almost within minutes of seeing it, Morris knocked on my door to tell me he was home from the Service. How he found me in that new location, I'll never know. I only knew that with a new step-son at my side, I could not console him. Knowing how much he loved his mother, I knew he was there because he knew I would share his grief… and I did. To have made this effort in such anguished hours ten months after our separation!

After four years, Hugo's dependence on alcohol became more and more a problem in our marriage. Richard's mother had begun driving by the school yard at recess time to see him. Richard had never asked to spend time with her. Finally, she promised him a car (at 14) if he would come live with her and her new husband - the friend with whom she had lived when she left Hugo. Richard had been the center of our life together. I had grown to love him and he was a very responsible child. Reluctantly, we agreed to let him go be with his mother. We both felt helpless, but the loss was devastating to Hugo.

I sought medical help for depression and for weight control. The medical doctors all knew Hugo at Brecklein's. For weight control, they gave me pills that worked for a time. The pills helped me lose weight at first and then they left me pregnant. My body, after thirty-five years, was behaving like a female body should. On April 23, 1947 our son, Bill, was born. I rationalized that without Richard, this never would have happened. But by this time, Bill was the only bright spot in my life. Four years later, Hugo and I were divorced. He continued to be a part of our family as he went from job to job. He and Bill were close until his death in 1967.

Betty Brackman letterhead from WIBW

Jobs for mature women were fairly plentiful, for so many men were in the Service. A kitchen cabinet manufacturer contacted me and offered me a job with a Topeka dealer who needed help in bidding several hospital and university installations. In Topeka, I had a modicum of success; primarily because my bids on large veterinary laboratories at K-State were successful. With cooperative advertising available, WIBW encouraged my boss to use it on TV advertising. Betty Brackman's Home and Garden Time became an enjoyable effort, even though TV was live and in its infancy. Interviews were great fun but live commercials were a bore. My heart returned to "romance mode" one day when I received a copy of the ad for my program that had been torn out of <u>TV Guide.</u> In the margin was a note from Morris. It wasn't until a luncheon at the Coates House several months later that I saw the post-war Morris replete with flashing black eyes and now with a black mustache. Of course, he came to our table before he left.

In these "scrapbook" years, each time I returned to Kansas City, as I reached the city limits I'd say out loud to myself: "Now I'm under Morris' sky!" The business news carried an item saying that the Yeddis' family headware business was moving from Broadway to 1150 Elmwood and that Morris' brother, Al, would share the building with them. Al had ridden back and forth with me from Fort Riley when I was dating Morris pre-war.

In my job, I sought materials for kitchen remodeling, counter tops and specialty millwork. Limpus Woodcraft in Kansas City invited me to join them and offered to warehouse specialty millwork items that I was finding in short supply. The Limpus connection rewarded my energies with money and took me back to Kansas City. By this time, I was enjoying not only the selling but the promotion of this new addition to the Limpus service. Mr. Limpus believed in me and my abilities.

It was during these happy Limpus years that Taylor, a longtime family "uncle", returned from Florida. He wasn't surprised to learn that Hugo and I had been divorced, but for six years! He knew how turbulent the Brackman years had been. Taylor also knew that I had always felt that my love for Morris had been a factor in my unhappiness. When Taylor asked me to marry him, I told him I would not make a good wife for I would always compare my life to what I thought it would have been with Morris. I also told him I still carried Morris in my heart. Taylor simply said, "Oh, let's try." My son was eleven and had known Taylor in an "old uncle" fashion all his life. Taylor was sixteen years older than I. With Bill's blessing, Taylor and I were married in the Presbyterian manse at Excelsior Springs with his friends, Clyde and Ruth Parker, as our attendants.

Taylor and I were married twenty-seven happy years. The age difference just may have been an asset. He knew how much I had loved Morris and he knew how much I had suffered during the Hugo years. Taylor joined Limpus Woodcraft and worked there until his retirement. Then he drove a school bus in Belton with Mr. Limpus' brother, Paul. I returned to college, completed an MA in Education and began teaching. The education field is much like the legal field; eventually you get into the specialty that is most fulfilling for you. Mine was remedial reading and library development. Taylor was welcome every place my work took me. For twenty-seven years, we were a couple. He simply wanted to make my dreams come true... and he did.
By 1980, we were in Hermann with The Calico Cupboard when my Hermann

doctor insisted that I see a specialist to treat my high blood pressure and my thyroid problem. My son urged me to first see his doctor and he made an appointment for me. As I waited in his kitchen to keep that appointment, I wondered if Morris was still alive. It had been twenty-two years since I had told him I was planning to marry Taylor and wanted his blessing. I called Pioneer, confident that his brother would ask me who I was and tell me that Morris had passed away years earlier. Instead, Morris answered his phone and seemed excited to hear from me. By the time I got back to Hermann two days later, there was a lovely note saying that he hoped the doctors would be able to help me and asking me to stay in touch. I remember the last line of that note vividly: "I know you're just as sweet as you always were." I felt so guilty about renewing my acquaintance with him that I kissed the note, tore it into teensy pieces and put it in the bottom of the trash can (along with a tear drop or two).

Taylor never expected me to forget Morris and I never expected him to forget Daisy. He had allowed me to keep Morris in my heart as we fashioned a world for ourselves. Taylor also knew that you couldn't discard real loves and that without them you are not a whole person. Our guests always remarked about how lovingly Taylor and I greeted each other when we came back to the res-taurant. I never thought it was unusual. We loved each other for who we were at that stage in our life… and we knew that our lives had been blessed. Calico Cupboard was our home and it was full of love; our guests never failed to tell us so.

Approximately a year later, Morris called me collect to tell me he had had a heart attack. He told me he was in the hospital and that he "just had to hear [my] voice." I promised him I would keep in touch with the hospital and told him to call me at any time. That evening, I took a long walk. The Van Kamps were on their patio but they never had seen me walking. They invited me to sit with them and my silence disturbed them. Something was wrong. I finally told them about this wonderful old friend whom I had carried in my heart for years and who had inspired me to be the best that I could be wherever I was. The Van Kamps were also sensitive to my anguish, for they knew Taylor was in the VA hospital at Columbia. We had just opened Der Klingerbau to great reviews as a bed and breakfast inn - a first for Hermann and great for Missouri tourism. I couldn't do Calico Cupboard without Taylor and, with throat can-cer, Taylor was no longer his happy self.

Without Taylor and with my son, Bill, and my grandkids in Kansas City; I knew I would be moving back. We had had enviable publicity and if we were going to sell the properties, now was the time. I also knew that I could never break up the furnishings of each house, for each had been decorated for the period in which the house was built. I would sell everything fully furnished.

On April 3, 1985, Pop Yeddis died and on May 2, 1985, Taylor died. Morris had been divorced since 1984. Taylor and I had had twenty-seven great years together and his friends had just showered him with cards on his 89th birthday. I had visited him at the hospital in Columbia every day. He was a wonderful husband and a wonderful companion. The Antique Taylors of Peculiar had become the Antique Taylors of Missouri.

Morris' ready wit, his beautiful voice and his quiet reassurances blessed my seventies. His planning for me blesses my eighties. Morris died at home in January, 1996 after a series of illnesses. Salina Davis and Myriam Guiterrez cared for him daily. Our granddaughter, DeAnn Warren, became a nurse as she saw our needs developing. I still hear from Salina regularly and Myriam and her husband bought our townhouse in Overland Park.

Morris is part of every hour of my life. His thoughtful brothers join me every Sunday morning for breakfast at Ari's Pumpernick Restaurant, just as they did when Morris was here. I am close to his daughter, Sandra. Morris now has a great grandson, Julian Alexander, the son of Violet and Bradley Jones in England (another Jones family!). I know his parents will tell him what a wonderful great grandfather he had.

Our family breakfasts have been of great help to me in adapting to a world without Morris. Our breakfast conversations may touch on sports news of the day, the stock market, or friends who may be in ill health. Eventually we get to unusual incidents in our own lives and, sometimes, someone has a new story worth repeating. This week, Abe and President Clinton had been in China at the same time so that prompted a lot of remarks. Occasionally, Abe's longtime friend, Chester Kaplan, joins us. As our family attorney, he adds a sobering influence if our conversations get carried away. I'm sure Al and Abe know how much these breakfasts mean to me. Frequently, people tell me how nice it is to see the Yeddises together each Sunday morning. Abe's travels take him away many weekends, but we just know that the next Sunday will be full of a lot of new experiences.

It was Morris who suggested that I retain "Taylor" as my middle name, for he knew that Taylor had given my life meaning and creativity during the years he and I were separated. He also knew that our life together would build on that happiness. I revere the years with Taylor but I'm "in love" with Morris… just like I told Taylor years ago. Sometimes I think God planned for me to "serve" forty-five years before joining Morris in order that I would be properly conditioned to spend the rest of my life without him. Morris planned for me to live and enjoy these later years. It is appropriate that I have dedicated the book to this wonderful man. It was during a recent hospital stay that I realized what influence his parents had had on my life. Morris took me with him on several visits to his Dad but, since Morris was then divorced, his father thought Morris "boarded" with me. He always hugged me and kissed me good-bye, but a bit of my heart remained with him. So today I have added Jacob and Sarah Yeddis to the dedication of <u>Recipes, Recollections and Reflections.</u>

Morris was so proud of his parents and his family. He related in detail how his dad and his mother had adapted themselves to life in America and the Midwest. His father worked for Empire Cap Company to support his young wife and son just months after having decided to leave Russia and settle in Kansas City.

Jacob knew that he was at the top of his trade. As a cap maker in Kiev, he had had to get special permission from the government because Jews were not allowed to live in Kiev. Because of his "good fingers" and the fact that the Czar and his officers needed his needle skills, he had been allowed residency. "Sonya was a first-class hat saleslady. She was the best." he said. So he married Sonya and together they decided to escape the impending pressure from Russian government. When they boarded the ship in Bremen, Germany for America, they both had relatives already established in their new country.

Sonya's mother had died when she was born. Her father had been in the Russian Army for forty years. Jacob's father, a Rabbi, encouraged their going to America and regretted that he had not had that opportunity. As a Rabbi, he fasted 52 days a year and taught the village children Hebrew - not for money but because he was a committed Jew. Sonya's relatives were settled in New York and Jacob's brother and sisters were in Missouri. Sisters Mary and Fanny were in St. Louis and brother Morris was in Kansas City in the produce business. After visiting both cities, they decided on Kansas City. Within four months, Morris was born. Within five years, they had three sons: Morris, Abe and Alexander.

Only Uncle Morris' son, Nathan, remained in Kansas City. His widow, Cyril Yeddis, survives. We see his son, Lew Yeddis a couple of times a year when he comes from Colorado. His daughter, Goldie, also lives in Colorado. Today I spoke with Jennie Gershenson in St. Louis. She is 91 and her voice reflects a healthy body. Before Morris and I became reacquainted, I tried to always attend the book sale of the St. Louis Jewish Federation. Morris had told me he had a cousin, Rose Londi, in St. Louis. Just possibly, I might meet her. When I asked if she was involved in their group, they said, "Rose just left here five minutes ago." I had come to the stage that I would have told her that I had

Photograph of Morris, Abe and Al Yeddis

Photograph of Morris with "Pop" Yeddis on his 95th birthday

known Morris in my twenties. One of the ladies had told Rose that I had inquired about her. After Morris and I were married, we went to St. Louis deliberately to renew these family connections. She greeted us lovingly and wanted to know if I was the one who had asked about her at the book fair. Unfortunately, this gracious and beautiful woman died a very few months later. Jennie Gershenson, at 91, had vivid recollections of Pop Yeddis' sisters, Aunt Mary and Aunt Fanny.

Morris remembered working for his Uncle Morris in the produce business at 31st and Main. This intersection was a busy transfer corner because the street cars fanned out in all directions to take people to their homes south of 31st Street. With good planning, a customer could pick up fresh vegetables or other items between street cars and get them home in time for dinner. When people complimented Morris on his voice, he happily related how he had been in the Kehilath Israel choir under the direction of his father. He would shake his head in disbelief as he recalled the "hard times" when his mother went from house to house selling caps and other items to supplement the family income. He was quick to add, however, that his mother was heartily in favor of the family's effort to own its own factory and invest in equipment that would improve production and quality. City Magazine published an article in 1937 that reminds us of just how determined Jacob Yeddis was in those early years; coming into the business and knowing that Sonya and his family supported his planning wholeheartedly. As a foreman at Brauer, Gressman and Cohen Cap Company; he was in a position to buy the cap business with his son, Abe, when the previous owners abandoned caps for the robe manufacturing business. Pioneer Cap Company became a reality in 1937 in the heart of the Great Depression. Abe served as president and Morris as vice-president and sales manager. Sonya died suddenly in the beauty shop in 1943, just months after Morris entered the service.

Under Abe's leadership, Pioneer Cap Company went through several organizational changes preparing them for a broader market. This was a period that took caps from utility wear for men to essential fashion headwear for both men and women. You will not be surprised to learn that Abe's grandson, Dan Saferstein, now leads Promotional Headwear International in serving a global market. Importing under the Sportsman label added materially to PHI's distribution. It has now become even more important to be working with overseas manufacturers that share their determination for quality and dependability. Dan and Caroline both take pride in the Sportsman label and its identification with style and quality, which the Yeddis family has always been known for. Between the two of them, they will keep PHI "fashion forward." Wouldn't Jacob Yeddis be proud?

When you remember that the pleasure of witnessing this success was denied

Dear Betty,

I can't help it, I just keep thinking about you and your book, so I had to write again. It's so exciting! I'm now re-inspired to pick up those "projects I don't seem to have time for" and make some time. Not to give you platitudes, but you are living proof that age is all in the mind and that there is no limit to what a person can accomplish in their life. To use my generation's terminology, you are extremely COOL!

It is only in having my own child that I know the real meaning of "devotion" and what it feels like to put another person's needs before your own. Now that I've experienced this love I can also recognize it and give gratitude to find it in others... Though I was too young to understand and give thanks at the time, I would like to acknowledge your ceaseless devotion to my grandfather and your selflessness. You deserve a medal! Morris was TRULY BLESSED to have you as a sweetheart. I'm only sad that I was too wrapped up in college and work to have participated in both of your lives a little more. And now I'm in England! C'est la vie, I suppose.

Keep the creative juices flowing! Love, Vi

Letter from Violet, Morris' granddaughter; photograph of Violet with her son

Sonya (Sarah in America) because she died so early, it becomes even more heart-wrenching to hear how Jacob and she made the trip from Russia with Morris cradled snugly in her womb. Pregnancy added to her misery and discomfort during the three week voyage and morning sickness marked each day. She had relatives in New York and Jacob's brother and sisters were in Missouri. Morris was born four months after their arrival in Kansas City. You know how proud they were. I was so happy Abe shared this picture of his mother with me. Now it joins the other women from whom I gather love and inspiration. (See photo on page 281)

Jacob and Sarah would have had a loving daughter-in-law if Morris and I had married earlier. But traditions and customs were at the heart of their strength, particularly in the new country. At this stage, as I reflect on how my life found direction, I know that it would have been completely different. I would have been in such awe of Morris' business ability that many of the activities I found fulfilling, I would never have dared suggest. Aside from the birth of my son, Bill, the most fulfilling event in my life was to be with Morris for the last eleven years of his life. That fulfillment continues to be enhanced by our

Photograph of Violet with her husband, Bradley
Violet graduated with honors as an Art Historian and has been living in Europe for a year.
Bradley was recently transferred to Japan.

Photograph of Morris' great grandson, Julian Alexander Jones (son of Violet and Bradley)

weekly family breakfasts. I have been so blessed to be a lovingly accepted part of the Yeddis family. I sometimes feel Morris arranged it all. Tonight I know he did.

Photograph of the Yeddis family at Ari's Pumpernick with friends

Few of us relish the thought of traveling across the Atlantic Ocean on a crowded boat while pregnant, but, that is what so many of our grandmothers did. That is what I visualize as I contemplate the great courage it took for my non-English speaking grandmother to come to America and then get on with her life. And on with her life she went as did my grandfather who went on to have a successful business and full life.

My father was the baby on the boat. Maybe that is why he never had a problem with seasickness! Raised in the old ways, my father believed strongly in the American Dream and also in being kind to others. The Jews believe in making the best of every day and he was indeed a hard worker and stoic individual. He set an example to us all by never swaying from his daily itinerary and by setting goals and reaching them.

A businessman can become hardened, but my father did not allow that to happen. He cherished the virtue of kindness and did not have a bad word for anyone. He applied his orthodox upbringing in decisions he made and left this world with a legacy as a role model for hard work and fairness.   Sandra Kowall

Letter from Sandra, Morris' daughter; photograph of Sandra and Johann,
her husband Johann is a distribution consultant for Gress Northwest.
Sandra continues to work with special needs children in public and private schools.

Morris and I were married on July 12, 1986; after being in love since 1941. The next ten years were "dream come true" years. We became acquainted with Martha Mirrer on our first cruise. With such enjoyable memories, we joined her Post Haste Travel group for later cruises. Just by chance, her husband had been in the hat-making business in New York. By the first night, everybody knew Morris and I spent my afternoons writing down the words to songs he had promised women he would sing that night. They told us that after they heard our beautiful love story, they enjoyed Morris' singing even more for they thought he actually felt how meaningful the lyrics were. He answered their questions night after night, cruise after cruise. But to us, the most important thing was that it was our story and we were who we were because we had believed in each other all those years.

Photograph of Al and Adele Yeddis
as they attend to final preparations for a Yeddis family Seder

Photograph of Betty's 80th birthday celebration:
Betty in center and from left; Abe, Adele, Al, Barbara, and Morris

Because...

you've touched our lives so gently and in so many ways, we

Betty Taylor
and
Morris Yeddis

want you to know that we will exchange wedding vows in

Rolla, Missouri
on
July 12, 1986

Our families lovingly share our happiness in this "new beginning" and the reaffirmation of God's love throughout our long and busy lives.

9425 Delmar,
Prairie Village, KS   (913) 642-1163
66207

Wedding announcement for Betty and Morris (1986)

Some people I find hard to be with.

you, I find hard to be without!

M. Y. (apt. 212)

Note form Morris to Betty. Morris was never at a loss for words - some of them quite unexpected! Personally, he preferred to let Hallmark express his feelings and sometimes, he sent the same greeting card on two different occasions.
I put all of his cards in a scrapbook. He always selected beautiful cards with beautiful messages and I loved every one of them. They only stopped when he could no longer walk with his friends at Ward Parkway. Sometimes, he chose to fashion his own message - like this one, which I found on my apartment door one evening.

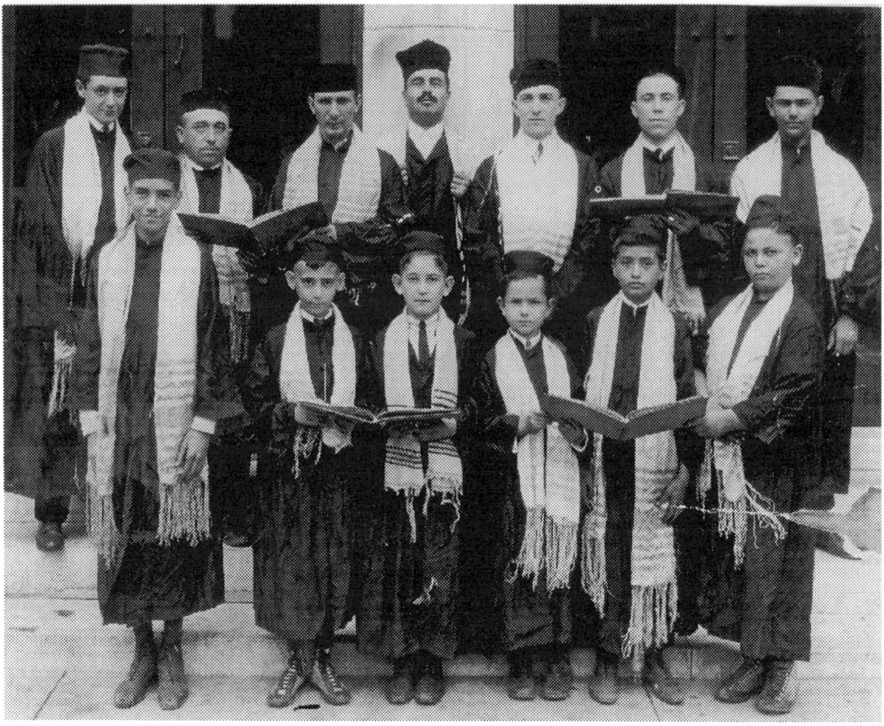

Photograph of the Kehilath Israel choir, under the direction of Jacob Yeddis
(back row, second from right) Morris Yeddis (front row, second from left)

Pioneer Cap Company logo

FROM CZAR'S CAPMAKER TO AMERICAN CAP CZAR

"When I came here, to Kansas City, the first few weeks wasn't so happy . . . When you come in, it's rough."

He could have stepped out of a Sholom Aleichem novel, this little capmaker from the Ukraine. And, indeed, the town in which Jacob Yeddis was born was almost identical to Kasrilevke, the small country town immortalized in the writings of the famous Yiddish author.

The difference between Jacob Yeddis and the Aleichem characters is that Yeddis and his wife, Sonya, boarded a ship at Bremen, Germany, in 1914 and, having left Russia forever behind, set sail for America, the promised land. He was 20 years old, had little money and could not speak a word of English. Two decades later, Yeddis founded the Pioneer Cap Company here and, during the following 30 years, watched his dream grow from a six-employee operation into one of the three largest cap manufacturing companies in the nation.

Why did he do it? How did he do it? The answer probably is that it was there to be done and Jacob Yeddis knew how to do it.

"I made caps for the Czar's army," he explained. "You've heard the saying, 'I played fiddle for the Czar?' Well, I made *caps* for the Czar's army. In Kiev, I was in a special class because I had good fingers and made caps by hand. In Kansas City, I got a job as a capmaker with the Empire Cap Company because I told the capman I was good. And I *was* good."

Despite his talents, Yeddis worked from dawn to dark in America, which had been described to him as having "streets paved with gold," just to make ends meet. For his efforts he received a $13 a week salary.

"Sonya, my wife, sold neckties and hosiery house-to-house when my earnings fell off during the horrible '30s," he recalled. "She had been a saleslady for a large department store in Kiev. That's how I met her. I delivered uniform caps for the schoolboys to her department. Sonya was a saleslady, *first class.* The best one. So I met her and I married her."

"When I came here, to Kansas City, the first few weeks wasn't so happy. I was making more money in Kiev. You see, naturally, when you come in, it's rough. You don't know the language. You want to know the American methods, and all

KANSAS CITY CAPMAKER: *Jacob Yeddis found that his long apprenticeship in self-sufficiency in the Ukraine paid off in the Midwest.*

that. But it didn't take any time."

Well, at least it didn't for Jacob Yeddis. His long apprenticeship in self-sufficiency in the Ukraine paid off in America.

"After 13, you go on your own, you see, you *GO.* After your Bar Mitzvah, you become an independent Jew. Right away, when I was 13, I left Picoff and went to Kiev. the capital of the Ukraine. A beautiful city of cathedrals. When there was snow on the steeples and all the bells were ringing . . . Ah, down there was beautiful!

"But Jews were not allowed to live in Kiev," he continued. "For a Jew to get the right to live in a big city, he had to perform necessary labor which would benefit the government. Well, my boss was playing for big stakes in Kiev. So he went to the police department and he said, 'Look, Yagoddis (in Russia, my name was Yagoddis) has to stay. You want to have caps for the Army? For the Czar's son? For the officers? Yagoddis has to stay in Kiev and work. If not, I can't make the caps. Go and make 'em yourself.'

"So," he sighed, "they gave me the rights."

Yeddis moved from his small country

town of Picoff to Kiev, which was about 100 miles away, returning to his native city only for holidays.

"The Czar did not bother us in the small towns but, in Kiev, they kept a close watch on you. You could say what you wanted, but you could say *nothing* against the Czar.

"I saw the Czar ride down the main street of Kiev. Nicholas de Roi . . ." (Nicholas II) ". . . in full regalia—with a crown on his head. Well, it wasn't exactly the *main* crown, but a sort of crown. He was *good-lookin'* and had a beard. The Russians were standin' along the street and they took off their caps and clapped. He waved and smiled. Oh. he was good-lookin'. dressed in a fancy uniform. With him was his son, Naslednik. pozhaluista, which means: He takes over after the Czar is gone.

"In addition to making caps for the Czar's army," Yeddis continued. "we—a few capmakers and I—also made caps for the Czar's officers for special parades."

Immersed in his work. Yeddis tried to forget the increasing violence around him. The czarist solution to the general

"It was 1937, the height of the Depression, when Jacob opened the doors of the Pioneer Cap Company..."

restiveness of the people was to create a blood bath. A campaign against the Jews would take the peasants' minds off their growing dissatisfactions, reasoned the royal government. So sadistic and brutal pogroms of Jewish villages began. Widespread and regular, the pogroms showed no mercy for even small children.

"They used to pass by Kiev's main street, Krishchtatuk, a beautiful street, with stores and everything. They know you're speaking Jewish—students hit you with a rope or anything they give them over there. They hit you over there with rope. Yah, *rope*. They didn't want to *kill* you . . . kill you in the street. They want to *hit* you . . . they want to *hurt* you."

It was in this atmosphere that Jacob Yeddis went about the business of learning to make caps. His appetite for learning was insatiable, and there, in the small Kiev cap factory, he became an expert in every phase of his craft. And, all the while, he dreamed of designing caps, as well as of America.

"My father used to talk about George Washington and Abraham Lincoln . . . there is two people I don't forget! He'd say, 'Oh, if I am younger, oh, I would go to America!'"

Yeddis followed his father's advice, arriving in America three years before the Bolshevik Revolution in 1917. It was a feat for a young man and his wife to come to America together in those days. Usually, the wife stayed behind until the husband had earned enough money for her passage. In the Yeddis case, however, there was an important reason for the couple to make the journey together: their first child, Morris, was born only four months after his parents set foot on Ellis Island, New York's famous port of entry.

With a family to support (Morris was followed by two younger brothers, Abe and Alexander), Jacob was concerned about keeping his head above water.

"I was making $13 a week but I had a philosophy," he confided: "A dollar goes into the postoffice at 9th and Grand before I come home." It was a savings plan that Jacob and Sonya agreed upon as a step toward starting his own company.

It was 1937, the height of the Depression, when Jacob opened the doors of the Pioneer Cap Company, which was so named because, according to Abe Yeddis, "We were pioneers in an industry just starting to grow with modern methods and machinery."

Beginning with six employees, Jacob supervised the factory, designed the hats and trained each capmaker in the various phases of capmaking. ("I made the patterns, one employee would do the cutting, another the sewing. I'd show them how to lay out the goods . . . economically, not to waste, to come out good. You can take ten yards of goods and if you don't put the patterns right, you lose a yard.")

When Jacob opened the doors of Pioneer Cap, it was in a sense a victory for his beloved mother and father who would never have the opportunity to come to America, the land they spoke and dreamed about during those dark days in the Jewish settlement.

Yeddis never saw his mother, father, brother, Meyer, or sister, Goldie, after he left Russia, although he corresponded with them and sent them money until 1941.

"Why don't you ask me what became of my mother and brother?" he asked, suddenly.

"During World War II their letters stopped coming. We contacted the Red Cross, exhausting every avenue to find them, but we were never to hear from them again."

It was Hitler's army and it was a massacre.

"Without any question," Yeddis said, "Hitler did that not only in Russia, but in other countries around Russia. He did so much bad to the French people. And to the Polish people. It's unbelievable! When there was the whole world. They didn't say nothing. They didn't do nothing."

He sighed, a great, long sigh.

"Well, you know, we've got one God in Heaven," he began anew, "and He's everybody's God. And there is in the Talmud, the Torah, the Bible, in the English books, too, you shouldn't kill, you shouldn't do it. But people doin' it."

Despite the tragedies he left behind in Eastern Europe, Jacob Yeddis remembers not the hard times, but the good times, the warm, happy moments with his parents, three brothers and two sisters.

"My father was a deeply devoted family man, a scholar," he explained. "He wore the *tallis* (prayer shawl) in the synagogue. We had to kiss the *Mezuzah* every time we went out of the house. We could not work on the Sabbath, not handle a writing instrument, not even tear paper. My father wore the ritual fringes and had to obey all 613 regulations of the Jewish code."

Yeddis credits his father and the years (from age 5 until 13) spent attending *chedar* (Hebrew School) with his success. However, he added, "I'll take myself credit for one thing. Here comes a greenhorn from Kiev, Russia. He can't speak a word of English. He started from A, the beginning on, and going into a country and opening up factories, and learning people, and buying the goods, and making the patterns, and now everybody's big shots." He chuckled, adding, "But you can't be lazy. You have to be ambitious. You have to sit down and think and do what you want to do." He rapped his knuckles on the end table for emphasis. "And DO it!"

And Jacob Yeddis did.

Today, Pioneer's 500 employees manufacture about 2,000 <u>dozen</u> caps a day, compared with the 12 a day Yeddis made in Kiev, everything from yacht caps to baseball, golf and fishing caps, ladies hats and tennis visors to utility and sport caps.

Purchased by National Industries, a subsidiary of National Recreation Products, in 1968, Pioneer now is one of the top three cap manufacturing companies in America, and also is the largest importer of men's and boys' headwear, buying from Korea, Taiwan, Hong Kong and Red China, with executive offices at 715 May St.

Until he retired three years ago (at the age of 82), Jacob Yeddis was the pivotal figure in the company's success. Today, his son, Morris, is president and Abe Yeddis is vice president and sales manager. No longer involved with the daily operation, Jacob devotes a great deal of his time to the Kehilath Israel synagogue ("I come from an extremely religious family. On my mother's side, there were six rabbis.") and with his family, especially his seven grandchildren and eight great-grandchildren.

And he reads. To Jacob, who arrived in America with only his education, faith and character, having time to read is truly a luxury. In Russia, he explained, there was ". . . time to read only on the Sabbath." In America, there was never time "to take it easy."

And he thinks about the old days—Russia, the *chedar*, the pogroms and his youthful quest for "streets paved with gold."

"My father used to *cry* when he talked about America, about George Washington and Abraham Lincoln. This is a free country. You can do what you want to as long as you don't do the wrong things. God bless America! All of us, especially Jewish people, should get up every morning and go out and kiss the ground!" ●

Article from the City Magazine in 1937,
includes a photograph of Jacob Yeddis at age 47

Photograph of Sonya (Sarah) Yeddis, Morris' mother

Photograph of Betty and Morris on a Caribbean Cruise in 1989,
their first cruise experience

Photograph of Abe and Barbara Yeddis (1998)

Photograph of Al and Adele Yeddis (1998)

Photograph of Henrietta Kay, Chester and Dorothy Kaplan in 1998.
Yeddis family breakfast celebrating Betty's 86th birthday at Betty's.

Photographs of Morris and Betty in 1986

In June, 1998, Betty entertained her "family" at the White Cottage Restaurant in Raymond, Illinois. Twenty-two of her relatives listened as she summarized her life, her dreams, her regrets and thanked them for joining her on a happy occasion. Only one cousin, Sister Anthony Boehler, is older than she.

Betty hosts relatives at Raymond, Illinois on June 20, 1998.
Photograph of Betty and her cousin, Norma Hampton (Aunt Alice's daughter)

Photograph of Betty with her sister-in-law, Betty Goby, and cousin, Anita Hall
(Uncle Guss' daughter)

They Can't All Come True

With arthritis, I'm doing what my doctors said I would have to do; live with it. Now is the time I should be engaged in Inch by Inch. The toning tables were very effective in maintaining mobility after surgery or because of arthritis. In 1988, the exercise emphasis was on jogging and walking and the younger generation opted for real physical exercise. Older customers came frequently, but their business alone would not support the expense of an open salon twelve or fifteen hours a day.

Frankie Packer and Kimbra Brackman did a great job and enjoyed the clientele Inch by Inch attracted. Many of our customers required gentle help in moving from one table to another. Fitness and rehabilitative services were just coming on the market and they were covered by Medicare. If you've been trained to read a profit and loss statement, you know when to acknowledge that you're in the right business at the wrong time. The Ranchmart location

"Inch by Inch" business card The dress form that became our logo was the one my mother had in her sewing room. It was padded to my size and, coincidentally, her size. I loved the dresses my mother made for me, even when I was in my 50's and a teacher in Belton.

had been very good to us and our advertising was well received. We arranged to give our tables to a nursing home and regretted not having access to them. Now, immobile from arthritis, I would be one of those people needing help in moving form one machine to another.

Inch by Inch was a postscript to an active 75 years, but it was only possible because other dreams had been successful. They can't all come true.

The Dale Purcells welcomed us to the Kingdom City area by being regular customers at the original Calico Cupboard in old McCredie. Dale was head-master at Westminster College at Fulton and Mary Lou was on the staff at Columbia Women's College in Columbia. Fascinated with our venture and its

Photograph of Jackie Krokson, one of my Missouri daughters

Photograph of Jackie's mother, Marge Postman who first coined me Jackie's
"Missouri Mother"

Jackie Kroksow and her partents The Postmans 1998 "Missouri Daughter"

apparent success, Mary Lou told her students about our undertaking. One of her students, Jackie Sicht (Krokson), followed up on her suggestions. After frequent and encouraging visits, Jackie became a part of our "Calico family." Jackie wasn't interested in our "down home" country cooking menus, but she always brought ideas for our decorating. She appreciated our simple foods prepared in new ways and she spread the word about Calico Country in all the other shops she visited in the Columbia area.

Jackie's flair for doing things with fabrics found a fertile field in Calico Cupboard and the shops that made up Calico Country Antique Village. She came repeatedly. Taylor and I tried to harness every ounce of her enthusiasm and vitality. We looked forward to her visits. Her mother called me Jackie's "Missouri Mother" and so it has become. Morris and I visited Jackie and her family in Madison, Wisconsin early in our marriage. Until then, Morris was not aware that women could build such strong ties independent of family relationships. By then, her Fashion Fittings was well on its way and has recently celebrated its 15th anniversary.

Jackie Krokson and her mother, Marge Postman, spawned Betty Taylor's "Missouri Daughters". From McCredie, we added Debbie Daro who as a teenager graced our Calico Cupboard with superb service. The list kept growing as the years passed. As I continued mothering, they continued "daughtering." At this date, there are six in my prayers every night. As you know, prayers do more for the pray-or than they do for the pray-ee. This book has given me an excuse to tell them how much they meant to me and Taylor and Morris all these years:

Jackie Krokson
Debbie Daro Craighead
Marie McCulley
Holly Horton Tyree
Sherry Hutson Staton
Frankie Packer
Salina Davis

Not all of them were a part of Calico Cupboard. Marie McCulley managed our antique shop very responsibly, which meant working all week. Sherry Hutson Staton was a sixth grade student in my first year of teaching in Peculiar. Her mother swears she has attitudes similar to my own. Salina Davis cared for Morris through several surgeries until the very end. She still keeps in touch.

If I ever decide to embark on a list of Missouri Sons, the first one will be Fred Besch, my caregiver since knee surgery. He doesn't need mothering, Heaven knows, but he shows genuine concern for my well-being; even calling periodically throughout the days he isn't with me. He came to me as a fill-in housekeeper. At DeAnn's request, he had driven my great-granddaughters and me to Illinois for a family reunion in the summer of 1996. At that stage, I was in a wheelchair. In October of 1997, he drove me to the hospital for a work-up before knee surgery. Upon release from the hospital, DeAnn asked him to do my housekeeping until she could find a replacement. When I told him my needs would grow as I became older, he sought CNA training. Now, in addition to being a retired Marine and chef, he is not only a CNA but he has established his own care service. All his patients share my appreciation of his thoughtfulness and quiet accomplishments.

Dream Realization Expectancy

Dream I: To get a college education.
Begun in 1931, interrupted in 1933.
Renewed in 1959 and realized in 1963
with a Master's Degree in 1965.   32 years

Dream II: To own a suburban home on a Missouri
hillside near a "babbling brook" like the one
I designed in Ada Foster's Home Ec. Class.
Dreamed in 1927, realized in 1962.   35 years

Little Dreams:

Began teaching like my mother, grandmother,
aunts and uncles; in Peculiar,
Cass County, Missouri.

Helped organize Cass County Historical Society.

Researched the "Burnt District" of Missouri
and wrote the history of Peculiar, <u>A Peculiar Heritage</u> in 1968.

Owned and operated an antique shop of
our own with William M. Taylor - The
Antique Taylors of Peculiar.

Dream III: To operate an inviting and interesting tea-
room offering my grandmother's Pennsylvania
style food to an appreciative public.
Dreamed in the heart of the Depression (1930's).
Realized in Missouri in 1973.   43 years

Little Dreams:

With Gibson Greeting Cards, prepared the
"Just Country Cookin'" calendar that sold 43,000
copies, with all photos shot at The Calico
Cupboard in Hermann, Missouri.

Being selected by <u>Missouri Life</u> for its Christmas issue.

To offer my home, Der Klingerbau, to bed and
breakfast guests in Hermann and make Bed &
Breakfast a part of Missouri tourism potential.

Encouraged Michaela Warner to establish a
reservation service for Missouri tourists,
"River Country Bed and Breakfast."

The Wurstfest - now Hermann's largest
festival. Dreamed in 1979. Realized in 1979.

To name the alleys in Hermann for different
flowers, like "Hollyhock Alley" and "Marigold Alley".
Dream fizzled, but still a good idea for Hermann's
beautiful alleys.

To host the Food Editors and Writers Association
to publicize Hermann and Missouri. Realized in 1981.

To introduce my grandchildren to the world that
once was revealed to me in its buildings, its
tools and its appreciation for quality in whatever
you made or undertook. "The Man Around the
House" grew from my son and my grandson's effort
to make the Third Street houses museum quality
bed and breakfast units.

Dream IV: To share my life with Morris Yeddis whose love
inspired me to be the best that I could be in
whatever I did. Dreamed in 1940.
Realized in 1986.   46 years

Little Dreams:

To record my grandmother's recipes, lifestyle
and values for my son and grandchildren. It
was the motivation behind The Calico Cupboard,
the Bed and Breakfast Inns… and now Recipes,
Recollections and Reflections. Realized in 1998.   52 years

<u>Recipes, Recollections and Reflections</u> has been five years in production, including four or five time-outs for a variety of reasons. It was my son, Bill, who begged me to record these recipes that he enjoyed. His death in 1993 found me blaming myself for his alcoholism. I really hadn't had time to mourn Bill's passing before Morrie's first of a series of little strokes.

The laundry basket of family memorabilia, photographs, clippings, etc. remained untouched until Fred Besch came to help me after knee surgery in 1996. DeAnn arranged for him to care for my house and other errands, but he soon learned that I needed attention too. He let me talk to him … he let me ramble. He let me cry. He let me sob. He restored my interest in doing the book and within a few weeks, he made it possible for me to think, Betty Yeddis style. A year later, Tim's wife, Roni, began putting the manuscript on computer, one section at a time, and my interest grew… but my energy did not. By this time, even without energy, I found myself mentally organizing the materials and memories that I had accumulated.

On February 17, 1998, as my grandchildren returned from their Christmas gift trip to Cancun, I lay in a coma at Saint Lukes North Hospital. I awoke as Tim came in my room the next morning. I was working on the book mentally as I lay there. This time, Carolyn Freeman, my masseuse, had noticed something wrong as I prepared to leave after my massage. She took me directly to the hospital and she waited for the kids to arrive at 8:00 p.m.

Three days later, I left the hospital with no diagnosis and no energy. I spent the days remembering the past and Fred kept the doctors advised of my vital signs. My favorite chokers would no longer fasten so I asked the doctor to feel my neck. "Goiter," she said and put me back on thyroid medication. May 22nd arrived with another coma. In reading about thyroid treatment, Fred found an article on Hashimoto's Disease. The article described all my symptoms, including a lack of iodine in my body. In March, Dr. Pheiffer (my chiropractor) had told me I didn't have a drop of iodine in my body. Based on this information, I asked my doctors to consider appropriate treatment. They didn't laugh at me… but they didn't made any changes either. Two weeks later, I decided that if I wanted to live and finish the book, I'd better take more initiative in my own healthcare.

It now has been three months of unbelievable energy and the book is "alive."

My doctor believes I did the right thing and when I told her I planned to consult an endocrinologist in Overland Park about my goiter, she said she would gladly give them any of my records. Based on past experience, I was due for another coma in September.

Working on the book, studying the replays of my life, decade after decade, has been great therapy. It also reaffirms my belief that there is a PLAN that leads you into decisions, opportunities and (sometimes) stone walls that force you to rethink the path you're taking. The other night, on a long distance call, Melva Beeler told me she knew I was happy for if I weren't, I would go out and find happiness. That may oversimplify things a bit!

The first forty-five years just furnished the groundwork from which I could choose to continue my life. I thank God for my son and his children. I revere the quiet but creative years with Taylor. Presently, my caring brothers-in-law allow me to still make the Morris years a vital part of each day. I do know, however, that I am responsible for my health and my happiness. I hope my grandchildren will find me a role model, for they will have a much longer life span in a world more brutal than the one I have known. These years I call the "now" years - no "past" to worry about and no "future" to plan for - just today. I have determination to make every effort productive and meaningful. I've had a great life. I'm *having* a great life. Thank you all for being a part of it.

As I write this afternoon, Ida Mae Limpus has called to tell me that Mr. Limpus has died quietly. As you read earlier, he was my old boss and alerted me to my ability to sell and promote. My devoted Fred has told me he'll accompany me to the funeral home tonight because "you need it." It's a beautiful October day and a fitting occasion to celebrate Mr. Limpus' quiet but creative life. Earlier in the manuscript, I told you about Mr. Limpus' idea of selling. I guess he saw the palms of God's hands when he slipped away quietly this morning.

Barrybrooke on the Lake was a perfect choice for Morris' and my last home. I chose it because the house was arranged to facilitate caring for loved ones and because my grandchildren were nearby. In addition, Saint Lukes Hospital is just across Barry Road. As we sped north to the airport, I didn't realize that nestled along the old highway (that became I-29) we would find tranquillity, caring neighbors and friendly businesses in an established area known as Platte

Woods. With my walker, I literally "invade" a business that I patronize. I am surprised at the times when customers hurry to open a door for me. You grow accustomed to warm "greetings" but warm "good-byes" are a special benediction every time you visit.

After Morris' death, I dared to brave the I-29 & Barry Road traffic congestion to find a darling drive-through donut shop that was carved out of a former teensy weensy filling station. I had had my life's quota of donuts years ago at Gaylord's in Belton (which is now in Excelsior Springs). But I brave the I-29 & Barry Road intersection two or three times a week just to hear Elisa say, "Good morning." or "You look great today, Betty." Sometimes it's her beautiful daughter serving me through the window and, if I'm lucky, it's her gorgeous husband. Fred stops frequently on his way to work, for he knows a message from them will give my day a great start. Sunday morning, I stopped for a cup of coffee and they asked if I was meeting my brothers-in-law for breakfast. They forget nothing.

This personal touch is not unique to Day-Light Donuts, Dirk's Bar and Grill customers sometimes get off their bar stools to hold the door for me and my walker. I never ate at taverns except at Mr. R's in Hermann, but now I look forward to Dirk's or 54th Street Bar and Grill. The food is excellent and the hospitality GREAT. LaDean and Regina are quick to catch up with me "health wise" if Fred goes in alone. They are always full but never noisy and they always make me feel very welcome. Denise at Winsteads no longer asks for my coffee choice and she thinks everyone who joins me is a grandchild.

While I'm planning to attend Mr. Limpus' wake tonight, I think this would be a good time to tell you how I have planned for my family to dispose of my lifeless body. There will be a "wake" at Louis Funeral Home, but there will be no burial. The funeral will be conducted by Reverend Mary Omwake with Rabbi Michael Zedek participating. There is no room for me to be buried beside Morris. My tombstone is already standing in Peculiar, for when I buried Taylor under the old pine tree he selected, I erected a double stone carrying my name and birth date also. The kids will complete the stone lettering and my cremated ashes will be thrown on Taylor's and Morris' graves, with some on the place Bill built at the lake where his ashes were thrown.

Daylight Donuts

You seldom see a "drive thru" donut shop and you never see folks as friendly as Elisa and Christy at Daylight Donuts

It's October 12th and I'm heading for an October 17th date to give Tom Leathers the manuscript. That is Morris' 84th birthday. Our plan is for Fred to take me to Taylor's grave in Peculiar where I'll leave plants and share the occasion with Wilbur and Lois Hutson, my Peculiar family. From there we will go to Rose Hill Cemetery in Kansas City and place flowers in recognition of Morris' birthday. If Abe or Al, his brothers, can join us; we just might continue to celebrate the occasion with a corned beef on rye at New York Bakery and Delicatessen. We'd like to see the Holzmarks there again.

As Chester advised me when we met with the publisher, "Your days are numbered, so don't put off getting the manuscript to Tom." I've always tried to be prepared for leaving this world, but in the hospital last week I realized that I hadn't planned for Joe and Casey, my beloved cats. Tim and Roni are already seasoned cat parents, so I'm leaving that up to them. I hope to get to see <u>Recipes, Recollections and Reflections</u> in print, but if I don't, know that it has made the last years of my life most enjoyable.

For months, I've carried my President and his problems in my heart. He's almost the same age as my son, Bill. Finally, the other morning, I said aloud to myself, "I forgive Clinton." After telling my masseuse, Carolyn, of this experience, I got off the massage table and went immediately to a printer where I ordered 100 bumper stickers that carried that very message. Few people would park close to my car for a few days. I divided them into packages of ten and gave them to businesses who know me well. Now they are getting calls wanting as many as 100 more. I believe in "putting your money where your mouth is." They can do the same. Forgiving is natural healing. Try it!

It was good to see Jerry Gaines' name in the business section of the <u>Kansas City Star</u> this morning in connection with Stanford's new location. Jerry is a contemporary of Morris and was his next door neighbor as they raised their families. We got to enjoy his restaurant at The Landing at 63rd & Troost.

I've always wanted a Mezuzah! Morris always told how Pop Yeddis kissed the Mezuzah every day. When I learned that it was a blessing on his home, I felt it appropriate for my home too. And besides, I loved Pop. Today in a fashion catalog, I saw a Mezuzah offered in three designs. Soon, with Fred's cooperation, it will remind me of just how blessed I am to enjoy this tradition.

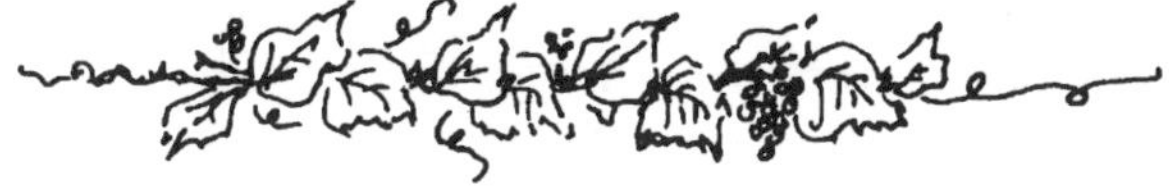

When I wrote <u>A Peculiar Heritage</u> in 1968, so many people were known as "Aunt Dode" Wills, "Aunt Effie", "Miss Clara", or "Miss Helen." "Uncle" was also popular. I often wondered if I'd ever live to have such a role. I guess I'll have to be satisfied with being "Granny" to all my grandkids' friends.

Mornings at Ari's Pumpernick Restaurant in Ranchmart find many of Morris' lifelong friends and old schoolmates — or B'nai Brith pals—enjoying a leisurely breakfast intermingled with the latest news on special people, retirements, sick friends or even over-night deaths. You just might get an opinion or two on what's going on in Washington… or today's editorial page in the K. C. Star. We include this photo through the courtesy of Joe Zenitzky, whom I met when the group was breakfasting at Leonard's on Gregory. Leonard's is no longer there and neither are a lot of that group but the concept of togetherness, of looking out for each other and concern for the problems of the community continue to have their attention. Their parents probably shared the same courage and determination that Jacob and Sarah Yeddis brought to America in 1914. Some of the group are shown here.

Left: Morris Merker, Ben Schanzer, Harold Levitt, Bob Raskin, Sid Carr.
Right: Joe Zenitsky, Bernie Fremerman, Seymour Robbins, Bert Schwendeman,
Len Selden. Obscured or missing: Jack Slade, Jack Farb, Herb Berman,
Elvin Klein, Lee Farb, Sam Taber

Ranch Mart Shopping Center at 95th & Mission Road is in the final stages of renovation and renewal and they've done it in the usual Regnier style. It's beautiful. I almost wish I was still there in "Inch by Inch." At Ari's Pumpernick Restaurant, on the day following Yom Kippur, Mrs. Barash found her way to my booth and gave me a warm New Year's kiss. Mr. Barash, a well known tailor, has been gone for several years but she is continuing the business. On other mornings, Morris' old friends gather for coffee and conversation. Tom Leathers met us there last week. Someone called it my "Johnson County office."

Ari and his wife have restored the jovial atmosphere and it is a most enjoyable place to meet old friends. Just meeting them in such an atmosphere makes it an occasion. Ari had a stroke recently and we all hope for his early recovery.

Blake and Fran Parketon owned the old Central Hotel in Hermann when I was there in Calico Cupboard. Now we both live in the Parkville area and I share my <u>Advertiser-Courier</u> from Hermann each week. They enjoy the reading at least as much as I, for they knew more local people than I did. Blake and I are severely disabled, but Fran is her same lovely self.

Nothing was pretty in my growing up years. Even Sears and Roebuck catalog was in black and white. My mother was very careful with my dad's resources, which in those farm days were strictly at the mercy of the weather. Even in our substantial home, my dad had not had the finish coat of plaster put on the walls. They were all gray and nothing could be changed without a lot of preparatory work. It was no wonder then that where I live has always been a major priority for me. The wrong color combinations have actually made me ill. At 86, I've finally achieved the atmosphere that will bless these last years - days - moments of my life.

In my next life, I'm going to do cards for Hallmark! Particularly for step-fathers and unexpected fathers. Dale Webber was such a great step-father for Tim and DeAnn and I can never find a suitable card to express my gratitude.

I just listened breathlessly to Donnie and Marie sing "Unbreak My Heart." I've only had one broken heart and it has almost healed. I'll bet those intermittent rapid beats that the monitors showed last week are when I'm remembering Morris.

The first thing we made in Home Economics cooking was Eggs al a Goldenrod. I thought it was great. When I suggested it to Tim and Roni, they said, "Yuck!" Today's <u>Time Magazine</u> pictures this pretty dish in announcing an up-dated Betty Crocker cookbook. The ad identified the old time with the 1950's. It made me stop to consider what cookbook era spawned me… the Marion Harland era? <u>Time</u> wouldn't dare!

Just when I thought no one else cared about family history, a second cousin (the granddaughter of my Uncle Lloyd) called from Washington in search of genealogical data. Now the Jones family adds Deanne Cross, 4721 Cumberland Avenue, Chevy Chase, MD 20815.

I know that Morris appreciated Cyril's and Nathan's Sunday afternoon hospitality over the years and he probably told them so countless times. Nathan Yeddis is gone now, but I want Cyril to know how important their personal concern was to Morris. Cyril was Nathan's wife, Morris' devoted cousin and is now my very dear friend.

The Taylor marker at Peculiar Cemetery

As Kim and I entered Nordstrom's yesterday the sight of the escalator reminded me of an incident during the years Morris and I were not in contact…it probably had been 15 years since we had seen each other.

I think it was in Macy's, We accidentally saw each other on the escalator. Morris was going up. I was going down. It was a great moment of surprise for both of us. As we continued we each kept looking back. His expression his black eyes penetrated my "soul." When he reached the next floor he threw me a kiss. I responded by silently forming the words "I love you." We continued on our separate ways. I know he cherished that chance encounter as much as I. We were still "in love" after all those years! For years afterward I relived that moment in my dreams. Now that Nordstrom's escalator has triggered this happy recollection maybe I'll be lucky enough to dream it again.

When I related the incident to Kim she said "that has to be in the book," But the book is at the publishers. When I told Tim & Roni, they asked "Is it too late to get in the book?" So I'm hoping the friendly folks at Leathers Publishing Co. will find a may. (They did). Reliving that happy day so many years ago will keep me remembering a few more years.

Abe, Betty and Chester at Morris' grave on his 84th birthday (1998)

ABOUT MY GRANDMOTHER

The following letter was written by Betty's granddaughter, DeAnn Warren:

Many of you know my grandmother, Betty Taylor-Yeddis. She's been talking about doing this book since I was in third grade and now my daughter, Anne', is in third grade. I used to spend time with her and I'd say, "Grandma, finish your sentences!" I still say this, for while she's telling me one thing, something else slips into her mind and takes precedence. But nothing ever diminishes her determination to recall her loving grandparents, her family or her friends.

Somebody wrote "an old retired school marm she isn't." Add her doctor's "not like any 86 year old I've ever treated. She's got the right attitude." You get a little insight into Betty Taylor-Yeddis' zest for living life to its fullest… while always aware of who she was, who she is and where she is.

Grandma has been hospitalized 5 or 6 times this last year. She has outlived her third husband and her only son, my Dad. She reminds me of the "Energizer Bunny," she just keeps going and going… and at full speed, tackling all those curves in her path, one after another.

In the Spring of 1998, she invited my twelve year old daughter, Amanda, and her friend spend the night with her. We planned to meet at Tippins on Noland Road at 2:00 p.m. to exchange the girls. After visiting with her for a few minutes, she was ready to "head North" for home. She asked me, "Just how far North does Noland Road go?" I said I wasn't sure. She said simply, "Well I will let you know." With that, she headed for home.

Grandma is choosy about where and when she drives, certainly avoiding high traffic times and darkness. I phoned her frequently that evening but received no answer. Around 8:00 p.m. I notified my brother, Tim, who lives only a few miles from her. He was also becoming worried not knowing where Grandma was. I told him she was last seen heading North on Noland Road into unfamiliar territory at 2:00 p.m. He went to her home and discovered that her car was not in the garage as he would have expected by this time of the night.

We decided to call hospital emergency rooms describing an 86 year old, white female with gray hair and glasses; last seen in a dark green Taurus. She would have been admitted as Grace Elizabeth Yeddis, but she might have gone by Betty Taylor-Yeddis like her checks. I mentioned distinguishing features, including hip and knee replacement scars.

We found no one matching this identity, yet there was still no sign of Grandma. The Missouri Highway Patrol was notified and on the look-out for an abandoned Taurus. Frantic by 9:30, we decided to file a missing person report so my husband, Jim, and I told our kids what was going on and we headed for the Independence Police Station. We weren't three miles down the road when Tim called on the car phone to inform us of Grandma's return home from a neighborhood meeting. She had recently become involved in the Barrybrooke Homes Association Board. The meeting had taken place in the cul de sac directly behind her house! What a relief! She was truly shocked by our concern and the urgency with which we had searched for her. She was taken aback each time someone we had notified questioned her about where she had been that evening. We had phoned everyone we could think of. She was surprised to learn what lengths we would go to seek assurance of her safety.

It is now October and Grandma is still going strong. She was in the hospital twice in September but this month its been impromptu luncheons for old friends, meetings with her publisher, artists, and her attorney; bed and breakfasting old teacher friends from the Belton years, University of Illinois reunions, and multiple doctors visits. When she's having a "bad day, its the same routine but without make-up and she lets Fred do the driving.

PS: I truly was shocked. As I opened the garage door, my grandson bolted out of the living room. "Do you realize the whole world is looking for you? Where have you been?" But before I could answer, "Bradford Court," he was busy reporting me "found."

On October 17th Abe and his life long friend, Chester Kaplan, joined me at Morris' grave to mark his 84th birthday and to say *Kaddish*, the Jewish prayer for the dead. As I placed the beautiful roses on Morris' grave, I realized that this traditional ritual to honor his death provides a perfect benediction for <u>Recipes, Recollections and Reflections.</u>

Photograph of DeAnn's family:
(clockwise from left) Amanda, Jim, Dustin, Devin, Dominic, Anne', and DeAnn

Tim and his wife, Veronica (Roni) who has been invaluable
as a typist / editor / organizer of this book

Tim and Cathy (his daughter) at her 16th birthday party (1997)

Co-authors: Casey and Joe

To the Reader:

Betty Taylor-Yeddis has been "Granny" to me for about four years now. From the very first time I met her, I have had a certain respect for the person she is and the life she has led. While working on this book with her, however, I have grown to admire and appreciate her to an even greater extent.

Aside from being Betty's granddaughter, I am also a licensed psychotherapist. In spite of all my education, I must admit that I had (at best) an incomplete understanding of the "mature" woman's mind. My non-clinical bias was that life after fifty was basically a period of "winding down" from life. I believed that, as I aged, life would become less stimulating and certainly less active. Betty has shown me how utterly ignorant those beliefs have been. I thank her for sharing her vibrant perspective on the human life cycle and for educating me on what it means to live courageously at any age.

Her passion and enthusiasm is truly infectious. When she delves into a project, she beams with inspiration. Her eyes sparkle with eager anticipation, because she knows how meaningful the finished product will be. This zealousness applies in every effort she makes; whether it be cooking, writing, decorating, or grandparenting. Betty Taylor-Yeddis is a remarkable woman with an endless capacity for envisioning possibilities.

Biologically speaking, I have no living grandparents. Betty's kindness and generosity, however, have made it easy to consider her family. In the short time that I have known her, she has profoundly influenced my life and my attitudes about many things. For her, this is nothing new. She has been profoundly influencing people for 86 years and will continue to do so for many years to come.

Veronica Brackman

It's over! Helping Betty get the book just the way she wanted it - extending deadlines - adding photos - when an unexpected telephone call from a long ago friend triggered pages of recollections! But I'll always be grateful for being her caregiver during these MONTHS. She's been an emotional uplift and a constant source of "therapy" that enabled me to stop and smell the roses from day to day. I know I'll be a better person and a more sensitive caregiver because she touched my life. Besides, it was Betty who said I had the sensitivity to be a "caregiver" and encouraged me to seek training. When I sought a "cutesy" name for my service, she reminded me that Besch offered the perfect name - Best Care - that I wanted to provide.

Fred Besch

Doerr Family Notes

As recorded by Etta Jones and Theodore Doerr, 1880-1907
Footnotes by M.D. Jones

"After The Thirty Years War, a man named Dorr (or Doerr, as it is now spelled) came over from the French border and settled near the Rhine in Hesse. The ravages of the war had left that country almost uninhabited. This man had twelve sons from whom are descended the numerous Doerr families of that region. He seems to have been a man of some learning and esteem, having held the office of Burgomeister. He was the great grandfather of my father, Phillip Peter Doerr, who was born on August 16th, 1820 in Sonnenberg by Wiesbaden, Hesse-Nassau, Germany on the upper Rhine. Four of his sons' first names were Phillip, but their middle names varied. Now known as Peter Doerr, he completed six years of public school and served an apprenticeship of three years as mason. As required by the law at that time, he traveled over a large part of Germany working in various cities. Workmen usually traveled in pairs, carrying tools and necessary clothing. Their passports were in book form and gave a description of the person, business, and home. Upon entering a town, they presented their credentials and themselves to the magistrate. If their credentials were approved and stamped, they were permitted to establish residence and look for work. If found begging, they were immediately arrested and fined. They were known as hand-werks-bursche or trade lads and were respected by everyone. This hand werks buche of my father, Peter Doerr, is in the possession of my son, M.D. Jones.

In 1842, Phillip Peter Doerr was twenty-one. He passed the examination for the national military draft, but was rejected on account of slightly in-bent knees. In 1844, he emigrated to America and worked in and about St. Louis, Missouri. He had been five weeks en route by sailing vessel."

Following my mother's graduation from high school, she worked in G.C. McLean's Dry Goods Store. It was there that she became interested in fabrics, beautiful laces and insertions, and the fine art of dressmaking. Aunt Grace Grotts, my mother's close friend, was a dressmaker. Every woman was trained to clothe herself and her family and quilting came from the scraps that accrued from those skills. I was named for "Aunt Grace" and my Aunt Elizabeth.

My grandmother was a teacher in Raymond's two room elementary school when she married Grand Dad Jones. He was a wagon maker and a blacksmith with a six year old son, George. The income from a blacksmith shop would not support their dreams of a college education for their family. As Presbyterians, they had access to Lake Forest College in Illinois and Park College in Parkville, Missouri. These were both "self-help" school where one could work in exchange for tuition. Uncle Milton, and later Uncle Lloyd, enrolled in Lake Forest first and Mother was accepted at Park.

Park College was just across the river from Kansas City, Kansas, where some of my grandmother's nieces lived. Being away from home with some relatives near was a great experience for my mother. Coming from the Illinois flatlands, she was impressed with her new surroundings. She marveled at her nearness to the river, the beautiful hills and bluffs on which the town was located, having classmates from near and far, and the sociability of dorm life. My earliest recollections are of her telling me about what happened at Park. In fact, for years we had waffles on Sunday evenings in remembrance of Sunday evenings at Park College.

I, too, was impressed; for I married Hugo Brackman in the chapel at Park College in 1943. I did this so my mother could feel a part of the service from a three hundred mile distance. It probably was a subtle influence in our moving to the Parkville area two years ago (1995). But the quaint village my mother remembered is now surrounded by Kansas City. Parkville and the historians are now restoring the river front area in the manner of the early 1900's. Mother would have loved that!

**The following notes are from A. Theodore Doerr,
"Uncle Thee," son of Peter Doerr**

The Shore School was over three miles distant. We had few books, but the parents were faithful and untiring in their home instruction. We spent the memorable period of the Civil War on this farm. We walked to school and sometimes traveled by pony. At this time, there were countless prairie chickens, ducks, geese, sandhill cranes, snakes, and even deer. There were no game laws at this time. One day, a large flock of prairie chickens alighted on the

Shore School fence. The teacher, Ely Brown, dismissed school, walked to the front door, and with one shot garnered seven of them. Theodore Doerr killed five one morning before school at his home place as they rested in the maple trees. The seats at Shore School were benches of saw mill plank on peg legs with no backs. Around the wall was a shelf for the reception of books, lunch pails, and a water bucket. Another school was built nearer to the farm and became known as Frog Pond School. This was low country and the last stand of ducks and prairie chickens. The chickens liked to nest in timothy hay. It was usually cut after the nests were made but before the eggs were hatched. The parent bird would abandon the nest and the whole clutch of fifteen or more chicks would perish. By this time, you were limited by the amount of game you could carry.

No family enjoyed family reunions more than the Doerrs. They were always well attended and they were always at the home place; near Harvel, Illinois. I hope I am correct, but I think the original farm was called Walnut Grove Stock Farm at one time. This name seems appropriate, since Grandfather Doerr had planted a windbreak of walnut trees soon after he acquired the land from the government and settled there. From Germany, he had come to St. Louis. A brick-mason by training, he had no problem keeping himself occupied. His wife, Johanna Vollbrecht Doerr, had brought her two children from a former marriage with her to America. Her sister had preceded her and her brother, Henry, was already established in St. Louis.

My grandmother, Henrietta Christina Elizabeth Doerr, was the first child of the Doerr-Vollbrecht union. She was born to them in St. Louis, but they soon relocated to Edwardsville across the river in Illinois. Three more children were born: A. Theodore (Uncle Thee), Emma, and Gustav. With the two step-children, Ludwig and Christina, they made a sizable family for prairie settlers. So family reunions were large even if all the relatives didn't attend. In my lifetime, Uncle Thee lived on the home place. As long as I can remember, we made a summer trip to see Uncle Thee and Aunt Alice, reunion or not. We usually visited during watermelon season.

Food was a major attraction for everybody, but mainly we enjoyed visiting with aunts, uncles, cousins, nieces, and nephews that you saw so infrequently. In this photograph, my mother and dad are not present because she was great with child as my birth approached. When I think about what effort we made to attend those events to see our kinfolk (in a horse and buggy at that) I am appalled at our indifference to maintaining family connections now. In the photo, the man at the far right was Roy Reineke, a young hardware merchant who happened to have one of the first automobiles in Raymond and was available for hire to transport people on such occasions. My grandfather and grandmother Jones are at the far right in the first row; my grandfather with his straw hat on his knee. To my grandmother's left is Uncle Thee and to his left, Aunt Alice. Aunt Alice Doerr was totally deaf but she was a delightful, gentle woman. Her son, Elmer Doerr, is at the far left of the first row with his daughter, Virginia, at his side. In my mother's generation, cousins were a vital part of a family.

From the time I was old enough to ask questions about my grandparents and great grandparents, I was always told that Great Grandmother Doerr had two children when she married Grandfather Peter Doerr. That was uncle Ludwig and Aunt Christina, according to my mother. They were always a part of the family. Of course they were older than the Doerr children, so they were married and gone by my mother's time. Aunt Christina married Ed Lebermann and moved to Seguin, Texas in the 1870's. Uncle Ludwig married Wilhelmina Walters and remained in the general area of the home place.

A few years ago, at the conclusion of a chance meeting of family members, Billy Doerr remarked," You know that Grandmother Doerr had two children when she married Grandpa Doerr." Without hesitating, I said," Uncle Ludwig and Aunt Christina," and he nodded that I was right. By this time, my mother was gone and I had no one with whom to explore the relationship further. From my point of view, it presented no problem, for they were simply stepchildren. Occasionally, I would wonder about their feelings about coming to America. Grandmother Doerr had been orphaned at the age of four. I had a feeling that the hardships she had endured gave her a valid reason for appearing stern and resolute in the few family portraits we had. But that too I excused, knowing how difficult it was for her to get to a photographer and accommodate the photographer's need for her to remain motionless.

In the last few months of my dad's life, he added to a casual Sunday morning conversation," You know Aunt Lil was not my full sister?" I didn't know, but she was the oldest Goby child and was much finer boned than the eight Goby children that followed her. Aunt Flora and Aunt Alice were the only two left. In a later visit, when I was at Aunt Alice's and Aunt Flora was there too, I told them of my dad's comment. I also recounted his tearful statement, "Aunt Lil was like a mother to me." Aunt Flora said nothing and Aunt Alice said that she had never heard that.

By the time of the Goby family reunion in 1990, Jack Goby's research reaffirmed Grandmother Goby's wedding date as February 14th, 1873 and Aunt

Lil's birth date as May 12th, 1873. However, all copies of obituaries of Grand Dad Goby list Aunt Lil as a daughter, deceased in 1924.

I mention these two genealogical items primarily to record the manner in which such occurrences were handled by families before the days of vital statistics and government records. Loving families found a way to expand family ties to include everyone under all circumstances, with no derogatory remarks. Love heals all. I know you have learned that just as I have.

Doerr family photograph

Milton Doerr Jones
1883-1959

Milton Jones started his college education at Lake Forest College, Illinois and later transferred to the University of Ilolinois in Champaign, Illinois where he gaduated.

On January 26, 1918 he married George Minnie Kein. At that time he was a Manual Training teacher in the Rockford, Illinois schools. He then worked for the National Carbon Co. in clarksburg, West Virginia, where their first child Robert was born.

In 1920 he was working for the Cleveland public school system as director of school housing, equipment and supplies. his next position was Principal of the Cleveland Trade School. later he returned to teaching, first at East Technical High School in Cleveland, and then in Collinwood High School. During this time he obtained a masters degree at Western Reserve University and continued graduate courses until he was qualified to teach all of the sciences at the high school level.

His two sons, Robert and John (who was born in Cleveland in 1923) graduated from Collinwood High School. It was after that time, in the early 1940s, that he requested a transfer to be in a school nearer home. He retired from teaching after WW II, in the late forties.

Milton Jones was an avid fisherman and hunter, and spent his summers caping and fishing in the eastern provinces of Canada and upper New England. All through the 1930s he hauled his family with him and they lived primitives lives until school resumed in the fall. Both Robert and John continued with their father's love of the out-of-doors, both becoming expert fishermen and hunters.

Manual arts was the hobby and recreation in the winter months. Milton created many useful and decorative pieces of art from wood, metals and ivory. A chess set carved from ivory and ebony won an honorable mention at the Cleveland art Museum show in the early 1930s.

Milton died at home October 7, 1959, after a long illness brought on by many years of high blood pressure.

John Paul Jones

John Paul Jones was born on June 8, 1923 in Cleveland Ohio. His parents were G. Minnie Klein and Milton Doerr Jones. he had one brother, Robert Jones.

John's father was a school principal, and the family spent summers camping in the eastern provinces of Canada, and Maine. John developed a lifelong love of the outdoors that he carried with all his life. He enjoyed fishing and canoeing most of all, which evidenced itself when he was first married to Minna and chose to buy a canoe prior to any other funiture purchasses.

John had a special rapport with animals, and a talent for imitating birdcalls. For most of his life, John went to Canada every summer and hiked into the wilderness with his fishing buddies. His favorite fishing spot was Gardner's Bay in Quetico National Park. He has passed on his knowledge and love of fishing to his grndson, Johnny, who is working to match his grandpa as "The Best Fishermand In The World".

John's passion for the outdoors continued when later in life he and Minna purchased property in Waushara County affectionally remembered by all as "The Drake".

The Drake inspired a new hobby which bean a new love – bee keeping. After the sale of the Drake, the bees were transferred to his daugthter, Paula's property and are still kept there by her husband, Vance, who has inherited the bug for bees.

John was a devoted family man. He married Minna in 1946 and remained married for 49 years. Together, they raised three girls, Magot, Paula and Alison. his devotion to family carried through strongly to the next generation of his five grandchildren whom he cherished: John, Jean, Claire, Anne and Lucia.

John was always very creative. he was successful in business, and designed innovative sales promotions for Mohawk Distribution Center, formally known as Neidhoefer & Co., his employer of 34 years. After retirement, he continued to use his business talents at Service Coprs of Retired Executives, where he counseled new businesses.

John's creative abilities were most appreciated at home. One of his creations, a Christmas Tree made of balloons, placed first in the Wauwatosa outdoor decoration contest. He made paintings, sang Rudy Vallee songs, and played ukelele.

John was very active in the community. He was an elected member of the Wauwato School Board; enjoyed performing in a barbership quartet; and juring 43 years of membership in the Wauwatosa Presbyterian Church, he sang in the church choir, served as an elder, and was a church school teacher and Superintendent.

He will be misse by us all, but for all of those he touched, in some small way, he will continue to live on. In our memories, our actions, and most commonly, in our hearts.

Margot, Paula, Alison and Minna

Ancestors of
John Paul Jones

Albert Milton Jones
b: Feb. 05, 1850 in Tuscartawas Cty, Ohio
m: 1882 in Mongomery Cty, Illinois
d: 1924 in Raymond, Montgomery Cty, IL

Milton Doerr Jones
b: Sept 16, 1883 in Montgomery Cty, Illinois
m: Jan. 26, 1918 in Champaign Cty, Illinois
d: Oct. 07, 1959 in Cuyahoga Cty, Ohio

Peter Doerr
b: Aug. 16, 1820 in Weisbaden, Germany
m: Oct. 10, 1848 in St. Charles Cty, Missouri
d: September 07, 1893

Henrietta Christina Elizabeth Doerr
b: Jan. 05, 1850 in Madison Cty, Illinois
d: 1926 in Raymond, Montgomery Cty, IL

Johanna K. Volbright
b: Oct. 16, 1819 in Schwartzburg, Germany

John Paul Jones
b: June 08, 1923 in Cuyahoga Cty, Ohio
m: June 22, 1946 in Cuyahoga Cty, Ohio
d: 1995 in Milwaukee Cty, Wisconsin

Lorenz (Lawrence) Klein
b: 1814
m: 1840
d: 1880

Johnson Andrew Jackson Klein
b: March 10, 1866 in Muscatine Cty, Iowa
m: October 04, 1888
d: Sept 25, 1945 in Champaign Cty, Illinois

Katherine Schmidt
b: in Dusseldorf, Germany

George Minnie Klein
b: February 22, 1891 in Muscatine Cty, IA
d: 1979 in Milwaukee Cty, Wisconsin

George H. Plitt
m: 1860 in Cambria Cty, Pennsylvania
d: Aug. 16, 1905 in Muscatine Cty, Iowa

Emma Eliza Plitt
m: Nov. 16, 1866 in Kearney, Clay Cty, MO
d: Nov. 29, 1941 in Champaign Cty, Illinois

Nancy Ramsey
m: 1842 in Westmoreland Cty, Pennsylvania
d: May 31, 1934

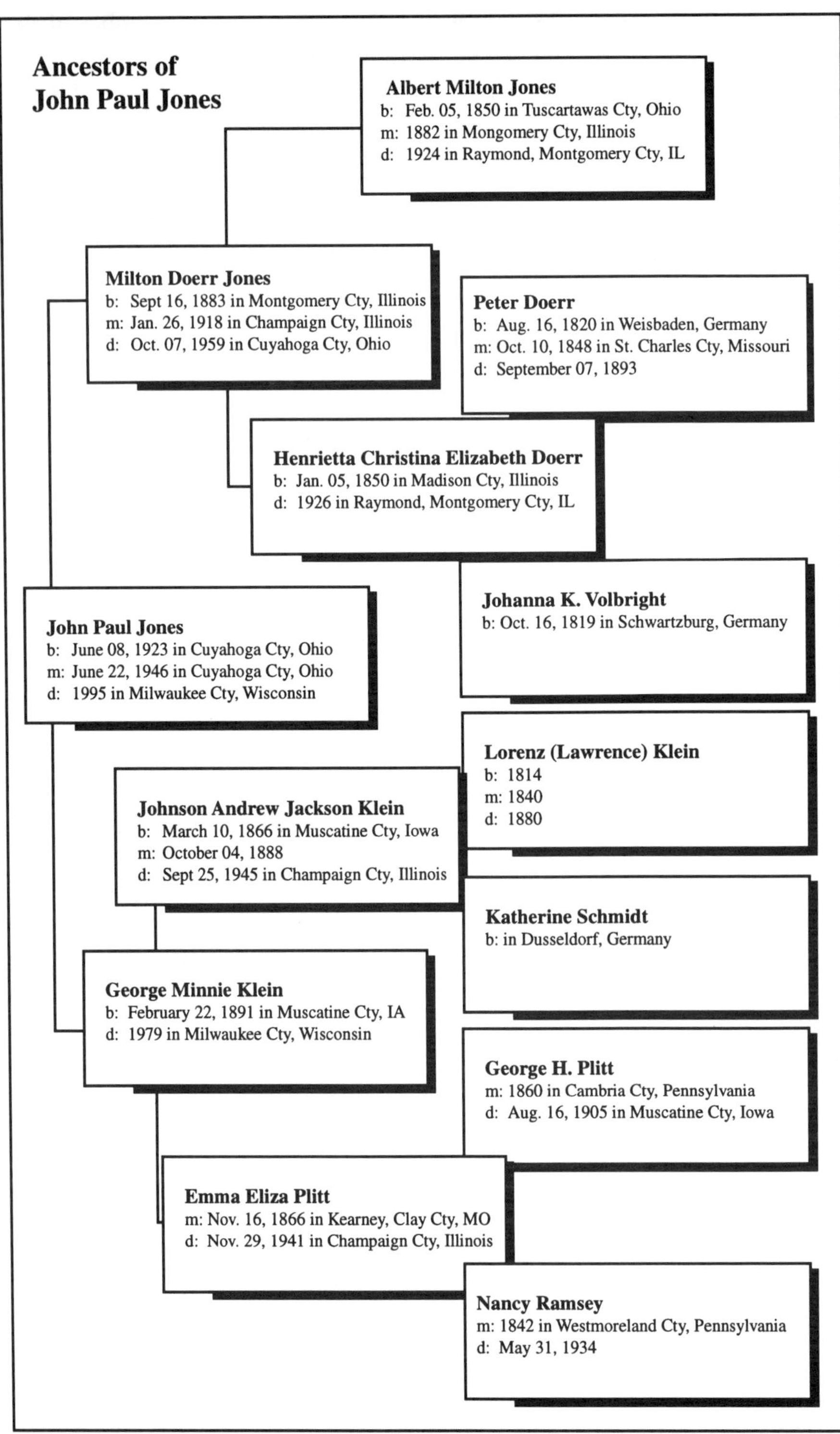

316

Reader's Notes